Publications of the

Minnesota Historical Society

RUSSELL W. FRIDLEY
Director

JUNE D. HOLMQUIST
Assistant Director
for Research and Publications

FOOD

ON THE FRONTIER

Minnesota Cooking
from 1850 to 1900
With Selected Recipes

By **MARJORIE KREIDBERG**

Minnesota Historical Society Press · St. Paul · 1975

Library of Congress Cataloging in Publication Data
Kreidberg, Marjorie.
   Food on the frontier.
   (Publications of the Minnesota Historical Society)
   Includes bibliographical references and indexes.
   1. Cookery, American—Minnesota. 2. Minnesota—
History. I. Title. II. Series: Minnesota
Historical Society. Publications.
TX715.K897   641.5'9776   75-34214

International Standard Book Number: 0-87351-096-8 (hard cover)
0-87351-097-6 (paper cover)

To my mother

Acknowledgments

MOST of the information in this history of food and cooking on the Minnesota frontier was yielded by the vast resource collections of the Minnesota Historical Society. Although the painstaking research was time-consuming, it was far from being a solitary enterprise, for much valuable assistance was readily and generously given by the society's staff.

The project began in 1964 when I discovered the collection of 19th-century cookbooks in the society's library. It gathered momentum during conversations with June D. Holmquist, assistant director for research and publications, who helped me move the simmering pot from the back burner to the front. For her guidance and encouragement I can never thank her enough.

All members of the society's manuscripts division staff were consistently helpful, and I thank in particular Lucile M. Kane, state archivist, Catherine Rafter, and Ruby J. Shields. Librarians James T. Dunn, Patricia C. Harpole, Waldemar F. Toensing, and Margaret J. Habermann repeatedly pointed the way toward answers to my questions. Both Faustino Avaloz and John Dougherty in the newspaper department offered smiles as well as assistance, and Janis Obst, curator of historic houses, set me on the right course on several occasions.

My everlasting gratitude goes to the staff of the society's research and publications division — June Holmquist and Jean A. Brookins, gifted editors; Mary D. Cannon, Carolyn Gilman, Bruce M. White, and Burton H. Cannon, tireless researchers; and June Sonju, able typist. I thank especially Alan Ominsky, production supervisor, who is particularly skillful in transforming lines of type, illustrations, and white space into book design.

I also want to acknowledge the generous assistance of Evie Mageli, librarian at General Mills, Inc., Minneapolis; Sharon Ross and Marianne Brueggemann at Webb Publishing, St. Paul; Mrs. Verner Claypool, Duluth; Mrs. Robert Rosenthal, St. Paul; and the Henry E. Huntington Library and Art Gallery, San Marino, California.

I am grateful in large measure to my husband, Irving B. Kreidberg, whose sustained interest and unremitting thoughtfulness allowed the pot to occupy the front burner until its contents could be "cooked until done."

St. Paul, Minnesota   MARJORIE KREIDBERG
October, 1975

Contents

CHAPTER ONE

Introduction

FOR AMERICANS a honeycomb of nostalgia has grown around the words "pioneer," "settler," and "frontier," and the word "cooking" conjures up the smell of baking bread, the sizzle of meat, the snap and tang of crisp pickles, or the special taste of a remembered childhood favorite dessert like mother's chocolate cake. These words call up images of the "good old days" when a family lived a self-sufficient, bucolic life in a log cabin or a claim shanty set under spreading trees, hunted the abundant wild game, fished in clear-running streams, picked berries, or gathered nuts when they were hungry. Or so we tend to think. And sometimes in some places, it was even true.

But not always. The image is, of course, incomplete and thereby false because many essential elements are missing. The letters and diaries of the men and women who peopled the forests and prairies of Minnesota from the 1850s to the early 1900s tell us in their own words of the harsh and abiding realities of life on the frontier. On now-faded pieces of paper of many sizes and colors, the pioneer housewives of Minnesota recorded in their own handwriting the everyday problems, the satisfactions, and the sadnesses that went into the frontier experience. In their writing, the women reflected the broad range of living conditions throughout the period. A few came from well-to-do families with elegant homes and household servants; some attained a comfortable life of adequate means and hired help a few years after reaching Minnesota; and many represented the large number of pioneers who struggled long and hard for a better life.

Two themes are paramount throughout this legacy of documents — a tenacious optimism and an underlying code of hard work and constant effort shared equally by the women and men who participated in the settlement of Minnesota over the 50 years from 1850 to 1900. Not unexpectedly the diaries of the women speak frequently

of food. That of Mrs. Susan M. Adams, who, with her husband Andrew, moved from a temporary and unsatisfactory boardinghouse in the young Mississippi River city of St. Paul to the prairies near Shakopee in April, 1856, is typical. Having "trudged along over & through the mud & water" on foot to reach the rough dwelling Mrs. Adams called "*our own* little shantee," she wrote: "We're glad enough to get into a place where we could feel at home. I made fire and we soon had a meal of nice pork and mush which we ate with thankful hearts." Neither a hard rain that "found its way into our shantee quite freely" nor a limited and repetitive diet of potatoes, salt pork, fried mush, and corncake with "nothing but pork fat on it" could diminish Mrs. Adams' sense of thanksgiving or her conviction that life had taken a turn for the better.[1]

Such personal stories, supported by 19th-century cooking literature, newspapers, account books, and other relevant records of past times and places provide the framework on which to reconstruct the life of the pioneer housewife, substituting the sharp edges of reality for the honeycomb of nostalgic legend. It is true that a homemaker on the frontier often turned out loaves of bread by the dozen, and the fragrant aroma of baking was a welcome part of her life — if she had available the ingredients for making bread. It is also true that she had to master the diverse arts of preserving, salting, pickling, smoking, drying, and canning foods. These and other skills were essential to a well-provisioned cellar without which a family had no protection against shortages, raw isolation, or the uncertainties of the seasons. But most of all, the pioneer housewife had to learn to adapt. She substituted, she altered, she "made do" in many ingenious ways. Her individual personal accounts graphically identify the conditions of life experienced by many settlers in a place where, and at a time when, the promise of a better life was much greater than the means to achieve it.

Living in the late 1850s on a farm near present-day Cambridge in Isanti County, Mrs. Harriet Griswold, a widow, helped support herself and her four children with the income she earned from boarders, many of whom were loggers on their way to the north woods. Some of the food she put on the table came from the land, grown from seeds her father sent to her. "People say we have a very good garden," she wrote to relatives in Michigan; "we have plenty of Water and Musk melons, cabbages, tomatoes, squashes, onions, turnips, carrots &c. Arnold [a son] has threshed out a little of the rye which we have had ground." Produce from the fields and garden, wild ducks, prairie chickens, a pig, and a cow to supply milk contributed to her resources. Game birds apparently were not a dependable source of food, however, for Mrs. Griswold remarked that in spite of the ice remaining on the nearby lake "there were thousands of Ducks in the open places but too far out to get a shot at them. We have had no game this spring except 2 or 3 Prairie chickens."[2]

The Griswolds, like so many others, felt the impact of the severe depression, or as it was then called, the Panic of 1857. "Every body is complaining of hard times here," Mrs. Griswold wrote, "money scarce, &c[.] Produce is very cheap[.] Corn 30 cts. . . . butter 15, Eggs 6 and 8[.] Flour costs me 5 dollars at Anoka and one dollar for freight." The barrel of flour had to be brought by wagon over some 35 miles of rough roads from Anoka to Cambridge. No expenditure of money was necessary for the family to enjoy an abundant supply of cranberries when the wild fruit ripened in the fall. "The first day I got about 12 qts[;] the last [day] 3 or 4 qts short of a bushel," Mrs. Griswold wrote, "but we have to stand in water ancle [*sic*] deep. . . . the ma[r]shes where we pick are about 4 miles from here and are very wet the water being about a foot deep all over them[;] we start soon after breakfast and get home about dark[.] Florence [*a daughter*] can ride horseback but I do not dare[.] I have walked out and back two days this week[;] it does not make me sick but I feel rather old and lame."[3]

CRANBERRY.

Although Mrs. Griswold regarded theirs as a good life, she was not unaware of the rough edges and genuine discomforts. For example, the family obtained its cooking and drinking water from a nearby lake, even though they had a well. Because no stones were available in the sandy Cambridge area, Mrs. Griswold explained, we "must have a curb made of boards for the well which gives a little bad taste to the water." She lamented that they did not have a wagon, nor was there one nearby that they could borrow. She would have liked a barn for the livestock, too, but somehow miraculously managed to get along without one in Minnesota's cold winters. "People who have always lived at the east know but little what hardships some of the pioneers endure and we as yet have seen but little in comparison with some," she wrote, for "we have so far had enough to eat and clothing sufficient to keep us warm[.] Arnold has got wood hauled enough for the present[;] we have killed our pig which would probably weigh 175 lbs and I have some venison so we are pretty well off for provision[.] I wish you could come in and eat some of our baked venison[;] it is very nice[;] apples I have not seen more than 2 or 3 since I was in St. Paul last Spring." St. Paul was over 50 miles away, too far to be considered a source of supplies.[4]

The Robert Andersons, an Irish family that settled in 1854 at Eden Prairie in southern Hennepin County after a stay at Galena, Illinois, brought with them seven cows, a sheep, a sow and its litter of pigs, a plow, a harrow, a supply of seed oats and corn, "quite a store of provisions — groceries, flour and hams," and a little money. Their house was a one-room log cabin with a loft that was reached by a ladder. "We made most of our furniture," Mary Jane Anderson later wrote, "and with feather beds, dishes and a small cookstove" bought in 1856 from the sale of 30 bushels of cranberries "we were quite comfortable. At first we had curtains to divide the rooms, the living room from the bed room, and afterward we built a partition across." During the 18 years they lived in the cabin, the Andersons added a lean-to kitchen to the original structure and seven children to their family. In 1872 they built a "good frame house" and moved into it. To Mrs. Anderson, life in the log cabin represented very happy years. "We had a home of our very own, we were young and hopeful, and with our little family and life before us, and always work to do and the strength to accomplish it, what more could we ask?"[5]

Oftentimes the work taxed the stamina of even the hardiest woman. Mary E. Carpenter, a farmer's wife who lived near Rochester in 1871, listed what she did in one day at harvesting time. "My hand is so tired perhaps you'll excuse penciling" she began her letter to a cousin. "I'll tell you what I did yesterday. I am too tired to write but may have to delay a long time if I wait till I am rested. . . . You see we are right in the midst of harvest-ing[,] the great *drive* of the year. Now for what I did yesterday. I got up before four, got breakfast (we have a hired man)[,] skimmed milk, churned, worked over the churning already on hand, did a large washing, baked 6 loaves of bread, & seven pumpkin pies, while I was bak-ing put on the irons & did the ironing, got supper &c — besides washing all the dishes, making the beds[,] sweeping &c — Mamie [*a daughter*] was not well so she didn't help me so much as usual. I was tired & lame enough at night, and feel miserable in consequence to-day. So you see I am giving you the dregs in writing today but this is the first *gap* in work I have had for weeks. We are now nearly through cutting the grain but it is all to be stacked & threshed. Then we may feel less driven I hope."[6]

For Mrs. Carpenter and many housewives like her, a concern for the here and now was foremost. They knew few of the conveniences that would, in time, make their lives easier, for they had as yet reaped little benefit from the accelerating settlement that had advanced Minnesota

Territory into a developing state. After the area was officially organized as a territory in 1849, land speculators as well as thousands of homeseekers poured in. So rapidly did the population grow that Minnesota was admitted to the Union as the 32nd state in 1858. Like their counterparts in other regions, Minnesotans played diverse roles in the unfolding drama of the American frontier experience. They built homes, organized communities, established institutions, founded businesses, and developed industries that transformed the empty reaches of prairie and forest.[7]

The advances that affected the quality of life in Minnesota during the half century from 1850 to 1900 developed sporadically as the population increased. In 1850, a year after the official organization of the territory, when the settlers numbered 6,077 persons, the editor of the region's first newspaper, the *Minnesota Pioneer*, wrote prophetically and buoyantly of the future. He anticipated a rapid multiplication of farms, new enterprises, buildings that would "leap into existence," and, most significantly, "thronging multitudes of immigrants" who would settle in Minnesota. By 1855 the population had grown to about 40,000, and two years later, when the territory was on the threshold of statehood, the number of residents had increased to over 150,000. The federal census recorded 172,023 persons living in the state in 1860; that number grew to 780,773 in 1880 and surged to 1,751,394 at the turn of the century.[8]

Although the motivations that inspired newcomers to settle in Minnesota varied, it was the availability of land that attracted many of them. The Homestead Act passed by Congress in 1862 generated a powerful impetus to settlement in Minnesota and elsewhere. The act granted a settler title to 160 acres of land in exchange for five years of continuous residence and the payment of nominal registration fees. Turning the spirit of the law into rhyme, a Rochester newspaper editor in 1862 issued this invitation:

> Then come along, come along, make no delay.
> Come from every nation, come from every way.
> Minnesota's broad enough, don't be alarmed,
> And Uncle Sam is rich enough to *give* you all
> a farm.[9]

And come along they did. The same poetic Rochester editor observed in June, 1862, that the "great share" of those taking advantage of the act in southern Minnesota were "Germans and Norwegians, nearly all of them having good teams, stock of cattle and money. They will make excellent Pioneers and contribute largely to the material wealth of our State," he noted. Other national groups also came in increasing numbers. Swedes, Irish, English, Scots, Welsh, Swiss, and Czechs crossed the ocean and half a continent to the new land. They were joined by more Norwegians, Danes, Bohemians, and Hollanders. Migrating Americans, primarily from New England, the Middle Atlantic states, and parts of the Middle West, joined their European counterparts in Minnesota, bringing with them family and cultural traditions which would enrich and shape the emerging character of the new state.[10]

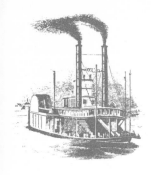

Hundreds of thousands of newcomers reached the Minnesota country aboard steamboats on the Mississippi River, a seasonally ice-locked route closed to navigation at least five months of each year, usually from late November until April. In spite of the limited navigation season, thousands of settlers arrived annually, disembarking from crowded vessels at such river ports as St. Paul, Red Wing, Winona, and Hastings. Gathering their worldly goods — the "old country chests, copper kettles for the manufacture of cheese, and other utensils that strewed the levee" — many of the new arrivals set out inland. Often they headed for communities where their fellow countrymen had already established homes, finding strength and security in the bonds of a common past.[11]

The often difficult last leg of the journey from the river towns to the outlying settlements gradually became easier as transportation improved. During the 1850s, fur trade trails were widened into rude roads that could accommodate wagons and the stagecoaches that then began to carry passengers and mail. More of the state's rivers became highways of travel for steamboats and smaller craft, and the ferries that transported people, wagons, and supplies across streams were soon replaced by bridges. To the great satisfaction of all Minnesotans, but especially of the newcomers looking for a way to reach the open lands of the state's interior, the railroad finally came to St. Paul in 1862. The 210 miles of track within the state's borders in 1865 grew to about 2,000 miles by 1872. Not only did the railroads take the immigrants to Minnesota at reduced rates, but several of the companies built large reception centers where they could stay while looking for farmland. Once the farmers were established in western Minnesota, they could depend on the railroad to transport agricultural products to market and to bring back needed supplies.[12]

While railroads and steamboats brought thousands of settlers to Minnesota, there were unrecorded numbers like Mr. and Mrs. Adams who went overland on foot or in wagons over rough roads or no roads at all. Typical of the pioneers' wagons was one noted by a newspaper editor as it passed in front of his office. It held, he wrote, "the usual plunder inside; on the rear of the wagon was tied a chicken coop, on the top of which, too big to go inside, sat a shang[h]ai rooster looking with surprise at the busy city around him; a man with a gun, and a boy driving three cows brought up the rear."[13]

Some settlers traveled in groups. Among them was a caravan of three families who left Wisconsin together to settle near Mankato. They had packed their household goods and a large supply of provisions into prairie schooners, readied "five yoke of oxen, several span of horses, and about forty head of cattle, among them a

number of milch cows," and set out on the four-week journey. "We found our way by compass," one of the men explained, "and made our own road west." Each Saturday they stopped to bake bread in a cookstove carried in one of the wagons. They set up the stove in the open instead of baking, as many other overland travelers did, in covered iron kettles over hot embers with more hot coals over the lid. When they reached their homestead, the family placed the precious stove near a tree and cooked out of doors for two months, sleeping in a hastily thrown up claim shanty until their log house was finished. To keep the shanty warm and to protect it from rain, they covered the roof with seven loads of hay and hung a quilt over the entrance.[14]

By contrast, other Wisconsin families moved expeditiously from Bay City on the east shore across the frozen Mississippi to the Minnesota side in the winter of 1865. Working together, they maneuvered each house onto broad, steel-shod runners so that half a dozen horses, hitched by ropes to a house, could pull it across the ice to the community of Lake City. There in a matter of hours they became Minnesota residents and householders simultaneously.[15]

The state's rivers not only served as the most important highways of settlement, they were also essential avenues of commerce. Dependence on river navigation and the growing demand for supplies were stressed by the *Minnesota Chronicle and Register*, a St. Paul newspaper, as early as March 2, 1850: "BUTTER, EGGS AND POULTRY. — We hope our provision dealers will see to having a good stock of these table essentials on hand by the 'first boat'. Butter of an inferior quality commands 25 cts. per pound, and eggs 30 to 35 cts. per doz. — scarce at that. . . . Poultry remarkably scarce at any price. Living is rather tough with us now that the venison season has passed; but the beef we have in our market is *tougher*." The absence of "wholesome food" in St. Paul in 1855 so profoundly impressed a woman from St. Louis that she recalled years later how difficult it was for her to adapt to such "vexations and privations." Fresh vegetables and fruits brought by boat from St. Louis were, she said, "often in such a condition upon their arrival at St. Paul that their use would have been deleterious to health." [16]

The arrivals of steamboats at the St. Paul levee were regularly reported in the newspapers. Both a welcome and a forecast appeared in the *Minnesota Pioneer*, on October 4, 1849, when it announced the arrival of "The old Dr. Franklin" after a 14-day trip up the Mississippi from St. Louis bringing "an immense cargo of merchandize and provisions. . . . There is needed in Saint Paul a much greater supply of provisions than we now have; of every kind. We are essentially, a hungry *beef-eating* people, who live by eating." That need increased as the coming of winter closed the river to navigation and the city's store of provisions dwindled.

Commission houses and grocers' advertisements heralding the arrival of new supplies each spring serve as inventories of the provisions carried upriver. Dried apples and peaches, spices, sugar, molasses, coffee and tea, barrels of oysters and boxes of herring and sardines, pep-

per sauce, and barrels of vinegar were among the supplies that arrived in 1849. Candy, pecans, filberts, almonds, and Brazil nuts were shipped, along with bourbon, wine, rum, gin, and brandy. Choice preserves, olive oil, codfish, sugar-cured hams, lemon syrup, raisins, chocolate, crackers, salt, rice, cheese, saleratus (baking soda), flour, corn meal, and barrels of salt pork suggest variety, and even a measure of luxury, for pioneer tables within the port towns.[17]

Although less ample amounts of provisions made their way to more remote areas over rudimentary roads and trails, it is apparent that food supplies in the river towns were indeed adequate at times. "We have now plenty to live on until spring," wrote the editor of the *Minnesota Pioneer* on November 20, 1851. "Let winter crack down. We have pork, beef, flour, butter, poultry, oysters, every thing that is good, and enough of it." From Rochester during the winter of 1855, when temperatures fell as low as 32 degrees below zero, Elizabeth Steere wrote to her sister: "We are all remarkably well and thriving in spite of the cold and capable of eating an allowance that would almost astonish an Arab. I never have been anything like as fleshy since I was married."[18]

Further evidence of the availability of food in the river towns is detailed in a "House Account" book kept by Elizabeth Fuller for her family of brothers and sisters in St. Paul in 1857. At that time the Fuller household numbered from eight to ten persons, and Elizabeth's record of store-bought provisions reveals that grocers and markets in the capital city on the Mississippi provided a variety of food. During January alone she bought 10 pounds of crackers for $1.50, 6½ pounds of salt pork for $1.10, 157 pounds of beef for $17.32, 10 pounds of codfish for $1.00, a gallon of vinegar at 25 cents, 5 pounds of dried apples for 62 cents, 125 pounds of venison for $13.75, mackerel at $5.50, 80 pounds of corn meal for $2.00, 5 pounds of rice for 63 cents, 2 hams totaling $3.66, 10 pounds of bear meat for $1.50, small amounts of olive oil, spices, and cream of tartar, and 20 pounds of butter for $7.00. One item apparently not available in continuing supply was eggs. Miss Fuller's account book indicates that she could not buy them from January, when she began the record, until April, when she purchased three dozen for $1.20.[19]

According to the accounts, the amount expended during January, 1857, for "Table" was about $58, while the total food budget for the entire year came to $884. Throughout the year the Fullers regularly purchased such essentials as fresh and salt meat, flour, eggs, vegetables, salt, cream of tartar, saleratus, and corn meal, along with walnut catsup, pepper, nutmeg, cinnamon, and vanilla, almond, and lemon extracts. Their kitchen stocks also held coffee (10 pounds for $2.00) and green tea ($1.00 a pound), molasses by the jug, sugar syrup, currants, citron, raisins, cranberries, pumpkins, onions, canned oysters, turkey, dried beef, pigeons, and elk meat.

Wild game, such as elk, deer, prairie chickens, partridge, and other fowl were taken by individual hunters or purchased from the town's meat dealers, who received their supplies from market hunters. Farmers, Indians, and others developed a source of income by selling the products of their hunting success to the merchants. During the winter of 1851, it was reported that Indians provided St. Paul markets with a five- to six-week supply of venison. The dealers sold the meat for nine cents a pound for the hind quarters and eight cents a pound for the remainder of the carcass. Two successful hunters earned over $200 a month from sales of game during a three-month period in the winter of 1853–54, and a meat dealer in St. Paul paid a market hunter $53 for a 311-pound buck deer.[20]

Passenger pigeons, once so abundant in the state they were a menace to crops, were killed "by hundreds and thousands" by both market hunters and farmers. The latter turned the destructive birds into a monetary profit by selling them to St. Paul meat markets. A family at Brooklyn Center during the 1850s snared pigeons by staking a net low to the ground and scattering corn under it to attract the birds. The pigeons "would stoop and go in under and pick up the grain," one woman recalled. "When they held their heads erect to swallow the corn, their necks would come through the meshes of the net and they could not escape."[21]

As late as August 22, 1880, the *Minneapolis Tribune* reported that market hunters were killing more prairie chickens than the citizens would buy from the merchants, albeit three days earlier the same newspaper had commented that the chickens were "unusually scarce" compared to previous years. Clearly there was no shortage of ducks on Heron Lake in southwestern Minnesota in 1885 when two brothers from Windom killed over 2,800 and sold them for a total profit of $700.[22]

Since the fur trade era, fish from Minnesota's inland lakes and Lake Superior had been a food staple also exploited commercially. As early as 1851 market fishermen caught pickerel through the ice, took them by cart and sled to St. Paul, and sold them at 20 to 25 cents a pair. The following year a group of men at Red Wing were providing salted catfish, buffalo fish, and carp to St. Paul buyers at $6 a barrel. By 1860 fisheries on Lake Superior had some 40 vessels plying the Minnesota shore bringing in fish for the St. Paul trade. Thus grocery stores in the Twin Cities of St. Paul and Minneapolis after 1850 offered not only the ever-popular salted codfish from the East, but fresh and dried fish as well. At Rochester, too, suppliers carried halibut, mackerel, herring, cod, trout, and whitefish.[23]

Largely uninhibited by laws limiting fishing, Minnesotans in the 19th century took as many fish as they could by hooks and line, spears, seines, even guns. Reports of catches that are almost unbelievable today dot the records between 1850 and 1900. For example, two men with hooks and lines took over 2,000 pounds of bass, pike, and pickerel in six weeks during 1851, and anglers in 1882 caught "exactly five hundred fish in four hours." With such abundance, fish was hardly ever in short supply, summer or winter.[24]

Like fish, wild fruits and wild rice augmented the early Minnesota town dweller's stock of store-bought provisions. Anyone interested in picking the wide variety of

fruits that grew wild throughout the state soon discovered the best nearby strawberry meadows, raspberry patches, cranberry bogs, and plum trees. Each summer Dakota Indian women brought wild gooseberries into St. Paul, where they sold them to the townspeople in 1851, for example, for about six cents a quart. Wild plums were sold in the towns, too, bringing $2 to $3 a bushel in 1855. Apparently wild rice was a new taste that had to be acquired by the white pioneers. In 1855 it was reportedly not too well liked by settlers, but by 1868, according to the *Sauk Rapids Sentinel* of September 25, the crop harvested by the Chippewa Indians was available for $4 to $5 a bushel — "a cheap article of diet and everybody likes it."[25]

While the general availability of food supplies gradually improved, some settlers continued to know scarcities caused by individual economic circumstances, remoteness from markets, and isolation intensified by weather conditions. The supply and demand equation, then as now, resulted in "good prices" for scarce foods in the market place in spite of protests from housewives. The unexpected closing of river navigation by an early winter immediately cut off the flow of provisions brought in by steamboats. Such recurring natural disasters as grasshopper plagues, hailstorms, and destructive winds also contributed to the shortages of homegrown foods. A hailstorm that struck Dodge County in 1855, reducing a subsistence farmer and his family to a winter's diet of rutabagas, wild tea, and whatever game could be killed, was not an isolated incident.[26]

Shortages and the total absence of some food supplies were characteristics of an era that many settlers in various parts of Minnesota experienced throughout the decade of the 1850s and well beyond. Thus the gradual improvements that eased the stringent conditions of their lives were all the more welcome. As the population increased so did the acres of land brought under the plow; subsistence farmers advanced to suppliers of produce for the market. Yields from the "luxurious soil," wrote a Mantorville editor in 1857, would abundantly supply the needs of "all the emigration that may flow to us before another harvest." Such natural optimism, and the editor's recognition of the value of his newspaper in encouraging immigration, were partly responsible for many roseate comments in the early press. Some editors, however, mixed a measure of realism into their appraisals of food supplies. "So far as flour, corn meal, buckwheat, and the bread staples generally, are concerned, our town and the country are abundantly supplied for the winter," recorded a Winona editor in 1857, "but we apprehend the pork, butter, and some varieties of groceries will be scarce enough ere the spring returns. . . . With plenty of good flour as ever the Genessee valley mills produced — potatoes in abundance, and 'hard to be beat' in quality — a pretty heavy 'sprinkling' of fresh beef — and as much game as our hunters can bag, we isolated Minnesotians can laugh and grow fat at a rapid rate this winter." Heartening evidence of an expanding agriculture appeared in the *Daily Minnesotian* of St. Paul on November 20, 1858: "For the first time in the history of Minnesota, we have raised enough to largely satisfy all home demand, and export to the amount of $300,000 to markets below." The following year cattle were exported from the state for the first time.[27]

The value of wider distribution of farm products was recognized as early as 1852 by the editor of the *Minnesota Pioneer*, who pointed out the growing need for a city market. He predicted that such a central establishment would double the produce brought into St. Paul for sale. Perhaps more important, vegetables, eggs, and other food products that were "brought from below, and sold at a profit by the stores, would soon be supplied from the country around us," and should the market be built "those who want to buy and sell would know when and where to meet together and trade." The city market did open a year later. Whether it fulfilled the editor's predictions is open to question. According to a St. Paul woman, the market at first consisted of "a two story almost square brick building without anything that would identify it as a place where food was sold. There were no stands or market wagons in the space around the building. The interior would have been entirely empty but for two stands where butchers were endeavoring to dispose of a poor quality of meat at a high price." The second floor served as a large hall for balls and public gatherings.[28]

The city market went through a period of struggle during its early years. Perhaps one reason for its limited success as a supplier of fresh produce was that many St. Paul residents cultivated home gardens and had ready access to wild fruits and game. With an economical source of corn, beans, and other domestic vegetables, as well as muskmelons, watermelons, and various fruit right in her own back yard, the St. Paul housewife had little reason to visit the market during the growing season. In addition, her abhorrence of waste and her desire for greater variety led her to take advantage of wild fruit. No doubt Sarah Fuller's "beautiful picking" in a patch of wild strawberries she discovered growing near the Fort Road (now West Seventh Street) was an experience shared by many St. Paul women. In any case, the market's "sorry aspect" in 1858 led one editor to ask, "Who depends upon our city market for supplies of vegetables? Yesterday, we could have taken all the vegetables in market away in a two bushel basket. A half bushel of onions, the same of turnips and carrots, and a few beets, made up the assortment. We noticed a handful of olive radishes, at the rate of 10 for a dime, and early lettuce at 5 cents a stalk." Despite its detractors, however, the city market represented another move to better serve consumers as well as producers, and it became an established institution as St. Paul grew from a rude river port into the state's capital city.[29]

As the steady increase in population created new demands for store-bought foods, St. Paul citizens also benefited from other innovations introduced by enterprising businessmen. Housewives could buy bread and cake at the Eagle Bakery as early as 1850. The owner advertised that all orders would be immediately attended to and that during the holiday season he would have fruitcake, poundcake and "Fancy cake" on hand. Refinements of another kind came two years later when residents discovered the confections offered at the newly opened soda fountain in the St. Paul Drug Store, and ice cream, one of the "new articles of luxury," became available at a bakery on Third Street.[30]

It is not surprising that ice cream — beloved since the heyday of the Roman empire — was among the lavish foods offered at the "Anniversary Festival in Commemoration of the Landing of the Pilgrim Fathers" held at the Fuller House in St. Paul on December 22, 1856. From the diverse menu, guests could select mock turtle or calf's head soup, followed by a choice of native fish — fried bass, stuffed pike, baked pickerel, or braised sunfish. Next came "Boiled" dishes that included chicken with egg sauce, leg of mutton with caper sauce, ham, corned beef, turkey with oyster sauce, and tongue. En-

FULLER HOUSE,

STEPHEN LONG, · · · · PROPRIETOR.

Saint Paul, Saturday, December 20, 1851

BILL OF FARE.

WINES.

WINES.

SOUP.
Vegetable.

FISH.
Baked Pickerel, Wine Sauce.

BOILED DISHES.
Mutton Caper Sauce.   Corned Beef Plain.
Ham, Wine Sauce.

ENTREES.
Culbert Heart,   Pork and Beans,
Venison Pie,   Hog's Head, Spice Sauce.
Lamb Chops Fried in Batter.

ROAST DISHES.
Beef, Pork, Mutton, Venison, Cranberry Sauce.

RELISHES.
Slaugh, Horse Radish, Beets, Walnuts, Celery

ALL THE VEGETABLES OF THE SEASON.

PASTRY.
Cranberry Pie,   Mince Pie,   Pumpkin Pie.
Plum Pie, Grape Pie, Brandy Jelly, Orange Jelly,
Indian Pudding,   Rice Pudding.

DESSERT.
Raisins,   Apples,   Almonds,   English Walnuts.

BREAKFAST, from 7 to 10 o'clock.   TEA, at 6 o'clock.
DINNER, from 11 2 to 4.   SUPPER, from 7 to 10 o'clock.
SERVANTS AND CHILDREN'S BREAKFAST, 8. DINNER 2 1-2, TEA 6 1-2.
Waiters are provided with   wine cards and pencil.
All articles not on the bill of   Fare will be charged extra

CHAMPAGNE.

Mumm & Co......3 00
Mumm's Imperial,3 00
Mumm's Cabinet, 3 00
Chas. Heidsick... 3 00
do. Cabinet..... 2 50
Piper Old Heidsick 2 50
Duc de Montabelle 2 50
De Brem't Verzy, 2 50
Anchor Grapes, 2 50
A. Du Temple A
Fils Fles de Raras 2 50
Sparkl'g Catawba, 2 50

**BORDEAUX,
RED AND
WHITE WINES**

St. Joseph Medoc 2 00
Le duc St. Julien, 2 50
Pichade Longaville,3 00
St. Julien, ... 1 50

**SPARKLING
HOCKHEIMER.**

Hochemier...... 2 00
Rudesheimer,.... 2 00
Johannesberger... 2 00
Sparkling Hock....
very superior,... 3 00
Sparkling Moselli.
Naterette.... 2 50

BRANDIES.

O. A. & Co. Pale, 2 00
do   Dark, 2 00
do   Nonpareil, 4 00
Pinet............2 00

SHERRY.

Amontillado, ...2 00
Fine Old Harmony 2 00
H. H. de Bashed, 2 00

PORT.

London Dock......2 00
Crown,...........2 00
Old White.........2 00

CORDIALS.

Anisei,...........2 00
Moraschemo......2 50
Absynth,.........2 00
Curteou,..........2 00

ALE & PORTER.

Alsopps, Rye India, 50
Younger & Son,....50
London Porter, ...50

trees were breaded veal cutlets with fried potatoes, chicken livers au gratin, blanquette of veal with capers, pork tenderloin with a sauce piquante, fricassee of chicken with oysters, boned turkey, ragout of giblets in wine sauce, Italian macaroni, or baked macaroni timbale. For guests who favored roasted meat or fowl, that, too, was available: beef, lamb, veal, saddle of venison with cranberry sauce, mutton, pork, young pig, turkey, and chicken.[31]

Nine kinds of pies — cranberry, peach, green apple, pumpkin, lemon, grape, plum, mince, and raisin — appeared on the dessert list along with such delicacies as ladyfingers, Madeira, rum, and brandy jellies, ice cream, blancmange, and jelly puffs. If those desserts lacked appeal, guests could request pound or spongecake, macaroons, wafer jumbles, raisins, apples, filberts, Brazil nuts, or almonds. Tea and coffee were available as well as an assortment of stronger drinks. The wine list included champagnes, Bordeaux, red and white wines, brandy, sherry, port, or sparkling Hochheimer. If interest still prevailed and a guest's appetite was not completely satiated, there were four cordials to choose from as well as ale and porter.

While special events were celebrated in the city with "great dinners," the service and setting of private gatherings were less formal. Social entertaining ranged in elegance from a housewarming at which "Supper was served on a work bench from victuals out of a wash tub" to Senator and Mrs. Alexander Ramsey's Christmas Day dinner in 1875 where guests enjoyed soup, roast pig, boiled turkey, oyster sauce, vegetables, mince pie, ice cream, fruit, and coffee. On other occasions Mrs. Ramsey, who was a native of Pennsylvania, served "German dishes" — a boiled dinner with sauerkraut, for example — when she knew her guests would particularly enjoy them. In between these two extremes was the dinner a farmer's wife prepared for friends in 1882 by dressing a turkey and baking pies and a cake.[32]

Some 30 years earlier one guest brought to a potluck sociable in Minneapolis a pork and dried apple cake; another furnished a "delicious" white cake that she was able to prepare only after an intensive effort to borrow the necessary white sugar. The party was held in the early spring, "always a scarce time" before the boats could get up the ice-clogged river and after the horse-drawn supply wagons had stopped their winter trips. In midwinter, 1849–50, a young housewife at St. Anthony (now a part of Minneapolis) learned to make cookies "without eggs, or even butter" and ate hasty pudding sweetened with molasses and lacking the milk she was accustomed to pour over it.[33]

Empty sugar bins were only one of many periodic food shortages the frontier housewife coped with almost routinely at the same time it was possible to hold sumptuous banquets in the capital of St. Paul. "We had company one Sunday when we first came and all we had to eat was a batch of biscuits," recalled Georgiana M. Way, who settled near Blue Earth in 1856. "They all said they was mighty good too and they never had a better meal." A Thanksgiving dinner in 1855 consisting primarily of fried cakes and rice pudding was recalled by a Faribault pioneer, while the family of a Martin County man that had endured a diet composed largely of potatoes happily greeted his return from a three-day, 40-mile trip to Mankato across the rain-soaked prairie in 1859 to bring home flour, meal, and other supplies.[34]

Within the compass of the half century between 1850 and 1900, improvements in home life came only gradually; progress was halting and uneven. Yet Minnesotans knew a great variety of changes, many of which they could not have predicted. The enterprising and innovative qualities responsible for the multifaceted advances in transportation, agriculture, and industry also generated a marked transformation in the home. At the beginning of the period, for example, the "first work" of a family that had traveled from the East to settle near Red Wing was to cover the bark roof of a one-room, dirt-floored cabin with "sods taken from our future garden, and to build a stone fireplace to warm our house and cook our food." By 1900 a family could enjoy a frame or brick house, indoor plumbing, linoleum-covered, wooden kitchen floors, a modern gas stove, and coal or steam heat to warm the rooms. Heavy iron cooking pots and kettles that had once hung over an open fire could be replaced with the new "pure aluminum" cookware, easily purchased from local stores or mail order houses.[35]

In the early years most provisions were stored in a cellar — many preserved by salting, drying, or smoking. Before the end of the period, perishable foods could be kept fresh in an icebox in the kitchen. The home water

supply, at first drawn from individual wells or hauled in pails from a lake or stream and poured into a water barrel, was in time brought directly into the house with a pump at the kitchen sink. The housewife who used stones or a washboard to scrub clothes could substitute the first awkward forerunners of today's washing machine. Rugs that had been beaten out of doors and then sprinkled with wet corn meal or damp tea leaves and swept with a dampened broom could by the 1870s be cleaned with a mechanized carpet sweeper. Some inventions that lightened the load of the housewife were as simple as the paper bag and the rotary egg beater (costing 9 cents from a mail order house in 1897). Others were vastly more complex. Home lighting, once dependent on candles, gave way to kerosene-burning lamps, then to gaslights, and lastly, for prosperous residents of urban centers, to electric lights. Well-to-do families in Minneapolis, St. Paul, and Duluth could also boast a telephone in their homes in the 1880s.[36]

More important to the women of the late 19th century than the laborsaving devices that lessened their work, however, were the major developments that greatly improved the well-being of their families, for these years also witnessed a growing recognition of the health hazards present in the food they ate and the water and milk they drank. Meat processed from diseased animals or butchered in unclean conditions, sanded sugar, butter "dotted with flyspecks," milk contaminated by chalk, careless handling, and dirty containers, ground beans mixed into coffee, headcheese made from diseased pork

"The Ideal Method of Sweeping."

— all were dangers to health. Some processors of commercially canned food added a variety of chemical adulterants — benzoic acid, borax, boric acid, salicylic acid, formaldehyde, and benzoate of soda — ostensibly to protect the contents of the cans. Contaminants such as arsenic, ammonia, or alum in baking powder, sulphate of copper added to processed green vegetables to enhance their color, and aniline dyes blended with fruit jam to improve its appearance presented additional threats. These practices clearly indicated the need for federal regulation that did not come until the Pure Food and Drug Act was passed by the United States Congress in 1906.[37]

Yet as early as 1855, St. Paul passed an ordinance requiring inspection of flour and "gauging" of liquors sold in the market. That action marked the beginning of a series of local regulations and official state public health inspections that were directed primarily toward adulterated dairy products, meat supplies, and water sources. Minnesota's first act to prohibit the sale or manufacture of contaminated and adulterated dairy products was passed in 1885. Violations — some as simple as adding water to milk — persisted, but offenses became less numerous as regulations were strengthened. From its outset, the act's low standard of a minimum 3 per cent fat content in milk generated agitation for improvement. Tuberculin testing of dairy cows did not begin until the 1890s, and even then the practice was limited to the Twin Cities and specific areas in the southern part of the state. As the program advanced, a safer milk supply became available in Minnesota, and it was further reinforced when pasteurization began in the century that followed.[38]

The effort to ferret out and condemn unsafe foods sold in Minnesota gained increasing support from its citizens and was encouraged by newspaper accounts and pointed editorial comments. A St. Paul health inspector in 1875 accused a butcher in the capital city of selling beef that was as "black as a hat." A perplexed citizen appealed to a St. Paul newspaper in 1877 for a method he could use to detect chalk or water in milk. Adulterated food and drink, lamented a St. Paul editor in 1879, was almost as general as food and drink itself. When Dr. William W. Mayo in Rochester analyzed and reported on the impurities he had found in sugars and syrups, one newspaper in 1880 heralded his efforts as the onset of "a war on adulteration, which can only benefit the public."[39]

Indeed the war was a continuing one, and its failures and successes were given wide currency in the newspapers. In Hutchinson during July, 1886, at least 40 persons were poisoned and several died as the result of eating locally made spiced beef. The following year the Minneapolis meat inspector condemned in one month more than 30,000 pounds of meat and poultry, prompting the *Minneapolis Tribune* to comment that "Meat Inspector [Thomas F.] Mea, if he keeps up the present racket, will reduce Minneapolis to a vegetarian diet." In the 1890s, a variety of spices, vinegar, and flavorings were confiscated because their adulterants proved injurious to health.[40]

Recognition that illness lurked in impure drinking water as well as in foods inspired health officers, public officials, and private citizens to install effective sanitation systems and to locate wells and cisterns so that water would be free from contaminating influences. A systematic survey of domestic water supplies in 1877 and 1878 revealed sufficient pollution to justify the initiation of an educational program by the state department of health. Still intermittent outbreaks of typhoid fever occurred to the end of the century and beyond, a fact that clearly demonstrated the continuing need to monitor urban and rural systems to eliminate sources of polluted water. Chlorination, the major treatment developed to safeguard public water supplies, was not used in Minnesota until 1910.[41]

The prevalence of botulism, a hazard to health not identified until 1895, cannot be measured.[42] The proliferation of commercially canned food and its greater acceptance following the Civil War prompted the editor of the *Stillwater Gazette* to remark on August 8, 1877, that "Now they have got canned Boston baked beans for sale at the groceries. If they keep on canning new things for the table, pretty soon a man will not need to get married at all. He can rent a room, buy a can opener, can live on the fat of the land, with a dog to lick off the plates."

That some apprehension concerning the use of canned foods existed, however, is shown by a column of "Household Hints" published in the *New Ulm Review* on October 14, 1885. "Few cooks appreciate as they should the necessity of draining and airing all canned vegetables," it read. "For canned peas (in tin), beans, tomatoes, or any other, always open them three hours before they are wanted. Drain off all the liquor and throw it away. Turn out the vegetables to evaporate and air upon a flat dish. Stir them up so that the air may reach them all through. A little trouble, to be sure; but it makes this kind of food much wholesomer; it gets rid of any gases that may have been formed in the can, as well as any of the corroded solder that may have dissolved out with the liquor."

Although the home-canning procedures described in the cooking literature of the period varied widely, greatest stress was usually given to "the exclusion of air [which] is the one thing needful to a successful result." Heating of the filled jars, which is fundamental to the destruction of harmful bacteria, was sometimes mentioned, and other related perils were recognized. The author of a book published in 1857 cautioned against the use of brass, copper, and bell-metal vessels for preparing pickles because of the disastrous effect of the metal on vinegar. She went on to applaud (and overstate) the fact that cookware made from these metals had been "nearly exploded from all kitchens; iron lined with Delft, (called porcelain,) being universally substituted." [43]

a, *Dover Egg-beater;* b, *Grater;* c, *Omelet Pan.*

That cooking and domestic life were changing, however, was demonstrated by a food exposition or, as it was also called, a "Pure Food show," held in the Minneapolis Armory during the first two weeks in October, 1894. The event was reported fully in the *Minneapolis Journal*, indicating that the housewife's interest in cookery had not diminished with the availability of processed foods. The show featured exhibits sponsored by local grocers and manufacturers of nationally distributed products. Highly touted was a gelatin "made by the same process our grandmothers used in making calves' foot jelly," which would bring "the same results without the labor of preparing the feet." Guests enjoyed free samples of gelatin desserts, baking powder biscuits, and coffee. A pyramid display of food was created from "thousands of good things from all parts of the world." Food in bottles and cans, delicacies of every kind — caviar, potted meats, foreign-made sausages, dried fruits, olives, and jellies — amply testified to the abundance and variety of foods available in Minnesota in 1894.[44]

Attendance at the exposition sharply increased during the hours each day when Sarah Tyson Rorer presented her cooking demonstrations. The prominent Philadelphia lecturer and cookbook author spiced her commentary with information on nutrition, suggestions on achieving artistry and skill in cooking, and her opinion that the best of the meat butchered in Chicago went to eastern markets. She also offered a liberal helping of gratuitous advice to the women of Minnesota on how to cope with the cold weather that had people shivering on the streets of Minneapolis. Knowing that Minnesotans were obsessively interested in the climate, she assured her audience that there was no need to fret about the weather or to be uncomfortable because of it. She advised her listeners to dress in loose clothing and low-heeled, broad-soled, heavy boots and "three pairs of stockings" for "comfort and health." She told them that "Well fed people never mind the weather," adding that careful attention to prop-

erly prepared food would ensure "an inch of healthy fat on the body" that was "worth more in keeping warm than a sealskin cloak."[45]

To the women who attended the food exposition, it must have seemed remarkable that housekeeping and cookery had come such a long way in 50 years. Those who had lived through the trying conditions of the frontier were especially aware of the changes that had taken place. It is the story of these changes — a less conspicuous but important part of our history usually overshadowed by "major" events — that we shall try to chronicle in the pages that follow.

Much of the information comes from the rich sources already mentioned. A good deal of material has been gleaned from household guides published between 1850 and 1900, most of which cover every possible aspect of homemaking. For local flavor, numerous cookbooks published by Minnesota church congregations, and prepared by dedicated ladies' societies as fund-raising projects, have been consulted.

The recipes and food-processing methods described in the text serve two purposes. First, they help us perceive the almost unbelievable amount of time and energy women had to expend just to keep food on the table. And second, when read in the context of today's world of advanced technology, fast foods, and women's liberation, they put into sharp focus just how much times have changed. Today's homemakers will wisely reject many of yesterday's preservation techniques as downright unsanitary and hazardous. On the other hand, the recipes presented may spur some readers to prepare foods in the recipe section "from scratch" just as their great-grandmothers did, thereby recapturing what many consider the best of "the good old days."

CHAPTER TWO

Bread — The Visible Symbol

FRESHLY BAKED homemade bread, the traditional symbol so much a part of our heritage, was frequently absent from frontier tables. During the financial disaster known as the Panic of 1857, for example, one Minnesotan observed that "people in the best condition financially were mighty glad if they had Johnny cake, pork and potatoes and milk and when they had these they thought they were on the 'top shelf.'"[1]

Many were not so fortunate. The late 1850s harshly tested the traditional optimism of Minnesota settlers, for recurring heavy rains and floods in the following summer of 1858 so badly blighted wheat ripening in the fields that few farmers bothered to harvest the crop. The small amounts of "soft and smutty" grain that were gathered and ground into flour at a gristmill yielded such a poor product that bread made from it was "almost black." One woman recalled that she had "no wheat to be made into flour, and no money with which to buy it . . . we did get

so tired of Johnny cake before the next wheat crop was harvested." Many families had no grain at all. One survived on a winter's diet of potatoes and maple syrup; another got along with a little milk, corn, and potatoes, "no flour, no meat." A woman spoke for many in this period when she said, "We went without many comforts heretofore deemed indispensable."[2]

The adaptability of frontier homemakers and their ability to "make do" was severely tried. Buckwheat ground in a coffee mill and made into cakes was a welcome supplement to one family's store of pork and wild game. To conserve virtually nonexistent funds, others who had wheat or corn also used their coffee mills to turn the grains into flour or meal. "Never shall I forget those long hours of grinding to furnish bread for five in the family," a woman recalled. "Never bread tasted sweeter. Some of the time I would grind corn for a change and make meal . . . we pronounced it good then. . . . While I was grinding the wheat we had bread only twice a day. At noon, for three weeks, there was nothing on the table except baked potatoes and salt. Finally the salt gave out." Another family picked corn when it was in the "dough grade" in order to grate it for use in bread.[3]

The absence of bread in rural or urban kitchens was as hard on morale as it was on health. Bread was not only a basic food, but the quality and goodness of the loaves that each housewife produced was considered the ultimate yardstick of her domestic accomplishments. The significance of the art of breadmaking was also nurtured and encouraged by cookbook authors, vocal pioneer home economists, and teachers in cooking schools of the time. Their voices united in a single chorus, so strong and sweeping that it submerged any other standard of the housewife's abilities.

"There is no one article of food of so great importance for the health and happiness of the family as bread," asserted Maria Parloa, author and cooking school teacher, in 1880. Therefore, she warned, "make it as nearly perfect as possible." A decade later Mrs. Willet M. Hays echoed the canon for the benefit of St. Paul women assembled at a cooking class held in a church in 1892. "There is nothing in cooking more important than bread making," she said. "Every woman should so thoroughly understand the principles involved in its preparation as to eliminate luck and always have perfect bread as a re-

sult of her time and labor expended, and the good whole-some food materials utilized in its preparation." These ladies were following the advice of such experts as Eliza Leslie, a prolific Eastern cookbook writer who had pointed out as early as 1857: "You cannot have good bread without good flour, good yeast, good kneading and good baking, all united." There it was — the challenge of breadmaking on the frontier.[4]

Whether such professional guidance was available to her or not, the Minnesota housewife facing the formidable task of baking day was best prepared if she knew exactly what "good flour" and "good yeast" were. A locally published volume entitled *Buckeye Cookery* described the former as that which "adheres to the hand, and, when pressed, shows the imprint of the lines of the skin. Its tint is cream white." Poor flour, the book explained, "is not adhesive, may be blown about easily, and sometimes has a dingy look, as though mixed with ashes."[5]

Up to about 1860, flour was generally made from soft winter wheat, although experiments in milling hard spring wheat were common. The winter variety produced flour with less gluten and was therefore not as good for making bread. Hard spring wheat, which was the type grown most successfully in Minnesota, produced a darker flour specked with bran, because the millstones were run close together in order to break the flinty, flour-containing endosperm. For years the milling industry struggled with the development of machines that would separate the coarse bits of the endosperm

called "middlings" from the unwanted bran with which they were associated. If they could be separated, the glutenous middlings of the spring wheat could then be reground into flour which was more acceptable in color.[6]

This revolution in flour milling came during the 1870s with the perfection of the middlings purifier, and thereafter Minnesota's spring wheat quickly replaced winter wheat in flour production. Hailing the "new process" flour in her cookbook, Maria Parloa called it "the equal of the best," and "so much superior in strength that one-eighth less is used in all recipes for bread and cake." Her comment on the flour's strength referred to its ability to make bread of acceptable shape, texture, and appearance — factors that depended on the amount and quality of protein in the wheat. Shortly after installing middlings purifiers, flour mills in Minnesota were able to replace millstones with rollers, and by 1880 Minneapolis became the flour-milling capital of the nation. The impact of this revolution was manifest in a variety of ways. To the local housewife, however, it meant a more accessible supply of an excellent, white flour made from Minnesota-grown, hard spring wheat.[7]

Formulas for the preparation of yeast, the other major ingredient in bread, as well as generous advice on its special care, appeared in many cookbooks published during the latter half of the 19th century. *Buckeye Cookery* told the housewife that potato yeast was best because "bread made with it is moister, and there is no danger of injuring the flavor of the bread by an excess of yeast." Soft hop or potato yeast would keep well for one or two weeks if stored in a cool place and for five or six weeks in cold weather if it was protected from freezing. The book cautioned readers not to add soda in an attempt to restore yeast that had soured, but acknowledged that soda would do as a starter for fresh yeast even though by itself it would *"never* make good bread." Mrs. Hays told her breadmaking class that she was partial to commercially made compressed yeast, but she allowed that homemade yeast was a satisfactory alternative.[8]

The 1881 edition of *Buckeye Cookery* furnished eight recipes for preparing homemade yeast. Essential to most were potatoes and hops, salt, sugar, and water. Pulverized ginger and flour were called for in some recipes. All but one formula required the addition of a specified amount of "good yeast" saved from the last batch as a starter for the next.[9]

The exception was "Yeast without Yeast," which had to be prepared two weeks before it was to be used. The instructions directed the cook to begin the process on Monday morning by boiling the hops in water, then straining the liquid into a crock. When the hop liquor had cooled to lukewarm, salt, "best brown sugar," and flour were added. Two days later boiled mashed potatoes were thoroughly mixed in, and on Thursday the mixture was strained into stoneware jugs with loosely set corks. After a day or two the corks could be put securely in place. The jugs filled with the developing yeast mixture were set near the fire, and their contents were stirred frequently for the next 14 days. Apparently the yeast became quite active, for the recipe cautioned the housewife to shake the jug before pouring out its contents and, once the cork was removed, to place "the palm of the hand over the mouth to prevent the escape of the yeast." An especially desirable quality of this "best yeast in the world" was that it would keep in a cool place without spoiling for "any length of time, improving with age." [10]

The attention to detail necessary in the home preparation of yeast of any kind was clearly outlined in a recipe for potato yeast. "Take as many hops as can be grasped in the hand twice, put one-half gallon water over them in a new coffee-pot kept for that purpose, boil slowly for one hour. Do not tie them in a cloth to boil, as that keeps the pollen (an important rising property) out of the yeast. Pare and grate half a dozen large potatoes into a two gallon stone crock, add a half cup sugar, table-spoon each of salt and ginger, pour over this a half gallon of the boiling hop-water, stirring all the time. When milk-warm, add one cup of good lively yeast, set in a warm place until

it rises, and remove to the cellar or some other cool place. The boiling hop-water must be added to potatoes *immediately* or they will darken, and darken the yeast. A good way to prevent the potatoes from darkening is to grate them into a pan half filled with cold water. As grated the potatoes sink to the bottom; when done grating, pour off the water and add the boiling hop-water."[11]

Dry yeast was also prepared at home from the same basic ingredients plus white corn meal, a thickening agent that allowed the yeast to be formed into cakes and dried. Success depended on rapid drying to prevent excessive loss of fermentation, a process that continued until all the moisture evaporated from the cakes. Although heat from the stove or the sun injured the yeast, the cakes had to be set to dry "where the air will pass freely." Sometimes they were crumbled to expedite the drying process. Since damp or hot weather also caused a loss in the "vitality" of the yeast cakes, they were stored in paper sacks in a dry, cool place. One small cake made "a sponge sufficient to bake five or six ordinary loaves." One yeast cake was supposedly the equivalent of two-thirds of a teacup of yeast crumbs, a pint of potato yeast, a teacup of hop yeast, or a piece of compressed yeast the "size of a walnut."[12]

No matter how excellent her yeast formula, yesterday's housewife also needed considerable experience to produce good bread. She had to take into account the vagaries of the seasons to avoid having the yeast sour in summer or freeze in winter. She needed to know that certain conditions which helped bread dough rise in the winter would cause it to sour in the summer. She must be aware that a freshly made batch of yeast would spoil if she failed to wash thoroughly the stoneware vessels used for storing it. She also learned that when "yeast smells sour but does not taste sour it is still good; if it has no smell it is dead."[13]

To produce good bread that made "the homeliest meal acceptable, and the coarsest fare appetizing," the housewife began by preparing a sponge of water or milk, yeast, and flour or mashed potatoes. The milk had to be scalded first to prevent souring; water, if it was used, had to be made "as warm as can be borne" when tested with the fingers. The warmth of the wetting agent was particularly important in the winter; in very hot weather the sponge could be made with cold water. If water were used, the addition of a small amount of lard or butter contributed to the bread's tenderness. Yeast was added last, with care to be certain the sponge was not so hot that it would scald and thus destroy the action. Fifteen minutes of beating "like batter for a cake" was said to improve the sponge. The cook was also warned to set the sponge in a stoneware container (large enough to accommodate the sponge as it rose) in order to maintain a "more steady" temperature, a condition impossible to achieve if tin were used. To keep its temperature as constant as possible, the housewife could also cover the jar with a clean blanket folded several times. The proper time of day for setting the sponge depended on the season — earlier on winter evenings when the kitchen cooled quickly, and later during the warmer months when the kitchen temperature was 80 to 90 degrees.[14]

Summer or winter, the housewife was compelled to rise "at the peep of day" if she wanted to be certain the sponge would not sour in hot weather or to get the flour properly heated before she mixed it into the sponge in cold weather. Such prudence, however, did not automatically guarantee good bread. Proper kneading, watchfulness in allowing the bread to rise to the right degree of lightness, and, lastly, care in baking in an oven "just hot enough" were additional hazards.[15]

Although wooden bowls might be used, a large, seamless tin dishpan was preferred both for mixing the flour and salt with the sponge and, with the cover securely in place, for the first rising of the dough. During the first step, care was necessary to avoid getting the dough too stiff before turning it out onto a breadboard. After adding the "rubbings" that were taken from the tin pan, the dough was kneaded for 45 minutes to an hour. The housewife knew that any pause or interruption in this process would adversely affect the bread. When the dough was thoroughly kneaded, it was shaped into a large loaf or "round mass" and placed in a tin pan in which flour had been sprinkled. Salted lard, butter, or flour was then spread lightly over the top of the dough, the cover was secured, and the pan was put in a warm place for one to two hours while the dough doubled in size.[16]

When it reached the proper lightness, the dough was kneaded again and cut into equal portions. The loaves were formed, placed side by side in a greased baking pan, and the tops lightly covered with butter or salted lard. They were then set in a warm place for the second rising — "the point where observation and discretion are so indispensable." The weather, the quality of the yeast, and the perfection of the first rising all influenced the time necessary for the loaves to expand "so as to seam or crack," which was the precise moment that they were ready to bake.[17]

Properly raised bread required two fermentation periods: "the saccharine or sweet fermentation, and the vinous, when it smells something like foaming beer." Any leavening action beyond that point — even if soda was added to redeem dough that had soured — was said to be destructive to the nutritious properties of the bread. If the loaves reached the third, undesirable "acetous fermentation" stage before they were put in the oven to bake, the inevitable result was loss of freshness, or souring of the dough, or an accelerated drying of the bread after it was baked.

Although it was to be avoided in yeast breads, the acetous fermentation stage was vital in the preparation of salt-rising bread. Containing no yeast, salt-rising bread was started with a batter of flour or corn meal, warm water or milk, and salt to form the "rising." The bowl containing these well-beaten ingredients was then set in a pan of water which had to be kept at a uniform temperature throughout the two to four hours needed for the batter to leaven. During this period of acetous fermentation, the mixture emitted a strong odor. While the smell might

THE LITTLE HOUSEKEEPER.

be objectionable, it was a source of comfort to the experienced baker, because it assured her that the bread would be sweet when baked. To encourage the development of leaven, coarse flour or "shorts" — a low-grade flour containing principally the germ and fine bran — were often used in the batter instead of finely ground flour.[18]

The making of salt-rising bread was a touchy business. In spite of the housewife's care to use coarse flour, to combine and beat the ingredients well, and to keep the water pan warm during the fermentation, the leaven was doomed to failure at the very start if the water used in the batter exceeded a temperature of 90 degrees. "The bread is simpler [than yeast-raised dough]," according to *Buckeye Cookery*, "but not so certain of rising." Indeed it was understood that few cooks could do well in making "sour emptyings bread." "It took judgment," a Minnesota housewife stated immodestly, "but everyone thought there was nothing like it." This woman had her own variation of the basic recipe. She stirred together flour, sugar, and water "until it was a little thicker than milk, then set it aside to sour. When it was thoroughly sour, I put in my saleratus, shortening and flour enough to make it stiff." Salt-rising bread did not require as much kneading as yeast dough, but warm surroundings and ample time for proper rising were as indispensable to its success as to that of yeast-leavened bread.[19]

Even if all had gone well up to the critical time of baking, a batch of bread could still be ruined if the housewife ignored the adage that "The little fairy that hovers over successful bread-making is heat, not too little nor too much, but uniform." A "steady, moderate heat" was required that could be sustained in the oven throughout the 45 minutes to an hour baking period. Moreover, just the right heat had to be available at the critical time when the loaves of bread reached the ideal stage of rising. This feat required that a woman be well acquainted with the idiosyncrasies of her stove, which was a major accomplishment in itself.[20]

Even though stoves in those days had no temperature controls, there were several ways to gauge the oven heat. The housewife could merely put her bare hand and arm into the oven, and if she could bear the heat while she counted to 20 at a moderate speed, the temperature was right. A more comfortable method was to place a small amount of flour on a bit of old crockery in the middle of the oven. If the flour turned brown in one minute's time, the heat was right for baking bread. Still another test was to place a sheet of ordinary white writing paper in the oven. If it turned buff or yellow in color, the heat was considered proper. An oven that was too hot caused the paper to burn, and the stove's dampers then had to be adjusted to reduce the temperature.[21]

Because "a *freshly-made* fire cannot be easily regulated," a hot fire using ample amounts of wood had to be kindled well ahead of time and allowed to burn down to a moderate, steady heat. A coal fire had to be big enough (but not too big) to sustain the oven heat throughout the baking period. To add more fuel during the baking process would cause irregular temperatures.[22]

Loaves baked side by side in a single large bread pan

CAST IRON
BREAD PANS.

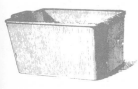

could be tested for doneness by separating them and gently pressing the side with a finger; "if elastic it is done, but if clammy, not done, and must be returned to the oven." The broomstraw method for testing bread was especially valuable for loaves baked singly. Before the straw was inserted into the loaf, its branches were broken off to expose the "little projections" to which insufficiently baked dough would cling when the straw was removed. Knitting or trussing needles were sometimes substituted for a straw in this test.[23]

After they were taken from the oven and removed from the pans, the thoroughly baked loaves of bread could be greased all over on the outside with melted butter and then set on edge to cool. Some housewives preferred to wrap the loaves in a slightly dampened towel called a bread cloth before tilting them on edge. After it was completely cooled, the bread could be kept in a tin wash boiler with a tight fitting cover, in a stoneware jar, or in a tin box. The receptacle needed to be well washed and dried before fresh bread was put into it.[24]

Eliza Leslie's basic recipe for "setting the sponge" was probably similar to those of pioneer housewives in Minnesota. "Sift into a deep pan, or large wooden bowl," she wrote, "a peck of fine wheat flour, (adding a large tablespoonful of salt,) and mix the water with half a pint of strong fresh brewer's yeast, or near a whole pint if the yeast is home-made. Pour this into the hole, in the middle of the heap of flour. Mix in with a wooden spoon, a portion of the flour from the surrounding edges of the hole so as to make a thick batter, and having sprinkled dry

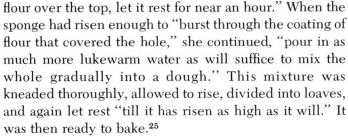

flour over the top, let it rest for near an hour." When the sponge had risen enough to "burst through the coating of flour that covered the hole," she continued, "pour in as much more lukewarm water as will suffice to mix the whole gradually into a dough." This mixture was kneaded thoroughly, allowed to rise, divided into loaves, and again let rest "till it has risen as high as it will." It was then ready to bake.[25]

Other recipes for making yeast breads of many types found their way into later cookbooks. *Buckeye Cookery* offered the contributions of several Minnesota women, including directions for "Bread Sponge" from a Minneapolis housewife. It called for "Six potatoes boiled and mashed while hot, two table-spoons of white sugar, two of butter, one quart tepid water; into this stir three cups flour; beat to a smooth batter, add six table-spoons yeast; set over night, and, in the morning, knead in sufficient flour to make a stiff, spongy dough; knead vigorously for fifteen minutes, set away to rise, and, when light, knead for ten minutes; mold out into moderate-sized loaves, and let rise until they are like delicate or light sponge-cake."[26]

A simple bread recipe for "six medium sized loaves" was written down by a woman for her church's cookbook. It told readers to "take four quarts of sifted flour, a teaspoon salt, and one cup yeast. Mix with warm water until stiff enough to knead. Work well fifteen minutes, and let it stand in a warm place over night. In the morning knead again, and make into loaves. Bake as soon as light, in a moderate oven."[27]

A variation on white bread was "Minnesota Rolls." "Rub one-half table-spoon of lard into one quart of flour," the recipe read, "make a well in the middle, put in one-half cup baker's yeast — or one cup of homemade — two tea-spoons sugar, one-half pint cold boiled milk; do not stir, but let stand over night; in the morning knead well, after dinner [*the midday meal*] knead again, cut out, put in pans, and let rise until tea time. Bake in a quick oven."[28]

A woman from Litchfield contributed her directions for "The Bread of our Forefathers" to *Buckeye Cookery*. This batter bread was, she wrote, "excellent when cold." To make it, "Put in a pan two quarts of [corn] meal, a half-pint of flour, stir up well; pour in the center a pint of boiling water, stir up enough of the meal to make a thin batter; when cool, put in a cup of yeast, a tea-spoon of salt and enough warm water to make a thick batter; let rise, then place in a deep, well-greased pan, cover with another pan, and place in a moderate oven. When nearly done, remove the cover, and bake slowly until done."[29]

To be found in most mid-19th-century cookbooks (and in those of today) were recipes for "Sally Lunn," the slightly sweetened yeast bread that originated in England and was named for the woman who, it is said, first made it to sell in the streets of Bath. A Minneapolis woman assured users of her church's cookbook that her recipe was for "the old fashioned Sally Lunn." It was made of "One quart of flour, four eggs, one-half cup melted butter, one cup warm milk, one cup water, four tablespoonfuls yeast, one teaspoonful salt, one-half teaspoonful soda dissolved in hot water. Beat the eggs to a stiff froth, add the milk, water, butter, soda and salt; stir in the flour to a smooth paste, and beat the yeast in well; set to rise in a buttered pudding dish, in which it is baked and sent to the table. It will not be light for six hours. Bake steadily from one-half to three-fourths of an hour, or until a straw thrust into it will come out clean. Eat while hot."[30]

On breadmaking day, part of the rising dough might be interrupted on its way to becoming loaves and made into fried bread. *Buckeye Cookery* called the result "Bread Puffs," though it was also known as "Pan Doodles," "Doughbellies," and other names as well. One recipe suggested that "If the wheat bread is light enough for the oven at breakfast time, have ready some hot lard in a deep kettle; with the thumb and two fingers pull up some of the dough quite thin, and cut it some two or three inches in length; as these pieces are cut, drop them in the lard and fry like doughnuts. At table they are eaten like biscuit; they may also be served in a vegetable dish with a dressing of hot cream, seasoned with pepper and salt." In many homes, the fried bread was eaten with maple syrup or molasses for breakfast.[31]

Should bread become dry or stale, it was used to make breakfast toast by dipping slices in sweetened milk and egg, frying it on a buttered griddle, and serving it with butter and powdered sugar. An "Excellent Toast" was to be made from "sweet, light bread, only a day old or less." *Buckeye Cookery* gave full directions, commenting "Although toast is commonly used, few know how to prepare it nicely." The reader was told to "Cut slices of a uniform thickness, of half an inch; move around over a brisk fire, to have all parts toasted alike; keep only so near the coals that the pieces will be heated through when both sides are well browned. If the slightest point is blackened or charred, scrape it off, or it will spoil the flavor of the whole. If covered with an earthen bowl, it will keep both warm and moist."[32]

The baked goods known today as quick breads — those that contained no yeast and required no period of rising — were widely used on the Minnesota frontier. Mixed in a manner similar to that for cake, the breads depended on "yeast powders" — as one authority called baking powder and tartaric acid — to give them lightness. Baking soda was used in combination with sour milk or buttermilk, as it is today, to release the carbon dioxide that causes the bread to rise. If sweet milk was called for in a recipe, an acid, such as cream of tartar with baking soda, had to be added to achieve the desired result. Other alternatives included pearlash, a purified form of potash, and hartshorn, a carbonate of ammonium also called *sal volatile*.[33]

To Eliza Leslie hartshorn was an "abomination"; its presence in bread and cake she felt rendered "the articles equally unpalatable and unwholesome." To underscore her revulsion, she asked, "Cannot the use of hartshorn in food be put down? Which of our *American* doctors will write a book on 'culinary poisons.'" Twelve years later Catherine Beecher and her sister, Harriet Beecher Stowe, described hartshorn in less harsh terms. It is a "volatile alkali," they wrote, "originally prepared from the horns of the stag or hart, but now procured from various other substances. It is known by the name of ammonia or spirits of ammonia." They considered pearlash a "common name for impure carbonate of potash, which in a purer form is called *Saleratus*." Cream of tartar, they explained, was developed from "crude tartar," an element "deposited on the inside of wine casks, consisting chiefly of tartaric acid and potass [*sic*]." The substance was "separated from all its impurities by being dissolved in water and then crystallized, when it becomes a perfectly white powder." Tartaric acid, they wrote, was a "vegetable acid which exists in the grape."[34]

Baking powder, a combination of baking soda and an acid salt such as cream of tartar, was a modern convenience first marketed in the middle of the 19th century. It was too new to be widely accepted, too suspect because of its questionable purity, and condemned as well for its high cost and poor performance. Thus it was conspicuously absent from recommended ingredients until late in the century. Plain soda and plain cream of tartar were better, according to some strong-minded authors. Over the years, however, natural prejudice slowly gave way to cautious, sometimes grudging, acceptance with scattered acknowledgments that "good" baking powder might be used in certain recipes.[35]

Minnesota housewives were correspondingly divided in their approval. For example, a Minneapolis woman's recipe for muffins called for "One quart of flour, one pint of milk, three tablespoonfuls of sugar, two eggs, two teaspoonfuls of cream tartar, and a small teaspoonful of soda, shortening the size of an egg." In the same cookbook appeared a recipe for "Hannah's Gems," which required "Two eggs, two large spoons sugar, a teaspoonful of salt, a small piece of butter, two small cups sweet milk, two teaspoons baking powder, and three tea cups Graham flour." Recipes contributed to church-sponsored cookbooks indicate that some Minnesota women continued to favor the separate additions of baking soda and cream of tartar over baking powder well into the 1890s.[36]

Even today the problems of determining equivalent amounts of the various types of baking powders now on the market have not been completely solved by modern cooks or cookbook authors. Irma S. Rombauer, coauthor of *The Joy of Cooking*, admitted that the complexities of baking powders became for her "one of life's major issues." In her ongoing experiments, however, she was able to determine to her own satisfaction the equivalent amounts of the three types of baking powders — tartrate, calcium phosphate, and combination or double-acting — for each recipe included in her cookbook. Another author helpfully stated that "one teaspoon 'double-acting' baking powder equals 1½ teaspoons of tartrate baking powder." But it should be noted that when following 19th-century recipes calling for baking powder, it is still largely a matter of experimentation to figure out how much to use.[37]

As early as 1881 the enterprising St. Paul manufacturer of Snow Flake baking powder sought to promote his product by publishing a cookbook of "carefully selected

and practical recipes" for biscuits, cookies, gems, waffles, rolls, popovers, doughnuts, and cakes. To stress the purity of his product and promote its acceptance by home bakers, he offered an award of $1,000 to anyone who could prove that Snow Flake's product was "anything but a Strictly Pure Cream Tarter Powder." The "recently improved formula," he claimed, "contains more carbonic acid to the pound than any other Powder made." At the same time, he emphasized the product's economy, asserting that a pound of Snow Flake baking powder would raise "Twenty Pounds More bread than any other in the market."[38]

Recipes for homemade baking powder were not uncommon late in the century. They called for bicarbonate of soda and tartaric acid with either flour or cornstarch mixed into the combination. A chemist's recipe for homemade baking powder, containing "Cream of tartar, 6 ozs.; bicarbonate of soda, 2⅔ ozs.; flour, 4½ ozs.," was claimed to be "a receipt for one of the best brands . . . sold by the trade."[39]

Biscuits, johnnycakes, popovers, waffles, griddle cakes, fritters, seemingly innumerable doughnuts, and even English crumpets were among the "Breakfast and Tea Cakes" made by Minnesota housewives. They also baked their own crackers following such simple recipes as this one from a Stillwater cookbook: "Two pints of flour, 1 pint of sweet cream, and the yolks of 3 eggs. Roll out thin and bake quickly." In that same collection, published in 1893, appeared a recipe for "Beaten Biscuit" which is nearly identical to that for "Maryland Biscuit" supplied by Eliza Leslie in 1857. The first recipe reads:

"To 1 quart of flour add 1 tablespoonful of lard and 1 teaspoonful of salt; mix with sweet milk in water; work or pound until they snap like cracker dough; make out small, stick with fork, bake in quick oven. Do not cut them, and be sure to stick them or they will be sad." Miss Leslie indicated that the kneading and pounding "must go on for two or three hours, continually," making the biscuit "the most laborious of cakes, and also the most unwholesome, even when made in the best manner. We do not recommend it," she added, "but there is no accounting for tastes."[40]

When each long baking day came to an end, the 19th-century housewife might comfort herself with the "old and true saying, that 'she who has baked a good batch of bread has done a good day's work.'" The writers of *Buckeye Cookery* assured her that she had performed "the most important task of the kitchen queen." A cook who regularly turned out "Light, crisp rolls for breakfast, spongy, sweet bread for dinner, and flaky biscuit for supper" could be certain that her efforts would "cover a multitude of culinary sins." In addition, she was reminded that there was "no one thing on which the health and comfort of a family so much depends as the quality of its homemade loaves."[41]

THE KEY TO A HAPPY HOME.

CHAPTER THREE

A Cool Dry Place

FOR ALL the emphasis given to breadmaking, it was only one of the 19th-century housewife's many activities. Almost everything she put on the table required special skills or special knowledge that the passage of time has since rendered not only obsolete but also unnecessary and in some cases dangerous. Perhaps the most important of the frontier homemaker's responsibilities was how to conserve and store food so that it did not spoil.

Among her most helpful aids were the springhouse and the cellar — words that have virtually disappeared from the vocabularies of people in many parts of the United States today. The old-fashioned functions of springhouses and cellars as places to store food have now been taken over by the development of electrical refrigeration and modern transportation systems which more efficiently handle food distribution. But a century ago they figured prominently in the efforts of both urban and rural housewives to keep food safe enough to eat over short and long periods of time.

59

For a frontier housewife, the problem of food storage was twofold — perishables had to be kept on a short-term, day-to-day basis, and supplies of staples as well as garden produce had to be stored in such ways that they remained edible from one season to the next. The short-term storage of milk, cream, and butter, particularly in the hot summer months, was an especially difficult challenge that remained until the end of the century, when iceboxes and icehouses came into general use. But many more foodstuffs had to be stored over the long winter, and most of these required a cool, dry place.

To early Minnesota settlers lucky enough to have a spring-fed pond or stream on their property, the springhouse was indispensable. The water provided a measure of cooling that was increased by the protective insulation of the structure's walls. Within the springhouse cans of milk, jars of cream, tubs of butter, and possibly some cheese could be kept for short periods of time even in warm weather. Some pioneer Minnesotans gave considerable thought to the construction of their springhouses. One farmer who lived near Minneapolis designed and built his in an eye-catching octagonal shape. In the infant settlement of Minneapolis itself, another man located his home so that the kitchen door faced Loring Lake, where he planned to build a springhouse. Thus it would be convenient for the family to fetch its milk and butter at the same time its members carried water to the house.[1]

Even wells or cisterns dug deep into the earth were used as places where perishables could be suspended by a rope to hang above the water in the cool hollow of the chamber. They were considered more desirable for storing dairy products than underground cellars or ground-level storage closets, where vegetables were kept along with other raw and processed foods. It was widely recognized that the "steam and vapor arising from the vegetables" affected the taste of the milk and butter.[2]

Nevertheless the most generally used food-keeping places were the underground cellar, the ground-level storage closet, and the root cellar. The latter was a cavelike structure dug into a hillside with good natural drainage; it was considered especially useful for storing raw garden produce or fruit. In the 1850s an Eden Prairie farmer was inspired to build a log "root-cellar in the hillside" to accommodate a "most remarkable yield of potatoes." His efforts were rewarded the following spring when he sold the crop for $1.05 a bushel and, as a result, accumulated enough money to buy two horses. Some settlers favored the root cellar over a cellar under the house, because it was unaffected by the "fires kept up . . . during winter" that encouraged decay or "commencement of growth in vegetables" kept below. Like the cistern, the separate root cellar eliminated the "gaseous substances of an unpleasant odor" that developed from the vegetables and were known to "pervade the dwelling."[3]

The cellar and the ground-level storage closet served the same purpose, but the latter had the added benefit of no "woman-killing stairs," as one authority called them. Unlike the usual pantry, a storage closet was built to certain specifications. The walls, for example, were double with an airspace between; there should be double windows and doors as well, and good floor drainage. It was desirable to locate the store closet so that it was "open from a kitchen," where the atmosphere could be kept dry, but never warm, from the kitchen fire to prevent "the articles stored from moulding, and other injury from dampness. . . . A *cool* and *dry* place," said Catherine Beecher, "is indispensable for a store-room, and a small window over the door, and another opening out-doors, is a great advantage, by securing coolness, and a circulation of fresh air."[4]

While ground-level storage closets were frequently used, more often the cool dry place for storing foodstuffs was provided by an underground cellar. "The cellar, when properly constructed and cared for, is the most useful room in the house, and no dwelling is complete without one," stated a household guide in 1881. Ideally it possessed the same attributes as storage closets and root cellars — good drainage, an adequate source of fresh air that could circulate freely within the room, cool storage conditions in the summer, and sufficient warmth in winter to protect the foods from freezing. There is evidence, however, that many cellars in Minnesota failed to meet these qualifications, especially during severe winters like that of 1881. "The contents of half the cellars in the city are more or less frozen," reported a Stillwater newspaper that year.[5]

Settlers devised several methods of retaining warmth in an effort to counteract Minnesota's extremely cold winters. One was to bank dirt against the house, but even that did not always keep the frost from penetrating the cellar. A Freeborn County resident claimed the best way to "frost-proof" the area was to apply four or five thicknesses of coarse brown paper or newspapers to the walls, "the bare joists overhead," and the windows. A thorough sweeping down of the walls had to precede the application of the insulating paper, which was secured with a "very strong size" or paste.[6]

That many homes, hastily built for the influx of new residents, were constructed without good cellars gave the *St. Paul Daily Press* reason to complain in 1863. Thus it is no wonder that an earlier resident of St. Anthony in 1850 proudly reported to the folks back East that he had "the best cellar in Town," remarking that it contained "the only Cistern in the Village" and had a floor of smooth rock. More often than not, cellars were merely dug out areas with dirt floors. Usually there was no source of heat, and they were unlighted except perhaps for a narrow window or two laced with cobwebs. If the walls were whitewashed, the cellars seemed brighter. According to Miss Beecher, the whitewash should be made of unslacked lime mixed with hot water and "nearly saturated with salt." Fine sand was sometimes added to the mixture to make it "thick like cream." *Buckeye Cookery* also suggested that the addition of carbolic acid would do away with disagreeable odors and that copperas would drive away vermin.[7]

Getting to the cellar could also be a problem for a housewife who lacked agility. Summer access was usu-

ally provided by a slanting outside door that covered a stairway. In winter, unless the home was exceptionally modern, entry was gained through an inside trap door in the floor that opened on steep steps leading downward. Many houses, however, had no inside access of any kind, making it necessary for the cook to slip and slide over ice or wade through deep snowdrifts to reach her larder. Woe be to the forgetful woman who failed to bring back all she needed and thus had to make repeated trips in the arctic cold.[8]

Whether of good or bad design, these underground rooms stored a variety of provisions. Writing in 1853, a St. Paul woman described the bounty in her cellar. It was "filled with potatoes, cabbage, Turnips, Beans, Molasses, Onions, Apples, 8 Turkeys, 3 barrel flour, 20 lbs. sperm candle, 4 of chicken, 50 dozen Tallow Candle for the kitchen, 7 pound sage, 10 pound dried pumpkin, 2 bags Buckwheat, 10 dz Eggs, 30 pound butter."[9]

The importance of the cellar and the housewife's need to maintain it as a dependable storage place for food were clearly evident in the advice that regularly appeared in the helpful hints columns of the newspapers. Detailed instructions for the care of the cellar were also included in the domestic guides published both before and after 1900. On July 20, 1887, the *New Ulm Review* printed a timely article on "The Cellar in Summer." It warned readers that "At this season the cellar must be kept cool, dry, ventilated and clean. The doors must be kept closed as much as possible during the day, but they may be opened about midnight, and remain open until early morning. During the latter half of the night the air is cool, and air must be admitted to keep the cellar dry and pure. If kept clean, not a great deal of airing will be needed.

"If the cellar is damp, fruits and vegetables decay sooner, and it is more unhealthful than is generally supposed. Many attacks of fever, and diptheria, or other diseases, result from damp, unventilated, unclean cellars. Keeping the cellars clean and ventilated, is the best way to keep it dry; it may be necessary to use other means. Lime placed in the cellar will absorb moisture and noxious gases, and thus help to keep the air pure. Charcoal is also a great absorber of gases.

"The temperature of the cellar may be lowered by putting a tub of broken ice and salt in. The rapid melting of the ice cools the air. This will be convenient when a considerable quantity of fresh meat or fruit is to be preserved. It is impossible to keep the cellar in good condition unless the drainage is efficient, and there is a proper arrangement of doors and windows. Double ones are needed to keep the temperature at the right point in summer as well as in winter."

Catherine Beecher issued a similar warning on the dangers of decaying vegetables. She urged that they be disposed of immediately to prevent development of a "miasma, that sometimes causes the most fatal diseases." Other threats to the safekeeping of foodstuffs were mold, rodents, and insects, a combination that required the housewife's ceaseless vigilance in a period when aerosol sprays were unknown.[10]

It helped to know what quantitites were judged safe for

MOUSE TRAP.

long-term storage, the proper vessels in which to store certain foods, and the wrappings each kind required. For even if "miasma" failed to develop, waste surely would. Thus the knowledgeable housewife avoided buying brown sugar by the barrel for it was "apt to turn to molasses, and run out on to the floor." The loaf sugar she used for tea was wrapped in papers and stored on a shelf. Crushed or granulated sugar for sweetmeats, raspberry vinegar, or "for the nicest preserves and to use with fruit, nice brown sugar for coffee, and common brown for cooking and more common use" in pies, fruit cakes, or Indian puddings were stored in kegs with securely fitting covers or in other "covered wooden articles made for the purpose." Minnesota commission houses in the 1850s offered a number of varieties of sugar for sale, among them "prime," "loaf crushed" and "powdered." The latter was to be used, said *Buckeye Cookery*, for "light colored" desserts and cakes."[11]

Grades and types of sugar in the 19th century were confusing, because the terminology was not standardized and varied with the whim of the writer. The white sugar that many Minnesota housewives bought was shaped in loaves or in solid five-pound cones wrapped in blue paper. To use it, the cook chipped off as much as she needed and then rewrapped the cone. When all the sugar was gone, one housewife added the blue wrapping paper to boiling water to produce a "lovely lavender shade" that she used to dye silk crepe and other delicate fabrics.[12]

Some dry stores, such as salt, required attention before

they were placed in the cellar. The importance of salt and its care made so strong an impression on a 12-year-old girl who arrived at Mankato with her family in 1853 that years later she recalled "The want of salt bothered the pioneers more than anything else." Then as now salt was considered a necessity and the demand for it often exceeded the supply in early years. The cost of transporting salt to Minnesota from Syracuse, New York, and Saginaw, Michigan, (the principal sources during the 19th century) resulted in high prices that made salt a dear commodity for most settlers. Several grades of salt were available from the grocers — coarse for curing meats, fine for table use, and dairy for curing butter — and none of it was to be wasted. Rock salt, considered by some best for table use, had to be "washed, dried, pounded, sifted," and then stored in a covered glass jar in a dry place. If the salt became damp in spite of her care, the housewife set it near the fire to dry, pulverized it again, then returned it to a dry box or glass container.[13]

Even more injunctions governed the storage of flour, which was generally purchased by the barrel, containing 196 pounds. Ideal conditions dictated that the barrel have a close-fitting cover to "keep out mice and vermin," and that it be placed in a cool room where it would not be subjected to freezing temperatures or to intense summer heat. Even artificial heat above 70 to 72 degrees Fahrenheit was considered undesirable over an extended period of time. Since flour was "peculiarly sensitive to atmospheric influence," storage areas where the odor of onions, sour liquids, or fish affected the quality of the air had to be avoided. Frequently the flour settlers purchased arrived in a less than fresh state. A Lake Crystal family discovered a barrelful so "musty" it had to be chopped from the container with an ax and grated before it could be used. Because flour would settle and pack down during storage, housewives were advised to sift it, and when all the "particles thoroughly disintegrated," to warm the flour before it was used for baking.[14]

Normally a supply of wheat flour adequate to meet a family's needs for a year was considered a safe amount to store. But to keep large quantities of corn meal or rye flour on hand was to invite the development of musty or sour conditions in them. Fifteen to 20 pounds for a single purchase was judged to be safe. The housewife who periodically stirred the store of corn meal she kept in a keg or a tub in the cellar lessened the chance that it would turn bad. Supplies of buckwheat, rice, and hominy also had to be limited and examined regularly because, according to Miss Beecher, each was susceptible to infestation by "small black insects."[15]

Other staples often used to prepare "delightful dishes for desserts" — arrowroot, sago, tapioca, pearl barley, macaroni, oatmeal, and isinglass, the "American gelatine" — were best bought in small quantities of 8 to 10 pounds or less and stored in either covered glass containers or in covered wooden boxes. "All of them are very healthful food," opined Miss Beecher, and valuable to keep on hand. Isinglass, particularly, served the dual purpose of making "elegant articles for desserts" as well as dishes that were "excellent for the sick." The useful sweetener, molasses, was stored in barrels or half-barrels in the cellar. Housewives were warned that the bung or cork of a full barrel had to be removed until the quantity was reduced or the contents would "swell and burst the vessel, or run over."[16]

Far more perishable were eggs, which were also stored in the cellar. For Minnesota settlers, particularly during the 1850s, hen's eggs were in limited supply. A Fillmore County housewife made do with the eggs of prairie chickens for cooking, claiming they "answered well." While advice on methods of keeping eggs for an extended period seemed at times more abundant than the supply, a cool, dry place for storing them was essential.[17]

One recommendation was to plunge fresh eggs into boiling water for one minute. Afterward, each egg was to be greased "all over the outside with *good* melted fat, and wedge[d] down close together (layer above layer,) in a box of powdered charcoal." Another suggestion was to set fresh eggs pointed ends downward on top of a two-inch layer of salt spread in the bottom of a stoneware jar. More salt was then sprinkled between each layer and over the top, and the jar was covered and stored in a cool place. Still other alternatives offered the options of coating each egg with a weak solution of gum, melted wax, flaxseed oil, or lard, and packing them into boxes in a bed of oats or bran. The suggested coatings rendered "the shell impervious to air" but affected the color; therefore the treatment was to be employed only on eggs for family use.[18]

As late as 1891, methods for preserving eggs for eight

to ten months were being advocated. One of them called for placing "a small quantity of salt butter in the palm of the left hand" and turning the egg around in it "so that every pore of the shell is closed." While any oil would do, salt butter was the best choice because it "never becomes rancid." The coated eggs were to be packed in layers of bran, well-dried in the oven. In his book, Dr. A. W. Chase listed a dozen other methods that purportedly preserved eggs for periods ranging from six months to two years.[19]

Care of an uncertain supply of eggs, particularly during the early years of settlement, was of less concern to housewives than the proper storage of usually more dependable food supplies from their own gardens. Both in

towns and in the country, the planting of vegetable and herb gardens was probably second only to building a shelter in the newcomers' priorities. Especially in rural areas gardens were a vital source of a welcome variety of foods. Some of them were eaten fresh; roots and more durable vegetables were put away for winter use; others were canned or dried. Cucumbers, green peppers, tomatoes, onions, beets, and even nasturtium seeds were transformed into pickles of all sorts, pepper hash, or a variety of catsups and relishes to spice a winter dinner. Cabbages by the basket were shredded, salted, and fermented to ensure a generous supply of sauerkraut. One woman recalled, "The turnips grew so enormous on our virgin soil that we could hardly believe they were turnips. They looked more like small pumpkins inverted in the ground." Another housewife liked the rutabagas that "grew tremendous" and were "so sweet and tasty" her family ate them raw as well as cooked, calling them "Minnesota apples." [20]

Such abundance was not always the settlers' lot. Instead unpredictable nature at times supplied devastating hailstones, torrential rains, destructive winds, occasional droughts, prairie fires, or unexpected grasshopper plagues. In Minnesota many farms suffered from swarms of so-called grasshoppers (really Rocky Mountain locusts) in 1856, 1857, 1864, and 1865, but the heaviest and most widespread destruction occurred in the summers between 1873 and 1877. Anyone who witnessed an attack by the voracious insects never forgot the experience. Years later a woman in Nicollet County recalled the day she "went out to the garden about ten o'clock to get the vegetables for dinner and picked peas, string beans, onions and lettuce that were simply luscious. The tomatoes were setting and everything was as fine as could be. I felt so proud of it." During that midday meal, the sky darkened with "myriads of grasshoppers," and by midafternoon when they left, "Everything in that lovely garden was gone." While the disastrous "grasshopper years" when vegetable bins in cellars stood empty and glass jars and stoneware crocks could not be filled were an indelible memory, usually Minnesota gardens yielded the housewife ample provender to put up for winter use.[21]

The cookbooks of the day advised the homemaker to store "roots and tubers" (carrots, turnips, potatoes, etc.) in "dark, *dry* places, where the temperature does not vary, and where neither light, warmth, nor moisture are present to invite germination or decay." The temperature considered ideal to maintain maximum quality of the stored foods was 50 degrees Fahrenheit. Vegetables to be eaten fresh but stored in the cellar until wanted were put into bins and covered with a wooden lid or with carpeting, "old clean blankets," or newspapers — anything that would shut out the light. Several thicknesses of newspaper were especially useful because they could be thrown away and replaced if mildew developed. Blankets and carpeting were to be aired frequently, and if mildew appeared, they had to be washed and dried. To keep vegetables fresh longer, they were gathered on a dry day and packed between layers of moss in boxes or barrels. The moss kept the vegetables moist and clean, absorbed excess moisture, and at the same time inhibited shrinkage.[22]

Some settlers merely spread onions over the floor of a dry, warm room, buried turnips in the ground, and left parsnips and salsify in the earth where they had grown, or packed cabbages "root up" in a barrel. If they succeeded in raising celery so far north, it was put into dry sand as were carrots, parsnips, and beets. The latter were also sometimes stored simply by covering them with straw or dirt.[23]

On the other hand, onions might be laid out on shelves or put into "well-aired baskets," where they stayed firm if the cellar was not too damp. Some housewives strung the onions in bunches and suspended them from the rafters of the house, where they not only kept well but were easily accessible for kitchen use. To prevent the onions from "growing," the roots were singed with a hot iron.[24]

Pumpkin and squash, particularly some varieties that were especially dependable for longer-term storage, required a dry place, but one as cool as possible without the danger of frost. On farms, they might be put into the granary, buried in oats or wheat to keep them from freezing. Sweet potatoes, a tuber with limited keeping qualities under the best conditions, were packed in dry leaves and stored in a warm place.[25]

The editors of a Minnesota horticultural magazine described an unlikely storage place for white potatoes. "An old ice house fell in and buried several bushels to the depth of six feet. Not being needed by the family, they were allowed to remain, but on throwing out the earth some two years later the potatoes were found to be perfectly sound, and quite as good as those that had been raised the same season." In another account a farmer merely buried potatoes "to the depth of three and a half feet . . . and all came out in fine condition after two or three years." On the strength of the two experiences, the editors recommended that a special place "be made in the corner of the cellar or root house, and covered with sand, from which enough [potatoes] could be taken in a few minutes to last a week or two."[26]

Potatoes were also put into boxes, barrels, or sacks, or merely "laid in heaps" on the cellar floor. Minnesota householders knew that potatoes kept better and longer if stored with the soil that clung to them after they were dug from the ground. They left them in the sun to dry for an hour or two before they carted them to the cellar. Even so the potatoes usually began to sprout before spring. In this state they became unfit for food "because sprouts draw their substance from the starch cells which make the healthy tuber mealy." To destroy "the germ" responsible for the inevitable spoilage, housewives were told to put old potatoes that were "likely to sprout" into a basket that could be lowered into a vessel filled with boiling water. After an immersion of from one to three minutes, the potatoes were dried and returned to the cellar. It was claimed that this procedure prevented waste "without injuring the rest of the potato for subsequent cooking."[27]

In a century before vitamins had been identified and named, it was said that green leafy vegetables or "salads" were never to be "laid in store in large quantities, because many of their wholesome qualities are lost with the evaporation of their moisture." Without refrigeration or even blocks of ice, keeping these vegetables fresh was impossible. Juliet Corson, however, did suggest a way to store head lettuce for up to two days. Her method was to wash the lettuce thoroughly in cold salt water, "then wet a towel and lay the lettuce in it, fold it loosely up over the roots" and put it in a tight wooden box or a thick paste-board box. These were to be stored in the coldest part of the cellar; each morning and night the towel had to be made thoroughly wet. The more durable cabbages, how-ever, could be placed with the root end up in bins or barrels and protected by a thickness of the outer leaves spread over them before the wooden cover was set in place.[28]

Vegetables that could be stored without processing complemented other dishes during the cold months when restricted supplies often gave a quality of sameness to winter meals. Equivalent methods of keeping fresh fruit, however, were far more limited. Cranberries would "keep all winter in a keg of water" and lemons lasted longer and stayed more juicy when they were put into cold water that was changed weekly. Apples, when available, were sometimes placed on open, slat shelves in the cellar or packed in barrels of sand, sawdust, or grain. But most fruits — and many vegetables, for that matter — had to be canned, dried, or otherwise preserved before they could be added to bounty in the settler's cellar.[29]

By late autumn, if the family was lucky, its cellar would be crowded with many kinds of food — some fresh, set directly on the floor or arranged in boxes, bins, and barrels; some in stoneware and earthenware crocks and jars in various stages of preservation; some wrapped in paper or put into cloth bags hanging overhead; still more canned in tin or glass, carefully sealed, and standing row upon row on shelves in the darkest part of the storeroom. From season to season and from year to year, the content and amount varied, but whatever was put by contributed to a more healthful and balanced diet and allowed for a *"successive* variety" of good food that "pleases both the eye and the palate." [30]

CHAPTER FOUR

Canning and Drying Fruits and Vegetables

FRUIT is "an indispensable ornament to an elegant dinner-table," announced one 19th-century cookbook, while another declared that properly cooked vegetables marked "the difference between an elegant and an ordinary table." Alas, such opinions were academic to most housewives in early Minnesota. Quantity was usually more important to them than elegance, and hearty meals to feed hungry families took precedence over other considerations. Good use was made of fresh fruits and vegetables in season, but their short-term abundance and inevitable overripening established the implicit need to put by as much as possible for the months ahead to ensure a safe, dependable reserve supply.[1]

Housewives preserved fruits in sugar, vegetables and nuts in salt and spices, and both kinds of perishables in vinegar brines. They canned some and dried others. It was demanding work, requiring both vigilance and physical stamina. "The secret of success in canning and preserving," one author noted, "is the observance of all the *minutiae* and not 'wearying in well doing' toward the last and spoiling all by undue haste to finish the task." The assortment of conditions deemed necessary for success was staggering, both in special methods and techniques to be applied in treating foods and the vessels in which they were stored.[2]

Preferences for containers varied among cooks. They put up food in stone and earthenware crocks, tin cans, and glass jars and tumblers — each requiring a different method of sealing. With the introduction of John L. Mason's revolutionary self-sealing zinc jar lid and glass jar, patented in 1858, there was a steady proliferation of patents and a corresponding increase in the manufacture of glass containers for canning. It was Mason's shoulder-seal jar, the easiest and least expensive to produce, that became popular throughout the country. These jars were hand blown until 1896, and even as late as 1915 some were still being produced that way without glassmaking machinery. A significant improvement in Mason's zinc cover was made in 1869. That year Lewis R. Boyd patented a lid with a glass lining that prevented canned foods from coming in contact with the zinc, which had imparted a metallic taste and in some cases contaminated the contents. The vitreous material Boyd used was made of opal glass, although it came to be called "porcelain," a name that persists.[3]

The inexpensive Mason jar won rapid acclaim. The

Daily Minnesotian of October 1, 1859, announced that the self-sealing containers were available in St. Paul in numbers "sufficient to preserve many bushels of fruit." The newspaper pointed out that they cost "but a trifle," and that they "may be used from year to year; thus securing families a means of having on hand a delicacy, at a season when health and scarcity make it almost indispensable." The *Minnesota Farmer and Gardener* in 1861 also urged its "lady readers" to use glass jars. "Since the introduction of the glass fruit jars," the editors wrote, "canning fruits is getting to be quite common. Every well regulated household in the land should have some of these cheap luxuries." They particularly recommended canning gooseberries and currants, which could be "put up with safety" with "but little or no sugar," and strawberries, which "are not easily kept unless preserved well in sugar."[4]

"A Utensil for the Ordinary Range."

In spite of these "cheap luxuries," many housewives were still using the full range of other vessels long after the Mason jar and Boyd's safer lid came on the market. Mary F. Henderson's 1881 cookbook offered a recipe that assumed the use of tin cans for tomatoes, a vegetable she considered "invaluable in a household." It also illustrates the "minutiae" that had to be observed. The recipe directed housewives to take an indeterminate amount of "entirely fresh" tomatoes. "Put scalding water over them to aid in removing the skins. When the cans with their covers are in readiness upon the table, the red sealing-wax (which is generally too brittle, and requires a little lard melted with it) is in a cup at the back of the fire, the tea-kettle is full of boiling water, and the tomatoes are all skinned, we are ready to begin the canning.[5]

"First put four cans (if there are two persons, three if only one person) on the hearth in front of the fire; fill them with boiling water. Put enough tomatoes in a porcelain preserving kettle to fill these cans; add no water to them. With a good fire let them come to the boiling-point, or let them all be well scalded through. Then, emptying the hot water from the cans, fill them with the hot tomatoes; wipe off the moisture from the tops with a soft cloth, and press the covers on tightly. While pressing each cover down closely with a knife, pour carefully around it the hot sealing-wax from the tin cup, so bent at the edge that the wax may run out in a small stream. Hold the knife still for a moment longer, that the wax may set. When these cans are sealed, continue the operation until all the tomatoes are canned.

"Now put the blade of an old knife in the coals, and when it is red-hot run it over the tops of the sealing-wax to melt any bubbles that may have formed; then, examining each can, notice if there is any hissing noise, which will indicate a want of tightness in the can, which allows steam to escape. If any holes are found, wipe them, and cover them while the cans are hot with a bit of the sealing-wax. There will be juice left after the tomatoes are canned. Season this and boil it down for catchup."

Mrs. Henderson acknowledged that self-sealing glass jars could be used, but she warned that they had to be "put on the fire in cold water with a plate or piece of wood in the bottom of the kettle. They should not be filled until the water is boiling" to prevent breakage, and they had to be sealed as soon as possible after filling.

Buckeye Cookery advocated a glass jar with a grooved ring at the top like that designed for tin cans and patented in 1855. Wax or putty had to be forced into the groove to completely seal the lid. If putty was used, it was made pliable by warming it in the hand. Then it was shaped "into a small roll, and pressed firmly into the groove with a knife, care being taken to keep it well pressed down as the can cools." The special advantage of using putty instead of sealing wax, according to the book, was that the covers could be "opened readily with a strong fork or knife."[6]

Using the self-sealing jars with their zinc covers and rubber rings was much easier. The procedure was to place the rubber ring firmly in place, then completely fill the jars, put the caps on at once, and screw them down tightly. As the jars cooled and the glass contracted, the screwtop lids had to be turned down "again and again until perfectly air-tight." The rubber ring had to "show an even edge all round, for if it slips back out of sight at any point, air will be admitted." One disadvantage of the self-sealing jar covers was that "heat hardens the rubber rings, which are difficult to replace, so that in a year or two they are unfit for use."

Other glass jars in use during the latter half of the century were designed to accommodate a variety of lids. Many required a wax seal to make them airtight. One needed a disk of paper impregnated with beeswax. Some had glass or metal stoppers that made use of rubber disks

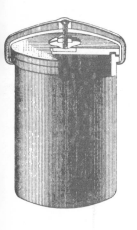

to secure them in place. One style had a core of cork; another was constructed so that a hand pump could be fitted into the stopper to draw air out of the jar. The togglestyle closure first appeared in the late 1860s and other metal fasteners followed, all constructed to keep the covers airtight.[7]

Before "doing up" fruits and vegetables in season, the careful housewife prepared well ahead the vessels she intended to use. She inspected tin cans for leaks, discoloration, and other flaws. Leaking cans had to be discarded or repaired by a tinsmith. The problem of discoloration inside a can intended to be used for fruit could be overcome, according to one author, simply by lining the can with writing paper. The housewife who was partial to the use of stoneware for canning looked for glazing imperfections that could cause the contents to "become poisonous."[8]

If she used glass containers, she examined them for blisters or other weaknesses, since defective glass was certain to "crumble off in small particles when subjected to heat." To check the perfect seal of a glass jar dependent on a rubber gasket to make it airtight, she was advised to partly fill the jar with water, put the rubber into position, and screw the cover on tightly. The simple test of turning the jar upside down for five minutes to see if the "water oozes out" determined the perfection of the seal. If imperfect, she was told to try changing the top or using a different rubber gasket that might "render the jar perfectly safe."[9]

Even if canning vessels were safe and properly sealed

after carefully prepared fruits and vegetables were put into them, the contents of some still might spoil if a housewife failed to store them properly. Most canned foods required a "dry, cool [storage] place free from light." Cookbook writers agreed that light was injurious to fruit and that warmth caused it to spoil. Unless the housewife possessed a *"very dark"* place to store glass jars filled with fruit, the cooking authorities suggested that she wrap them in brown paper to protect them. Strawberries were known to "keep their color best in stone jars," but if the fruit was put into glass ones, they should be buried in sand. Exposure to light was particularly injurious to tomatoes canned in glass jars, for it was said to contribute to "the formation of citric acid, which no amount of sugar will sweeten."[10]

When cans were opened so that their contents could be used, certain precautions were strongly recommended. Once opened, tin cans were to be emptied immediately into a glass or earthenware dish. Unused portions required additional cooking before they could be safely kept for a day or two. The "less perishable fruits" would keep a little longer, but figuring out just what was "less perishable" was left to the housewife's judgment.[11]

"No economy of trouble" governed the enterprise of transforming fruits into jams and jellies, or simply preserving them in cans. Rules abounded. Preserving kettles had to be large, porcelain lined, or made of graniteware or brass. Tumblers or glass jars had to be free of cracks or chips. The jelly bag was to be made of coarse flannel, linen, or cotton. Wooden or silver spoons were thought

Can opener

best for stirring, and an earthenware cup or a silver soup ladle were recommended for skimming and dipping the jelly from kettle to waiting vessels. If a tin dipper was used, it had to be bright and new, for "old and rusty" tin or steel utensils were said to discolor the fruit.[12]

Only "the best refined or granulated sugar" would do for fruits or juices. Some housewives warmed the sugar before adding it. Even the weather was considered critical by some jellymakers. It should be bright and clear, since damp, cloudy weather was widely believed to affect both the clarity and proper congealing of the jelly. To obtain good results in jellymaking, canning, or preserving, the fruit had to be gathered on dry days when it would be free of any moisture that thinned its "glutinous substance" and presented still another possibility for failure. Many women avoided handling a container once it was filled, sealed, and set away, because "any shaking of the jars is likely to be followed by fermentation of the fruit."[13]

Minnesota's wild and cultivated fruits reached the peak of flavor — intense, but not overripe, and "tasting of the sun" — from the end of June well into September. During those months, Minnesota farm women, and a good many who lived in towns as well, were regularly occupied in the work of gathering, picking over, washing, and preserving fruit. "Am so dirty," lamented a rural wife after spending a week picking berries and currants. But her diligence provided many jars of jam and jellies. Later in the summer she harvested more fruits to make apple jelly and butter, plum butter, and fruit sauces.[14]

The procedures she followed were as familiar to her as the ritual of brewing tea. If she made currant jelly, she mashed and boiled the currants and strained the juice. The sugar — one pound for each pint of juice — was sifted and heated "as hot as possible without dissolving or burning" it. Once heated, the sugar was stirred into the juice that had first boiled for five minutes, then the mixture was boiled for one minute longer.

The jelly, like jams and preserves, was poured into glass jars or tumblers. Preferences varied in the choice of protective coverings for the containers. Some women favored white paper dipped in brandy or rum and cut into circles to fit closely over the preserves. Others chose a covering made with "tissue or writing-paper," and then added a second cover of thicker paper brushed with egg white and secured to the outside of the glass. In 1858 Catherine Beecher suggested tying "bladder covers" over the filled jars, and the author of a cookbook published in 1891 recommended the use of melted paraffin poured on top of cooled jelly to prevent mold from forming. "When serving the jelly," the latter advised, "remove the wax, wash it with cold water, dry, and save it for a second season."[15]

When fruits were abundant, housewives could put up a wide variety of jellies and jams. Minnesota cooks made preserves of crab apples, strawberries, peaches, plums, currants, grapes, pineapples, quinces, raspberries, gooseberries, rhubarb, cherries, oranges, and even wine. Limited supplies of fruit, and often the absence of some traditionally used ingredients of jams and jellies, produced combinations born of necessity. Thus in order to be certain she would have preserves for her family, a woman with only crab apples and citron cooked them together. During the early years of settlement, anyone who had access to sources of supply and sufficient funds could buy a variety of dried fruits. St. Paul and Galena commission houses advertised dried peaches, apples, raisins, currants, figs and prunes — luxuries that would extend household fruit supplies. The listings also included commercially produced red and black currant jelly and raspberry jam.[16]

Certain fruits were more readily available to some early settlers than to others. For many families, fruit — like Christmas tinsel or Easter eggs — was associated primarily with festive days. To give Thanksgiving and Christmas dinners a special quality, one housewife cooked dried wild crab apples in water with soda, then sweetened them with molasses. The children in a family living at Sauk Rapids looked forward each year to finding "a few raisins" in their Christmas stockings. One such holiday became the most memorable of all when their father crossed the Mississippi River to St. Cloud and exchanged a load of firewood for a barrel of apples.[17]

The fresh apples may have reminded them of the wondrous variety of wild fruits they picked in Minnesota during the summer months. Many early settlers recalled finding on the prairie "wild and spicy" blackberries "as large as the first joint of a man's thumb." There were "delicious wild, red plums, half the size of an egg." One thicket yielded plums that were blue, others red, and still others yellow and red. "Some were sour, some bitter, others tasteless, while others still, were sweet and of an exquisite flavor." There were crab apples, chokecherries, gooseberries, raspberries, and strawberries in "quantities." On the prairies around Sauk Rapids wild strawberries ripened "with all the sweetness and flavor we used to so much love when we picked them in good old New England," the editor of the local newspaper reported in 1860.[18]

In some areas blueberries were abundant, and as many as five varieties of wild grapes were said to grow in the Minnesota Valley. Ground cherries were used in pies with cranberries or currants added to "render them a little tart." They also would keep through the winter, stored in a barrel with their husks on. In the fall, cranberries "by the hundreds of bushels" ripened in the swamps. Such bounty provided food that many settlers would otherwise have gone without. A guest at a New Year's Day wedding held near St. Anthony in 1844 remembered the sweet, tart taste of the bright crimson cranberry sauce that was served at a simple celebration dinner of fish, bread, and butter.[19]

Minnesota's early residents were not content to use cranberries only in preparations that could be poured into molds or spooned into sauce dishes. They baked the berries in pies and stewed them, strained them, added the grated rind and juice of an orange and a lemon, liberally sweetened the mixture, and froze it into a pleasing confection. One housewife was particularly proud of her never-fail recipe for a molded jelly made with two quarts of cranberries. Over the berries she poured "enough boiling water to cover well; this plumps out the good ones and shrivels up the bad ones; when cool pick them over and wash. To 1 quart berries add 1 pint boiling water and cook very fast for 20 minutes (mash with a silver or wooden spoon while cooking), add a heaping coffee cupful sugar at the last and let boil up once; then put into molds, or if liked, strain through a colander to remove skins, then put into molds. Never fails to jelly."[20]

The women of Minnesota who developed special ways to make distinctive jams, jellies, and preserves sometimes divulged their methods in the recipes they contributed to church cookbooks. One such collection revealed the secret of a subtle flavor imparted to a Stillwater housewife's "Crab Apple Jelly." It came from the addition of several rose geranium leaves to the boiling juice just before it was completely cooked. Another woman advanced the idea of using crab apple jelly as the "foundation" (since "apples are cheaper, and never fail to jell") to which small quantities of scarcer fruits could be added to give a variety of flavors — a method still widely used in commercial jellies today.[21]

The same moneysaving thought was expressed in the following recipe for quince jam: "Boil fruit in a little water until soft enough to break easily; pour off the water and rub with a spoon until smooth. To one pound fruit add ten ounces light brown sugar. A mixture of quince and apple would do as well and be less expensive." Quince, an acid, applelike fruit which is no longer widely available in Minnesota, was very popular in the

19th century. Numerous recipes incorporating it were contributed to local cookbooks.

The standard procedure for canning fruits was to clean them thoroughly, peeling and halving the larger ones, cooking them in a porcelain kettle, then placing them in a jar and covering them with a hot sugar syrup before sealing. This is what is now known as the open-kettle method of canning. Then as now, it had variations.[22]

All of the "small berries," including raspberries, blackberries, currants, and gooseberries, could be canned "plain." One set of directions told the cook to put clean berries "in a porcelain kettle on the stove, adding a small tea-cup water to prevent burning at first. When they come to a boil, skim well, add sugar to taste (for pies it may be omitted), let boil five minutes, fill in glass, stone, or tin cans, and seal with putty unless self-sealers are used."[23]

Peaches, pears, plums, and pineapple were cooked in a sugar syrup until they were soft enough to be "easily pierced with a silver fork." They were then ready to place in cans and seal. Ripe currants mixed with "a pound sugar to every pound fruit" were heated through and spread on plates or platters for a day or two in the sun, "when they will be nicely jellied." Then they could be sealed in cans, where they would keep "for years."[24]

By the 1890s, the canning process now called the water-bath method was being promoted. Although it was more complicated than the open-kettle method, it was said to be the best way to preserve the flavor and shape of fruits and berries. Briefly, the process as described in one cookbook was to fill the glass jars with whole berries or halved large fruit. Then, using the handy table provided, a sugar syrup was heated in a saucepan. When hot, it was poured into the glass containers and the covers were loosely screwed on. The jars were placed in a boiler or kettle, which was filled with lukewarm water to within an inch of the jar tops. After the water had boiled about 10 minutes, the fruit was tested for doneness; if it could be pierced with a fork, each jar was removed from the boiler, filled to overflowing with boiling water, then quickly sealed.[25]

During seasons when inadequate supplies of white sugar restricted canning and preserving, some house-wives "made do" by putting up fruits in other ways. Uncut plums in wide-mouthed jars with loose fitting corks were set in a "very slow oven (nearly cold)" for four or five hours until the fruit began to shrink. The bottles were then taken from the oven, tightly corked, and stored in a rack or basket "with the mouth downwards, and they will keep good several years." Currants, cherries, and gooseberries could be preserved in the same manner.[26]

In the absence of sugar, a housewife with three bushels of apples and abundant personal stamina or will-ing helpers might prepare apple butter following this rec-ipe: "Boil one barrel of new cider down half, peel and core three bushels of good cooking apples; when the cider has boiled to half the quantity, add the apples, and when soft, stir constantly for from eight to ten hours. If done it will adhere to an inverted plate. Put away in stone jars (not earthen ware), covering first with writing-paper cut to fit the jar, and press down closely upon the apple butter; cover the whole with thick brown paper snugly tied down."[27]

Pumpkins, too, could be preserved without the addition of sugar. This recipe for pumpkin butter required no sweetener, but it demanded a very long day's work: "Take the seeds out of one pumpkin, cut in small pieces and boil soft; take three other pumpkins, cut them in pieces and boil them soft, put them in a coarse bag and press out juice; add juice to first pumpkin, and let boil ten hours or more, to become of the thickness of butter; stir often. If the pumpkins are frozen, the juice will come out much easier."[28]

One acceptable alternative to refined white sugar appeared in Eliza Leslie's cookbook. "The best brown sugar" if properly clarified "will make a good syrup," she noted. The clarifying process called for one beaten egg white and a half-pint of cold water for each pound of sugar used. The water was poured over the sugar and allowed to stand until it dissolved. Then the beaten egg white was added, and the mixture was boiled and carefully skimmed. Just before the boiling syrup was removed from the fire, a half-cup of water for each pound of sugar was added. It was allowed to settle before it was strained and bottled for use. Molasses and brown sugar were substitute sweeteners for some fruit preserves. Plums put into an empty brandy keg with a generous ladling of molasses over them needed only a cover kept firmly in place and a daily turning of the keg to preserve the fruit for winter use.[29]

Whether frontier housewives used it fresh or put it up, wild and cultivated fruit like everything else was not to be wasted. Yesterday's cooks were as knowledgeable concerning ways to recover foods going bad as they were regarding procedures to preserve them. Remedies to correct potential ruin — fermentation, failure to jell, the development of mold — were all aimed at sparing needless waste. Freshly made jellies which were insufficiently firm were set out of doors in the sun for several days "covered with bits of window glass" or mosquito netting for protection while the jelly solidified. The vigilant housewife routinely inspected her filled jelly glasses near the end of the summer for "signs of fermentation" in order to correct the condition by reboiling their contents in time. Preserves and jams might be saved if mold specks were removed and the filled jars scalded in a bath of boiling water.[30]

While fruits seemed to be the most popular food put up in cans and jars, vegetables, too, were preserved in this way, especially later in the 19th century. The process used in canning "perfectly fresh" vegetables of "the best quality" was similar to that employed for fruit, since the primary goal was to exclude air from the sealed container. Both the open-kettle and the water-bath methods were used.[31]

The *New Buckeye Cook Book* supplied a basic recipe that could be used for preserving corn, peas, or string beans — which, with tomatoes, were the vegetables most often canned. Using corn as the example, the directions were to "cut the corn from cob, pack in glass cans, pound the corn as hard as possible without breaking cans [to pack it tight]; screw on top [without the rubber] but not tight." The jars were then put into a boiler of cold water, rising to within 2 or 3 inches of their tops, and the water was gradually brought to a boil. After boiling for 15 minutes, the container was drawn "to the back of the stove to let steam pass off." One by one the hot jars were then removed, the covers taken off, the rubbers put in place, and the tops screwed on tightly. The jars were returned to the hot water, where they remained overnight or until cool. After the covers had again been tightened, they were ready to store away.[32]

The same book suggested combining corn and tomatoes or lima beans before processing by the open-kettle method. Lima, butter, or case-knife beans, cooked for one hour as "for the table," could be seasoned with salt and pepper before putting them into hot jars or tins and sealing carefully. "They will keep the year round," according to the authors.[33]

Another book added asparagus to the list of vegetables that could be canned, and it also included a simple method of keeping rhubarb, a "vegetable . . . delicious for pies in Winter." The housewife was instructed to remove the skin from the rhubarb, cut it into inch-long lengths, and pack it closely into glass jars. "Fill the jars to overflowing with cold water and screw the top on tightly. Invert the jar to disclose any leak. If the jar is perfect, this canning, simple as it is, will be successful," the writer promised.[34]

Expedients in preservation, adopted whenever necessary, were combined with traditional procedures in the

constant battle against spoilage. One standard method —
drying certain fruits, vegetables, and herbs — needed no
additional ingredients to safeguard the foods. "To be
successful in drying food of any kind the one thought to
be kept in mind is that every particle of moisture must be
dried out." All that was necessary was long exposure to
the sun and air or to heat in a "very delicately tempered"
oven to prevent scorching, yet allow proper drying.[35]

To achieve the desired result, the housewife spread
the fruit in a single layer on boards in the sun or dried it
in the oven until it assumed a "leather-color." Fruits or
vegetables set outside were to be covered with netting,
turned a minimum of three times a day, and moved indoors before sunset. Care was to be taken so that fruit,
especially, would never be exposed to the air on a damp
or cloudy day lest mold set in. Completely dried fruits
and vegetables were to be "put in paper sacks and hung
in a dry place." Apples were peeled and cored and cut
into eighths before drying; plums were never peeled, but
cut in half and the seeds removed. A "dark, rich-looking
pumpkin" was considered ideal for drying; in fact, the

"more knotty and rough is the skin of this vegetable, the
surer is the possessor that it is full of richness." To ready
the pumpkin it was cut into strips and peeled, and the
seeds and "soft meshes which hold them" removed. The
strips were cut into two-inch lengths and then completely dried.[36]

Peas and lima beans required no special procedures for
drying, but recommendations for parching corn differed.
In 1877 *Buckeye Cookery* suggested cutting it from the

cob and drying it without preliminary treatment. About three quarts at a time were to be spread in a large pan lined with "flour-sack paper" and put into a moderate oven for 15 or 20 minutes while being stirred frequently. The corn was then spread on a cloth-covered table outdoors in the sunshine and brought in before sunset. The next day it was heated in the oven again and set outside. The corn "will be thoroughly dried on the evening of the second day, and when shaken will rattle," the writers noted. Another authority advocated first boiling the ears for two minutes "to harden the milk." The kernels were then cut from the cob, set on a cloth spread over a "baking board," and put into the oven or taken out in the sun to dry. To reconstitute the dried corn, it was soaked overnight in a bowl of water. Parboiled string beans were dried in the same way as corn.[37]

Housewives who grew herbs gathered them at the time most advantageous for drying — on a clear day just before the plants were ready to flower and were "full of juice." With dust and grime removed and the roots cut off, the herbs were spread in a flat pan lined with brown paper. To best preserve the delicate flavor and aroma the herbs imparted to cookery, the more rapid method of oven drying was favored, although herbs were also tied in small bunches and dried in a Dutch oven set in front of an open fire. They were turned frequently during the drying process, which continued until the heat released all of their moisture. Lastly the leaves were separated from the stems, put into a mortar and pounded and rubbed to a powder, then placed in labeled bottles with securely fitting corks; or the bunches of dried herbs were put into paper bags and stored in a dry place.[38]

It was no doubt true that "with the first signs of Spring many housewives are reminded that another Summer is at hand, and the work of the household is nearly doubled by the 'doing up' of fruit" and vegetables for the coming winter. But surely when the colorful jars of preserved foods stood row upon row in the cellars, a woman could stand back and feel justifiably proud of her accomplishment, knowing that she had completed yet another in her lengthy list of 19th-century housewifely duties.[39]

CHAPTER FIVE

The Useful Art of Pickling

A GOOD PORTION of the 19th-century housewife's effort to put by food for later use was devoted to the useful art of pickling. It was generally acknowledged that the "ambitious housekeeper should never be content until she learned to do all kinds of pickling." Fruits as delicate as strawberries and vegetables as traditional as cucumbers and beets were thus endowed with keeping properties. Some vegetables and fruits were mixed in seemingly endless combinations limited only by the yield from the garden augmented by wild fruits and nuts, the cook's ingenuity, and her supplies of salt, spices, sweeteners, and, most important, vinegar.[1]

While sugar and most spices had to be purchased, vinegar was one essential item that could be produced at home. Quantities of vinegar went into pickling of all sorts, but the pungent liquid had other household uses as well. It was called upon to tenderize meat, to turn sweet milk sour, or to prepare a zestful drink made with raspberries, brandy, and sugar. It was used to pickle oysters and pork hocks, and, when flavored with tarragon, it gave an added dimension to red cabbage soup. Sweet basil immersed in vinegar was revealed as the "secret" ingredient for successful mock turtle soup. Vinegar also added authority to homemade mayonnaise and salad dressings. It was essential for the preparation of molasses candy, and a piquant supplement to an onion, water, and salt basting for roast goose. In company with olive oil and spices, vinegar was basic to the preparation of potted herring and indispensable as the preservative for pickled fish. With so many uses, making vinegar at home was a sensible, moneysaving custom among frugal frontier housekeepers.[2]

In 1857 Eliza Leslie also strongly urged housewives to make their own vinegar in order to avoid the hazards of questionable commercial products. "So much of the vinegar sold in stores is concocted of pernicious drugs," she declared, adding that "What is shamefully called the best white wine vinegar is frequently a slow poison." Oysters cooked in it turned to "rags, and are soon entirely eaten up, or dissolved into a thin whitish liquid, fit for nothing but to throw away." Pickles reacted in the same way, she wrote. So vehement was her denunciation of commercially made vinegar that she called for a law to punish the manufacturers who sold the "deleterious compounds."[3]

Minnesota women could buy vinegar from local merchants who advertised it regularly in the newspapers. But housewives who were suspicious of the commercial products, motivated by economic considerations and long distances from a source of supply, or simply used to traditional ways prepared their own vinegar. The uncomplicated formula for "American" vinegar required only water, molasses, and yeast in proper proportions put into a cask, set by the fire for 24 hours, then exposed to the late spring and summer sun for three months to allow fermentation to take place.[4]

An alternative was to save "all the currants, skimmings, pieces, etc., left after making jelly" as a base for "Cheap" vinegar. The remnants were covered with pure water and allowed to stand in a stone jar for several days before they were strained. The strained liquid was added to more water that had first been boiled with apple peelings, then drained into a stone jar; "rinsings" from molasses jugs and "all dribs of syrups, etc." also went into the jar until it was full and ready to pour into a vinegar keg that contained "some good cider vinegar to start with." If the mixture was not sufficiently sweet, molasses or brown sugar was added before the bunghole was covered with coarse netting and the keg set either in the sun or by the kitchen stove.[5]

If a supply of gooseberries was at hand, a housewife might combine them with yeast, water, brown sugar, and treacle (a type of molasses), to yield a very strong vinegar in a year's time. Another strong vinegar of "excellent quality" could be prepared from honey mixed with water and exposed to the warmth of the sun. Still another formula made with "Good brown sugar," yeast, and soft water in the right proportions yielded vinegar in two to four weeks, if the sun was hot enough or the kitchen warm enough and if the action was helped along by shaking the barrel and its contents daily. Substituting shelled corn for the yeast worked well, as long as the vinegar was drawn off after three weeks. Neither corn nor yeast was necessary to the success of the mixture if enough good vinegar was available to fortify the water and brown sugar. A ratio of one gallon of vinegar to five gallons of liquid in the barrel was recommended.[6]

Producing the highly desirable apple cider vinegar at home became practical only with the gradual development of apple orchards. Seeds and young trees brought by settlers from states to the east were planted in Minnesota in the 1850s and 1860s. An increasing number of apple trees transplanted from Wisconsin and Illinois were growing well at Red Wing in 1861. The Wisconsin trees especially were making "a good growth" and bearing fruit after six or seven years in Minnesota soil. Some apple trees at St. Anthony that were "all grafted sorts" were producing fruit; and apples were grown near Chatfield of "good size and beautiful" appearance. "Let the 'croakers' who are forever lamenting the fear that 'apples won't grow in Minnesota,' now dry up," wrote the editor of the *Chatfield Democrat* in 1861. The orchardgrowers' persistence and determination to produce varieties that could survive the severity of the winters yielded a record crop of some 10,000 bushels of apples in 1869. Production continued to increase in spite of the damage to trees during two severe winters in 1872–73 and 1874–75.[7]

Greater supplies of home-grown apples doubtless encouraged the home production of cider vinegar. The wife

"*Vinegar by the Quick or German Process.*"

of then Senator Alexander Ramsey kept a recipe for it in her "Book of Receipts," dated 1865, that called for molasses and yeast to be added to cider in a barrel. Nearly 30 years later directions for an inexpensive, simple method of preparing cider vinegar were printed in the *Northwestern Farmer and Breeder.* In its entirety, the recipe read: "The cores and peelings of apples make the best of vinegar if placed in stone jars and just covered with soft water and a plate and kept in a warm place for two weeks or more. When drying apples is the time to make vinegar." [8]

General principles to be followed in the preparation of homemade vinegar, regardless of the ingredients used, were published in *Buckeye Cookery.* Requirements included ample space for air within the cask, preferably one made of oak, and "plenty of material, such as sugar, molasses, etc., to work upon." Further, the book included a reminder that vinegar should never be allowed to freeze and that alum and cream of tartar should never be used in its preparation. Nevertheless tartaric acid headed the list of ingredients in a Taylors Falls housewife's recipe. Her "Cider Receipt for 10 Galls." also called for soft water, brown sugar, and yeast. A Wayzata housewife made vinegar from maple sugar and, according to her family, "none could be better." [9]

Whatever the source — store-bought or homemade — and whatever the ingredients, the strength and pungency of vinegar varied significantly. An awareness of the unpredictable differences compelled some cookbook authors to include more specific adjectives in their recipes.

"Take one gallon nice vinegar" was a commonly used phrase. Others specified strong or weak vinegar. A recipe for mock mince pie warned that "if vinegar is very sour put in less." Only the housewife's experience could help her determine the quality and quantity of vinegar needed.[10]

Mistrust of commercially prepared vinegar prevailed at mid-century and beyond. A corresponding skepticism obtained toward commercially prepared pickles. That suspicion led *Buckeye Cookery* to suggest that "Pickles are not famous for wholesome qualities, even when made with the greatest care, but if they must be eaten, it is best to make them at home." The book explained that cucumber pickles "sold in market are often colored a beautiful green with sulphate of copper, which is a deadly poison, or are cooked in brass or copper vessels, which produces the same result in an indirect way." The desired color could be achieved safely in homemade pickles, the book suggested, by placing a lining of cabbage leaves in the kettle in which the cucumbers were scalded.[11]

The basic ingredients of common pickles, *Buckeye Cookery* explained, were cucumbers, coarse salt, strong vinegar, peppercorns, allspice, stick cinnamon, cloves, mustard seed, and gingerroot. "A lump of alum size of a small nutmeg, to a gallon of cucumbers, dissolved and added to the vinegar . . . renders them crisp and tender," the book noted. Readers were also cautioned to prevent air from reaching the pickles by making sure they were always covered by at least two inches of vinegar; to use a dry, wooden spoon or ladle to handle pickles; to replace vinegar that had lost its strength with some that was hot and strong; and to avoid "insipid" pickles, which were the consequence of insufficient salt or weak vinegar.[12]

Minnesotans' recipes for cucumber pickles generally agreed with *Buckeye Cookery's* basic rules, but the addition of various spices and sugar or different techniques in preparation made each unique. A St. Paul woman's recipe called for "Three hundred small cucumbers, one quart onions, one gallon cider vinegar, one pound brown sugar, one ounce cloves, one of allspice, one of mustard seed, one dozen small green peppers, alum size of an egg, one pound horseradish. Place cucumbers in a large jar with onions and layer of salt, then pour boiling water over them. Next day pour off brine, boil and skim and scald cucumbers again, and repeat the third day. The fourth day wipe cucumbers and onions and place in a jar with horseradish and peppers. Scald vinegar, alum, spices and sugar, and pour over them." Other recipes included olive oil, gingerroot, celery seed, dill, garlic, or nasturtiums.[13]

PICKLES AND PRESERVES.

Many Minnesota housewives lined their cellars and store-closets with an imaginative variety of pickled vegetables, fruits, nuts, and even eggs. Besides cucumber pickles, they made vegetables into crisp relishes and flavorful catsups, all spiced and infused with special flavors. In one season, they might pickle such vegetables as cucumbers, sweet red and green peppers, beans, cabbages, cauliflower, tomatoes, and onions, as well as apples, cherries, peaches, pears, plums, and other fruits.[14]

The rule that "Sweet pickles may be made of any fruit that can be preserved, including the rinds of ripe melons and cucumbers" put few restraints on home pickling. Spices and vinegar supplied the vigor, and sweetness was provided by "'coffee C,' best brown, or good stirred maple sugar." A mingling of vinegar, spices, and sweeteners with such fruits as currants, grapes, berries, watermelons, muskmelons, or gooseberries yielded a mixture often called simply "spiced" fruit or fruit "pickle." A recipe that transformed gooseberries into a spicy preserve "as thick as apple butter" appeared in *Buckeye Cookery.* "Leave the stem and blossom on ripe gooseberries, wash clean," the directions read; "make a syrup of three pints sugar to one of vinegar, skim, if necessary, add berries and boil down till thick, adding more sugar if needed; when almost done, spice with cinnamon and sugar."[15]

"Pickled Blackberries" were made by a Minneapolis housewife from "Five pounds of fruit, three pounds sugar, one pint vinegar. Cinnamon, cloves and allspice to taste. Boil hard until reduced one-half." This recipe was also said to make a "nice" but authoritative pie filling when more sugar was stirred into it.[16]

In those days, catsup was a generic term applied to spicy "table sauces" made of many things besides tomatoes. One housewife cooked nine quarts of gooseberries in a quart of vinegar until the fruit was tender. She strained the liquid, added one "box of cinnamon," a tablespoon of cloves, and three pounds of sugar, then al-

lowed it to boil until it became a thick syrup she called "Gooseberry Catsup." In 1880 Maria Parloa offered a recipe for a savory table sauce she called "Barberry Ketchup." It was made of "Three quarts of barberries, stewed and strained; four quarts of cranberries, one cupful of raisins, a large quince, and four small onions, all stewed with a quart of water, and strained." These ingredients she mixed "with half a cupful of vinegar, three fourths of a cupful of salt, two cupfuls of sugar, one dessert-spoonful of ground clove and one of ground allspice, two table-spoonfuls of black pepper, two of celery seed, and one of ground mustard, one teaspoonful of cayenne, one of cinnamon, and one of ginger, and a nutmeg. Let the whole boil one minute. If too thick, add vinegar or water." These quantities produced about three quarts of the robust sauce.[17]

Recipes for classic tomato catsups that often included vinegar found their way into local cookbooks in goodly numbers. One that produced a catsup that would "keep any length of time without sealing" was favored by a Buffalo, Minnesota, housewife. It read: "One bushel ripe tomatoes. Boil until soft and press through a sieve. Add ½ gallon of good vinegar, ½ pint salt, 2 oz. cloves, ¼ pound allspice, 1 tablespoonful cayenne pepper. Boil from 4 to 6 hours." [18]

Good pungent vinegar was also an indispensable ingredient in catsups made of walnuts, cucumbers, currants, elderberries, or plums. Doubtless many housewives agreed that "catsup properly made and seasoned is truly a delight, especially when cold meat or fish is to be served." Catsups were used not only as a condiment, but also to flavor soup, gravy, and prepared sauces.[19]

The importance women gave to transforming nature's bounty and garden produce into pickled combinations is indicated by the numerous recipes they contributed to church-sponsored cookbooks. A St. Paul housewife sparked her recipe for "Piccalilli" with grated horseradish added to green tomatoes, cabbage, onions, green peppers, and celery, which she chopped and put into vinegar sweetened with brown sugar and spiced with cinnamon, allspice, cloves, and mustard seed.[20]

A Stillwater woman took pride in her sweet and sour "Cabbage Pickles." She combined chopped cabbage with onions and gave the mixture piquancy with a blend of vinegar, brown sugar, black pepper, ground mustard, cinnamon, allspice, turmeric, celery seed, salt, and "a small lump of alum."

Another recipe outlined how to pickle eggs: "Boil quite hard 3 dozen eggs, drop in cold water and remove the shells; pack them in widemouthed bottles or jars. Take as much vinegar as you think will cover them entirely, and boil in it white pepper, allspice, ginger root. Pack in the jars and occasionally put in black and white mustard seed mixed, a small piece of mace, garlic (if liked), cloves, and a very little allspice, 2 or 3 small green peppers put in in very small quantities." The eggs would be "fit for use in 8 or 10 days."

Green, half-grown muskmelons, emptied of their seeds through long, narrow wedges cut into the flesh, became sweet-and-sour containers for an assortment of vegeta-

bles, some sharpened with vinegar, some with salt, and all with spices. The melons, each bereft of seeds and with one end of the wedge stitched back into place, were put into a salt brine for 24 hours. The wedge was then lifted to admit a stuffing. First chopped tomatoes and cabbage, previously immersed in vinegar, were put in. Then cut up cucumbers, onions, and nasturtium pods, all cured in salt brine, were added, along with green beans that had been boiled in salt water until tender. A pungent combination of cinnamon bark, chopped horse-radish, whole cloves, mustard seed, and cayenne pepper contributed more zest to the stuffing.

After this mixture was solidly packed into each melon,

the wedges were securely stitched into position with strong white thread. Then the melons were put into a large crock and submerged in weak cider vinegar. The following day the melons and vinegar were boiled for a half-hour, and reimmersed overnight in strong cider vinegar. Next day that liquid was drained off to be boiled with sugar before it was poured hot over the melons. After three or four repetitions of the boiling process, the stuffed melons were ready to eat. They were called "Mangoes."

Often found in the pages of church-sponsored cookbooks were recipes for "Chow Chow," a relish usually made of cucumbers, onions, cauliflower, vinegar, and spices. One book included three such recipes, each a little different. Digressing from the other two, the third recipe told the reader to chop "1 peck of green tomatoes, ½ peck of ripe tomatoes, 6 onions, 3 small heads of cabbage, 1 dozen green peppers (seeds removed), 3 red peppers (seeds removed); sprinkle with salt, put in coarse bag and drain over night; in morning put in porcelain kettle with 2 pounds of brown sugar, ½ teacup of grated horse radish, 1 tablespoonful each of ground black pepper, mustard, white mustard seed (whole), mace and celery seed, cover with vinegar; boil until clear; seal in jars."[21]

It was said that "any thing" except red cabbage and walnuts could be utilized in an easy-to-prepare, all-purpose mixture called "Indian Pickle." No cooking was necessary for the pickling brine made of vinegar, curry powder, salt, mustard powder, "bruised ginger," cayenne pepper, turmeric, garlic, and onions. Instead the ingredients were simply united in a bladder-covered stoneware jar placed in front of the fire and shaken thrice daily for three days. From the garden, the housewife could gather "every thing fresh, such as small cucumbers, green grapes, green tomatoes, cauliflowers, small onions, nasturtiums, string-beans, etc., etc. Wipe them, cut them when too large, and throw them fresh into the vinegar." [22]

A desire for variety could prompt a cook to convert immature, green plums into "Mock Olives." Heated vinegar seasoned with salt and mustard seed was poured over the plums. It was drained after one day to be heated again before being returned to the vessel containing the plums. After the combination cooled a second time, the imitation olives were ready to be bottled. A similar "cheap, easy, and palatable" substitute for capers was made from the green seeds of nasturtiums soaked in spiced vinegar when they were "full-grown, but not hard." [23]

pickling or salting trough

Immersion in a salt brine — usually "strong enough to float an egg" — was a preliminary to the vinegar and seasoning treatment accorded many vegetables. A salt-brine cure was also the first step in the preparation of pickled walnuts or butternuts. The nuts were gathered before they reached maturity while the shells were still "soft enough to be pierced by a needle." The nutmeats were soaked in their shells in a salt brine for eight or nine days, drained, and exposed to the sun for two or three days "until they become black." Lastly, vinegar boiled eight minutes with sugar, cloves, allspice, peppercorns, and mace was poured over the nuts. After an interval of three days, the vinegar mixture was drawn off, boiled, and again poured hot over them. The process was repeated once more three days later. The pickled nuts would be "fit to eat in a month, and will keep for years."[24]

The assortment of pickled produce and catsups turned out each season were assigned places in the cellar. Most catsups were bottled and tightly corked; stoppers and bottle tops were rendered airtight with a coating of melted wax. The vessels most approved for pickles by one authority were "wide-mouthed glass bottles, or strong stone-ware jars, having corks or bungs, which must be fitted in with linen, and covered with bladder or leather." Pickles stored in wooden casks or stoneware jars required a plate or saucer, often weighted down, to keep them well under the vinegar. However, *Buckeye Cookery* suggested that the "nicest way to put up pickles is bottling, sealing while hot, and keeping in a cool, dark place."[25]

No matter what type of container was used to store pickles, the standard practice was to "look at them frequently." If the vinegar developed white specks, it had to be drained, scalded, and "a liberal handful of sugar" added to each gallon to restore the liquid before returning it to the jar. A knowledgeable housewife, in an effort to protect the quality of the vinegar, sprinkled "bits of horse-radish and a few cloves" into each container just before she covered it. Nasturtium leaves or seeds were also said to inhibit the development of mold.[26]

Alongside the pickles in the cellar, some families stored a supply of sauerkraut — cabbage fermented in its own juice — a tangy vegetable well suited to serve with meats. One recipe for "Sour Krout" advised that a "little juniper" be burned in a "perfectly sound and clean" tub or cask. The seam at the bottom was to have "a little leaven" forced into it in the form of a mixture of vinegar and flour to promote fermentation. A layer of three or four handfuls of shredded cabbage was put into the treated tub, salt and caraway seed sprinkled over it, and the whole stomped down firmly with a wooden mallet. This procedure was repeated layer by layer until the cask was filled. Any excessive water that came to the top was taken off; the filled tub was loosely covered, and left in "a warm cellar to ferment." After three weeks, when the cabbage had "worked well," any scum that had formed at the top was removed, a clean cloth was spread directly on the sauerkraut, and the cover was replaced with several heavy stones set upon it to weight it down. With care to see that the "juice should always stand up on the top," the sauerkraut would keep for years in "a good cellar."[27]

Kraut fork

Another recipe called for simply lining a wooden tub or firkin with the washed large, outer green leaves of the cabbage and "beating the layers of [shredded] cabbage with a potato-masher." The only seasoning required was a pint of fine salt to each peck of cabbage. After six weeks it was ready to use. The author of a hydropathic cookbook made a point of not furnishing a recipe for sauerkraut. Although the fermented cabbage was "highly lauded by the medical profession, and by dietetical writers as

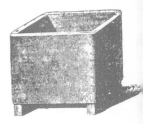

pickling tub or salting bin

medicinal and wholesome," he wrote, "it has nothing intrinsic to recommend it." There were many, however, who disagreed with that opinion. Among them was Louis Pasteur, who, it is said, "declared that sauerkraut was the most useful and healthful dish on earth."[28]

Pickling meats, seafood, and fish in vinegar as a method of preservation apparently was not widely practiced in Minnesota in the 19th century, if the local church cookbooks are an indication. None of those in the Minnesota Historical Society's collection includes such recipes, although a few do appear in the more general household guides of the period.

Buckeye Cookery offered two recipes — one for "Pig's-feet Souse" and the other for "Potted Fresh Fish." The first is a type of pickled pig's feet made by cooking cleaned "feet and toes" and packing them in a stone jar with pepper, salt, and good cider vinegar. To serve, the meat was thoroughly heated with more vinegar thickened with flour and water.[29]

To make the potted dish, a housewife soaked fresh fish in salt water for several hours, then sliced it, and put it in a jar alternating layers of fish with "spices, flour and bits of butter." The jar was then filled with equal amounts of vinegar and water, covered closely, and baked for six hours. The contributor of this recipe liked to slice the fish cold and serve it for tea.

A general rule for pickling "salmon, mackerel, sprats, herrings, &c." was given by Mrs. N.K.M. Lee in *Complete Library of Cookery*. After cutting the freshly cleaned, unscaled fish into "proper pieces," the housewife was to "make a brine strong enough to bear an egg," using just enough of it to cover the fish for boiling. The cooked fish was then drained, cooled, and packed in "kits," which were filled up with equal parts of the boiling liquor and "best vinegar." The containers were allowed to rest for a day, then they were struck on the sides "with a cooper's adz" to settle the contents, and filled again with the liquid before covering and storing.

Both Eliza Leslie and Maria Parloa included recipes for pickled oysters in their books. Miss Leslie's directions called for "five or six hundred oysters of the finest sort," which were simmered for 10 minutes in their liquor and fresh butter. While the oysters cooled, the liquid was strained and mixed with cider, vinegar, salt, peppercorns, powdered mace, and nutmeg. This combination was cooked down until only enough remained to cover the oysters packed in stoneware jars. Before covering, a tablespoon of salad oil was poured on top of the liquor, then the tops were secured with thick bands of white paper pasted all around.

Shrimps could be pickled after being boiled in water to which salt, cider vinegar, peppercorns, and mace were added. Miss Leslie suggested keeping them in a stone jar closed with a cork and sealed with a combination of beeswax, powdered rosin, and brick dust — "the usual red cement for pickle jars."

In a recipe for pickled herring, appearing in "*Aunt Babette's*" *Cook Book* of 1889, the writer directed cooks to "Take new Holland herring, remove the heads and scales; wash well, open them and take out the milch [*soft roe*] and lay the herring and milch in milk or water over night. Next day lay the herring in a stone jar with alternate layers of onions cut up, also lemon cut in slices, a few cloves, whole peppers and a few bay leaves, some capers and whole mustard seed." The roe was rubbed through a hair sieve, and, with a spoonful of brown sugar and vinegar added, poured over the herring.[30]

The importance of pickling in an age before refrigeration cannot be overestimated, for it ensured the presence of vegetables and fruit — as well as fish and meat — on the frontier table in winter. Cabbage made into sauerkraut, for example, could be served throughout the long months when many Minnesotans, isolated by deep snowdrifts and biting temperatures, had to subsist on the bounty of their cellars. The useful art of pickling made an important, but often overlooked, contribution to the settlement of the frontier and to the self-sufficiency of the frontier home.

CHAPTER SIX

The Challenge of Meat, Fish, and Poultry

AT MOST TIMES and places on the Minnesota frontier, wild game and fish were fairly abundant. "Our supply of meat for the first year or two," wrote a settler who arrived in the Zumbro River Valley in 1855, "depended upon our success as hunters and fishermen." He added that "During our first winter, we had a deer hung on every rafter on the north side of the house." In the early days putting meat on the table was often less difficult than keeping it there, for unless fresh meat was preserved in some way, it quickly became unfit to eat. Even after icehouses and iceboxes came into general use, the "putting up" of meat, fish, and poultry was a routine household practice that continued in the 20th century.[1]

Many settlers with access to markets duplicated the procedure of a family living in Minneapolis in the 1860s who purchased a variety of fresh meat, froze it with the

115

help of frigid winter weather, and then packed it in snow. "This worked well," one family member recalled, "provided we had no 'January thaw' and then we lost our supplies." An outdoor storeroom held a winter's supply of fresh, weather-frozen beef for the Reverend Edward D. Neill's family in St. Paul. Miss Minnesota Neill remembered that her father bought a side of beef in the fall and cut it up according to a diagram in her mother's cookbook. Abby Fuller, who lived at Crow Wing during the winter of 1860, also turned the cold weather to advantage by burying oysters in the snow to preserve them for a Christmas dinner of oyster soup, roast turkey, plum pudding, coffee, and "fixins."[2]

A well-stocked pioneer larder ready for winter might house game and fish preserved in various ways; a barrel of salt pork; a stoneware jar full of beefsteaks with salt, sugar, and powdered saltpeter sprinkled under, between, and on top of each; sausage seasoned and packed in jars

or hanging in natural casings; beef in a corn "pickle";
ham, bacon, and beef cured and smoked; and dried beef
hung in paper bags. While there were variations in individual settlers' methods of corning, salting, and curing
meats, the objective was the same for all — to prevent
spoilage.

In the 1850s certain techniques of preserving meat
were well known, but the dangers of botulism were not
as well understood as they are today. Many of the 19th-
century methods described in this chapter are now recognized as unsafe. Readers are warned not to attempt to
use the meat-curing processes discussed here, but rather
to consult the latest United States Department of Agriculture bulletins for safer and simpler methods.

For the inexperienced cook of yesteryear, the household guides of the era offered a multitude of instructions.
Mrs. Lee's *Complete Library of Cookery*, for example,
gave specific information on salting beef, a very widely
used method of preservation also effective for fish. "In
summer," she wrote, "the sooner meat is salted after it is
killed, the better; and care must be taken to defend it
from the flies." In her opinion, meat would "eat the shorter and tenderer" in winter "if kept a few days" after
butchering.[3]

Since most butchering was done in cold weather, she
cautioned the housewife to "take care the meat is not
frozen, and warm the salt in a frying-pan." She explained
that "The art of salting meat is to rub in the salt
thoroughly and evenly into every part, and to fill all the
holes full of salt. . . . A round of beef of 25 pounds will

take a pound and a half of salt to be rubbed in all at first, and requires to be turned and rubbed every day with the brine; it will be ready for dressing [*cooking*] in four or five days, if you do not wish it very salt." Mrs. Lee noted that the meat would retain its red color if the homemaker added half an ounce each of saltpeter and "moist sugar" to every pound of salt rubbed into the beef.

Pork salted in a similar way provided early Minnesota settlers with their principal source of meat outside of fish and wild game, although the pork had to be imported into the state until the 1860s. Hog raising on a large scale was not undertaken in Minnesota until local corn crops could be counted on for feed. Nevertheless a bride in Minneapolis wrote that before her marriage in 1858, her husband's winter diet consisted of "pork! pork! pork!" She believed that "if all the hogs he ate were stood end to end, they would reach to Fort Snelling." For a Northfield family that kept 16 to 18 boarders and also served "many extra" people brought by stagecoaches from Hastings and St. Paul in 1854, a 100-pound barrel of pork "would seldom last a week."[4]

The "nice pork" that flavored the corn meal Susan and Andrew Adams welcomed with grateful hearts in their Shakopee shanty in 1856 was almost certainly salt pork. Barrels of it were regularly unloaded at the river towns to be sold there or carried overland by wagon to outlying settlements. It was also put up by local butchers, as indicated by a St. Paul grocer's advertisement in the *Minnesota Pioneer* of November 11, 1852, announcing "PORK — Clear Mess, just put up last week, a superior article for families." More often, it was packed at home by Minnesotans for their own use.[5]

To prepare salt pork, the sides of a butchered hog were cut crosswise into strips. These were packed on edge in a barrel with the rind touching its sides. The bottom of the keg was covered with salt, which was also sprinkled generously between each layer of meat. A *"strong* brine" of soft water "sufficient to cover the pork" was boiled, skimmed, and poured into the barrel while *"boiling hot."* A board of smaller dimension than the barrel opening was set on top and weighted to keep the contents completely submerged in the liquid. If frothing or redness developed in the brine, it had to be poured off, "scalded, and returned while *hot."* Old brine, if boiled and skimmed, could be used on new pork, but cooks were adjured: *"Never put cold brine on old pork,* unless you wish to lose it."[6]

Even a self-proclaimed "decided prejudice" against pork did not prevent Mary Henderson from recommending that a "little salted pork or bacon should always be kept in the house." She believed pork to be both "unwholesome and dangerous" to persons who lived in cities "unless used in the smallest quantities." On the other hand, she wrote somewhat guardedly, "in the country, perhaps, there is less cause for doubt about its use, where the animal is raised with corn," and where the outdoor life of the people "will permit the taking of stronger food." Other cookbook authors were not encumbered by Mrs. Henderson's bias, but they were aware of the prevalence of contaminated pork. All

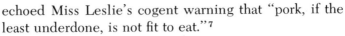

Pork.

1. Leg.
2. Hind Loin.
3. Fore Loin.

4. Spare Rib.
5. Hand.
6. Spring.

echoed Miss Leslie's cogent warning that "pork, if the least underdone, is not fit to eat."[7]

When pork was purchased from a butcher, great care had to be taken in its selection to avoid "ill-fed or diseased" meat. *Buckeye Cookery* told buyers to look for fine-grained lean and white fat. "The rind should be smooth and cool to the touch. If clammy, be sure the pork is stale, and reject it," the book stated. Bacon was checked for a thin rind, firm fat, and tender lean, and hams could be tested by sticking a knife into them; if it came out without a bad odor, the ham was considered good.[8]

A slaughtered hog yielded a variety of products — fine leaf lard to be rendered for cooking and baking use, low-quality fat for soap, casings for sausages, bladders for covering jars and crocks, and many types of pork cuts to be eaten fresh, salted, smoked, or made into sausages and headcheese. Entries in the diary of a farmwife living near Minneapolis in 1886 portray the extra work butchering made for women. Early on a cold Tuesday in February, the men of her family butchered the hogs, and in the afternoon she cleaned the entrails to use for sausage casings. The following day her husband cut up the meat while she cut and rendered the lard. She also began to fix sausage meat, a chore she finished on the third day. "What a hard tiresome week this has been," she wrote on Thursday. "Today finishes up my butchering work. We got sausage . . . have mixed and packed them, fixed head cheese[,] baked bread & ginger cake[,] churned & had to sit down to warm my feet & rest a while before pack-

ing away my butter. Am glad I was able to get it all done, it is a good job over with."[9]

Headcheese, normally made at butchering time, was especially valued for its good keeping qualities. Each cook's recipe differed from her neighbor's in some way, usually in the spices she favored or in the fineness of the cheese's texture. This recipe, contributed to a Minnesota church cookbook, clearly shows the frugal housewife's intention to make use of all parts of the carcass, including the hocks:

"Select a nice pig's head and hocks, soak them over night in weak limewater. In the morning scrape, clean, removing the ears, eyes and brains, and put into clear water. Take of tender, lean beef eight or ten pounds, which place toward the bottom of the vessel, as it requires more cooking than the pork. (Few housekeepers have one vessel of sufficient size, except the washboiler.) Cover with cold water. Several hours will be required to boil all tender.[10]

"When done, take from the liquid and remove every bit of bone. If the process of freeing from bones has not broken the meat rather fine, it all may be chopped a little. Mix the lean and fat thoroughly together while still warm, and while mixing add salt, pepper, and allspice, or sage, if preferred. Put it away in several shallow dishes, from which it can be sliced thin for the table, and then only a portion need be thawed at a time. As it will keep nice all winter in a cold place it is very convenient to have. It makes a pleasant change to warm some of it for breakfast. The hocks are nice seasoned by themselves, with the large bones removed, seasoned with salt, pepper, and allspice, covered with vinegar, and a weight placed upon them."

Sausage, like headcheese, reflected individual tastes. A St. Paul woman used ½ pound of salt, 2 ounces each of pepper and sage, and "a little ginger and a little sugar" to season 20 pounds of meat. Other cooks added nutmeg, lemon thyme, or a "glass of Rhenish, Champagne, Madeira, or other wine."[11]

The sausage meat was either put into jars or stuffed into casings. The latter had to be prepared ahead of time. Miss Leslie, who much preferred keeping the meat in jars, nevertheless included directions for fixing the "large entrails, whose skins are to be used for sausages." They had to be "cleaned out carefully, well scraped, and thrown into strong salt and water for two days, (changing the brine the second day,) and afterwards into strong lye for twenty-four hours. Lastly, wash them in fresh water."[12]

The casings, said Miss Leslie, were then ready to be stuffed with the following filling: "To fifteen pounds of the lean of fresh pork, allow five pounds of the fat. Having removed the skin, sinews, and gristle, chop both the fat and lean as fine as possible, and mix them well together. Rub to a powder sufficient sage-leaves to make four ounces when done. Mix the sage with two ounces of fine salt, two ounces of brown sugar, an ounce of powdered black pepper, and a quarter of an ounce of cayenne. Add this seasoning to the chopped pork, and mix it thoroughly. Pack the sausage-meat down, hard and

SAUSAGE FILLERS.

closely, into stone jars, which must be kept in a cool place, and well covered. When wanted for use, make some of it into small flat cakes, dredge them with flour, and fry them well. The fat that exudes from the sausage-cakes, while frying, will be sufficient to cook them in."

A combination of salted pork and salted beef was the basis for "Bologna" sausages. Boiled separately, the meats were cooled, chopped, and mixed with fat bacon, beef suet, black pepper, powdered mace, sweet mar-joram, sage, and, if desired, minced boiled onions. The mixture was stuffed into large beef casings which had been cleaned and scraped until almost transparent; then the sausages were tied and sewed at the ends. After a week of soaking in a brine of salt, molasses, and brown sugar, plus a few days of drying, and another week of exposure to oakwood smoke, the sausages were to be rubbed "over with salad oil, which is much the better for being mixed with ashes of vine twigs." Although these sausages were considered "equal to the real Bologna," said Miss Leslie cryptically, "Few ladies eat them."[13]

Ham Boiler.

Having completed her sausage making, a housewife who was not able to salt or freeze the remaining pork turned at once to other methods. To preserve a 5-pound piece of meat for five or six days even "in the hottest weather," it was sometimes completely immersed in souring skimmed milk that was "just getting thick" and set aside in a cool place with a cloth tied over the 3-gallon stoneware crock.[14]

An altogether different method of keeping uncooked pork or beef "fresh for weeks" during the summer required that the meat be sliced before it was put into a large jar which had been cleansed with a strong solution of salt and hot water. A combination of salt, pepper, and saltpeter sprinkled between the slices combined with the meat juices to make a brine. A cloth wrung out in water mixed with more salt and saltpeter was pressed closely over the meat. Whenever enough for a meal was removed from the jar, the cloth was carefully put back over the remainder. Occasional washing of the cloth in cold water followed by scalding in a solution of salt and hot water was suggested to keep it pure. In the absence of a "cool dry place" to store the jar, a two-inch-thick layer of melted lard was poured directly on top of the meat before the cloth cover was secured. Sugar, molasses, and spices supplemented salt in some recipes to achieve varying flavors.[15]

"A Coat of Melted Lard."

Lard was similarly used to seal "potted" meat, fish, or fowl. In this process, the meat was pounded to a paste, seasoned, baked, and covered with a protective sheath of butter or lard. One recipe for potted chicken suggested adding a cup of cold boiled ham to a quart of cold, boned, and skinned roast chicken. The two were chopped, pounded to a paste, then mixed with "four table-spoonfuls of butter, a speck of cayenne, a slight grating of nutmeg, and two teaspoons of salt." The result was packed "solidly in small stone pots," which were covered, set in a pan of hot water, and baked in a moderate oven for an hour. After the contents cooled, melted fat or butter was poured on top, heavy paper covers were pasted on, and the jars were put away in the cellar.[16]

While it was said that potted ham would "keep for months" in a good cellar, it was up to the cook to figure out how long it was safe to store other similarly prepared meats, poultry, or fish. When she wished to serve the potted meats, she removed the fat from the top of the jar, loosened the meat by running a knife around the inside, and turned the contents out onto a plate for easy slicing. If it was not rancid, the butter or lard that had sealed the jar could be reserved to baste other foods.[17]

A totally different technique, which called for a basic brine solution, was required for the preparation of corned beef, a traditional and dependable staple. One Minnesota housewife's recipe was especially detailed: "Take your beef, be it much or little; rub it over lightly with salt, and put it in either an earthern [sic] or wooden vessel; let it stand two or three days, then take it out, throw away the liquor, cleanse the vessel, and put it back again. Make a pickle of good salt that will bear up an egg; to about every four gallons of liquor add two pounds of sugar and two ounces of saltpetre; mix well together, and pour over the meat until it is covered; it must be kept under the brine." A variation called "Spiced Corned Beef" required that a mixture of molasses, saltpeter, ground pepper, cloves, and salt be rubbed into the beef daily for ten days; then the meat was said to be cured and ready to use.[18]

An acceptable alternative to salting or corning was drying. In this process the meat (usually beef or venison) was rubbed with salt and sugar, covered with a brine of soft water, salt, sugar or molasses, soda, and saltpeter, and soaked for three weeks. It was then transferred to a

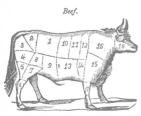

Beef.

1. Sirloin.
2. Rump.
3. Edge Bone.
4. Buttock.
5. Mouse Buttock.
6. Leg.
7. Thick Flank.
8. Veiny Piece.
9. Thin Flank.

10. Fore Rib: 7 Ribs.
11. Middle Rib; 4 Ribs.
12. Chuck Rib; 3 Ribs.
13. Brisket.
14. Shoulder, or Leg of Mutton Piece.
15. Clod.
16. Neck, or Sticking Piece.
17. Shin.
18. Cheek

tub of clear water for a day, removed, and hung from the kitchen ceiling (preferably over the stove or near heat from the fireplace) for another three or four weeks to dry. If the meat was placed instead on a frame behind the stove, it had to be turned each day to allow equal exposure to heat on all sides. When it was "well dried on the outside, and free from rawness to the center," it was sprinkled with ground black pepper — a recognized insect repellent — and either set in an empty flour barrel with a snugly fitting cover or tied in paper sacks and hung in a cool, dry, dark place.[19]

Jerky, the dried meat often used on the plains by both Indians and frontiersmen, could be made from beef, fish, or game. Some Minnesota families dried the breasts of prairie chickens during the summer for a winter meat supply. The procedure was to cut the boneless flesh into long thin slices, knead salt into them, and lay them aside under cover for about four hours. Then the slices were spread out in the hot sun to dry for a few days, or they were hung on a frame of green twigs over a good thick smoke for 24 hours. Fish cured in this way were skinned and boned before drying. When properly cured, the slices were dry to the touch and about half their original size. It was said that jerked meat would last for a year or more, and it could be eaten cold or fried.[20]

Smoking — the centuries-old, tried and true home method of preserving meats still used in some parts of the nation — involved several steps. Cuts of beef, venison, or pork, for example, were first treated with saltpeter and salt and then spiced with a pungent mixture that might include ginger, mace, black pepper, and cloves for two or three weeks before they were hung in the smokehouse and exposed for varying lengths of time to the smoke of a slow-burning fire. Smoldering chips of aromatic wood (oak, maple, and hickory were favorites) or even corn-cobs imparted a distinctive flavor to pork, fish, and wild game.[21]

Many cooking authorities of the era did not deal with the subject of smoke curing at any length, nor did they suggest how long an exposure was needed to be fully effective. Perhaps this information was so generally known that it did not occur to them to write it down. A revised and enlarged edition of the *New Buckeye Cook Book* which appeared as late as 1904 recommended that a large ham remain in a "good smoke" for 40 hours. A household encyclopedia published in 1909 allowed that "pork hams," which might be comparable in size to large cuts of beef or venison, should be smoked "8 to 10 hours or several weeks, according to the convenience and quality desired." The instructions warned that "Quick smoking merely coats the outside of the ham, but does not penetrate the fiber."[22]

Directions for constructing a farm smokehouse "That Will Give Satisfaction" appeared in the *North Branch Review*, a Chisago County newspaper, in 1891. "It is to be built of brick, well pointed, with no chance for the admission of flies," the article advised. The structure, which measured 8 by 8 feet and was 12 feet high, was fitted with a screen-covered ventilator at each gable to allow smoke to escape and hooks for hanging meat. The design also called for a pipe to bring smoke inside the house via an underground route from a fire source "at least 20 feet" away. The fire could be built, said the newspaper, in "any metal receptacle with suitable draft that may be properly opened or closed to prevent the actual breaking out of flame. Thus the smoke always enters the smoke house cool, and the meat may be hung even close to the ground."[23]

The house would hold 15 to 20 bars on which could hang 120 to 160 pieces of meat — more than enough for "an ordinary sized family." It was thought safe to leave meat hanging in such a smokehouse throughout the summer, for "a light smoke once a week or ten days will keep the meat in good condition, and no flies can possibly injure it."

The *New Buckeye Cook Book* provided directions for "a good and cheap smoke house quickly and easily made." The farmer was to "dig a trench about three feet long, and one half foot wide, cover it with brick, and then dirt; at one end of the trench dig a hole about two feet deep, and large enough to set an old kettle or something to hold the fire, at the other end of the trench, place a barrel, (with top heads out), put a stick across the top, on which to hang the meat; cover the barrel with old carpet, or anything to hold the smoke in. Or take an old hogshead, stop up all crevices, and fix a place to put a crossstick near the bottom, to hang the article to be smoked on. Next, in the side, cut a hole near the top, to introduce an iron pan filled with sawdust and small pieces of green wood, having turned the tub upside down, hang the arti-

"Hang up Under a Barrel."

cles upon the cross-sticks, introduce the iron pan in the opening, and place a piece of red-hot iron in the pan, cover it with sawdust, and all will be complete."[24]

"The best wood for smoking meat is oak, and, where a barrel is used, oak sawdust," wrote Juliet Corson. She also approved of green hickory and maple as well as corncobs. A charcoal fire could be used for small amounts of meat in a specially made smoking-closet that was probably much fancier than the homemade ones actually used on the frontier. Certainly the wood needed to make the closet and to burn for charcoal would have been impossible to come by on the Minnesota prairies in the early years of settlement. The smoking-closet was essentially a wooden box that usually measured about 3 by 5 feet. One of its four sides was hinged to allow access to the meat. The box stood on legs sufficiently high so that a small metal stove to accommodate the coals would fit under it. A thick layer of hardwood sawdust was spread over the live coals. The stove was ventilated by air holes to keep the fire smoldering. A funnel at its top allowed the smoke to flow into the chamber where the meat was hung on iron rods. Another funnel at the top of the closet functioned as a chimney "to carry off the smoke." It was said to take a week to cure "small joints" in this device, while "large ones" had to be smoked "from ten days to two weeks."[25]

That schemes of all kinds abounded to speed up the lengthy smoke-curing process was implicit in a stern warning issued by Miss Leslie: "Never allow yourself to be persuaded to use pyroligneous acid [*acetic acid and wood alcohol*] in curing dried beef or ham — instead of the real smoke of a wood fire. It communicates a taste and smell of kreosote, and is a detestable substitute, detected in a moment."[26]

Buckeye Cookery in 1881 offered a more acceptable short cut under the title "A New Way to Smoke Hams." A preliminary smoking of the inside of the barrel in which meat was to be "pickled" in a brine reduced the total curing time to eight or nine days. To smoke the barrel, it was inverted over a slow hardwood fire burning in a kettle. The smoked barrel was packed with hams which were then covered with a strong brine of salt, molasses, and saltpeter that had been boiled, skimmed, and cooled. According to *Buckeye Cookery*, if necessary the hams could be kept in the brine for a year "without damage."[27]

The brine in which various meats were soaked before smoking varied not only from meat to meat but also from cook to cook. A St. Paul family prepared an all-purpose brine of soft water, an ingredient referred to as "alum salt," saltpeter, and brown sugar. According to a recipe of the Rudolph H. Fitz family, hams had to be immersed in the brine for six weeks; beef and game required only 10 to 12 days. When the meat was taken from the solution, it was dried for a day or two and protected against freezing. Meanwhile a slow fire was prepared in the smokehouse to be ready when the meat was hung for the final curing.[28]

Another procedure called for rubbing the skin side of a fresh ham (or a slab of bacon) with a teaspoon of powdered saltpeter and the cut side with a teaspoon of cayenne pepper, followed by additional applications of a combination of salt and brown sugar. The bottom of a large tub was liberally sprinkled with salt before the hams were put into it. Salt was added between each of them and over the top of all. After eight days the hams were removed, the salt wiped off, and the tub washed out. They were returned to the tub and a brine of soft water, salt, molasses, and saltpeter — boiled, skimmed, and cooled — was poured over them. Hams required a four-week immersion for the necessary curing; bacon required three weeks. The pickling brine was then washed off and the meat was buried "while wet in a tub of bran to form a crust," thus preventing "evaporation of the juices." With a crust well formed and dried, the meat was immediately hung in the smokehouse.[29]

After the hams or other cuts of "fine pork" had been smoked for at least two to four weeks, they were usually liberally covered with ground black pepper, put into either a paper bag well secured at the top, or sewed tightly into a new cloth of coarse, thick cotton which was next whitewashed for additional protection. They were then hung in a garret or elsewhere within the house. Although she approved of the whitewash covering, Miss Leslie commented, "We have seen ham-covers, painted with flowers and gilded. Since California, gilding pervades the land." Whether California's gold discoveries inspired the artistic talents of Minnesota's housewives is not known.[30]

Some of them, however, chose not to hang the smoked hams and pork roasts at all, but to wrap them in brown

THE GAME FOR DINNER.

paper and put them in a box where they were completely surrounded with wood ashes that had been leached to remove the lye. Others simply put the cured meat without wrapping into a tightly covered box or barrel in the cellar where it could be covered on all sides with shelled corn, oats, or "clean, sweet hay, before flies come." Slices of cured ham, closely packed in jars, would "keep through the season" after melted lard was poured over the top of the jar to exclude the air. Housewives were warned to "*always be particular* to melt the lard and return it *immediately* to the jar" after some ham slices were removed.[31]

Because wild game birds — now regarded as gourmet delicacies — were a commonplace on the family table, housewives also sought ways to preserve them as security against times of shortage. Pigeons, geese, snipe, quail, grouse, ducks, wild turkeys, and prairie chickens were important food sources in pioneer Minnesota. For two years a family living in the southern part of the state in the early 1850s had "no meat but ducks and prairie chickens." Others enjoyed the now-extinct passenger pigeons, once so plentiful in Fillmore County, for example, "that they darkened the sky when they flew."[32]

Such birds, if killed during the summer, could be kept for two days provided they were drawn right after they were killed, washed in "several waters," then immersed in boiling water, and moved about in the pot for five minutes. After that they were drained, wiped dry, and cooled. The necks and cavities were rubbed with pepper before the birds were hung in a "dark cool place." An alternative was to wash them in soda water, rinse them in clear water, drain them, and insert several pieces of charcoal in the cavities before covering the birds with a cloth and suspending them in the cellar.[33]

In spite of the housewife's best efforts, fresh poultry and game often became "strong" before they could be used. The remedy recommended by *Buckeye Cookery* to "sweeten them when they are apparently spoiled" was to soak the birds for several hours in a solution of either charcoal or soda. Another formula, said to be so all-inclusive that it would rectify the condition of "Ill-Smelling Meats, Poultry[,] Fish, Butter, etc.," was offered in the one-volume, dual-purpose medical guide and cookbook prepared by Dr. Chase. It specified that an ounce of "Permanganate of potash" should be completely dissolved in a quart of water that had been boiled and allowed to cool. The housewife was instructed to add "from a teaspoon to a tablespoonful" of the solution to enough cold water to cover the meat. "Stir with a stick," the doctor cautioned, "as it stains the hand or clothing." Every part of the chicken, meat, duck, or fish had to be washed thoroughly and allowed to stand in the treated water for ten minutes before it was rinsed. Then "all 'taint' or ill-smell" would be eliminated.[34]

With a good supply of salted, fresh, and dried fish in the town markets and the abundant catches from Minnesota's inland lakes, rivers, and streams, housewives throughout the 19th century counted fish as a common staple. Minnesota's waterways were fairly alive with bass, pike, pickerel, sturgeon, dogfish, sunfish, buffalo fish, catfish, carp, and trout. Despite their general availability, fish sometimes were preserved in the home to augment supplies in the cellar or to add to the canned sardines, salmon, and oysters that could be purchased. A family living near Watertown regularly caught fish in a nearby lake in the 1850s and dried and smoked them to add "a nice variety to our somewhat same diet." An ever-present problem in storing fish was to prevent the transfer of its "fishy smell and taste" to other foods kept in the cellar.[35]

The easiest way to put up fish was to dry them. Some families no doubt followed the time-honored Indian method of simply splitting small fish lengthwise and laying them on the horizontal poles of a drying rack set outdoors. Larger fish were cleaned and cut along each side of the backbone, leaving the head attached, before they were placed on the rack. The drying process was often helped along with a small fire built below the hanging fish.[36]

Household guides provided more complicated directions for drying cod, salmon, mackerel, haddock, herring, pike, and trout, and Minnesota women could easily adapt the rules to whatever fish were available. In her instructions for drying salmon, Juliet Corson told readers to scale the fish, "split it down the back, remove the entrails, saving the roe; then rub the fish thoroughly with dry salt, and hang it by the gills to drain over night. The next day mix together two ounces each of powdered rock-salt and brown sugar and four ounces of powdered saltpetre; rub this mixture well into the fish, and lay it on

a large dish for two days; then drain the fish, rub it thoroughly with dry salt, hang it by the gills, and let it dry. After it is thoroughly dry, it will be ready for use."[37]

Early editions of *Buckeye Cookery* neglected the subject of drying fish, but the editor of that issued in 1904 saw fit to include these directions: "Fish may be simply salted well and dried in the air, afterwards smoking them if liked, or rubbed over with pepper and salt and cured by hanging in a dry place indoors, which is generally thought the better way." The writer went on to comment on the handling of specific fish. Cod was most often plainly salted, without being spiced or smoked; small fish required only 24 hours in salt. Large fish, such as pike and trout, should have the backbone removed before they were salted and hung up to drain for a day and a night; after that they were again rubbed with salt, moist sugar, and spices, then dried for 24 hours and cured with smoke.[38]

Salted fish was a familiar commodity to Minnesotans, and to prepare it at home the housewife could use this recipe for preserving salmon: "Cut the fish up the back, and cut out the bone; wipe it clean, and sprinkle it with salt; let it lay a night to drain off the liquor; wipe it dry, rub on it two or three ounces of pounded saltpetre; cut it into pieces; pack it close in a pot with a thick layer of salt between each layer of fish." If the brine did not rise within a few days, the cook was advised to "boil a strong one, and pour it, when cold, upon the salmon, which must always be covered with it."[39]

Along with fish, Minnesotans counted on deer and

other game to supply meat for the table. As late as 1856, several years after it was supposed that the buffalo had withdrawn to the Dakotas beyond the northern and western limits of Minnesota Territory, two very large herds wandered down to the St. Cloud area. In 1850, buffalo in the Red River Valley were hunted by métis from Pembina, and much of the spoils of that hunt reached St. Paul in the form of pemmican, which sold for 10 cents a pound. Buffalo tongues, considered a delicacy, also were for sale that year at $5 a dozen.[40]

As described by an elderly missionary who ate it as early as 1841, pemmican "was made by boiling the flesh of any edible animal, usually that of buffalo or deer, pounding it fine and packing it tight into a sack made of the skin of a buffalo calf, then melting the fat and filling all interstices. When sewed up, it was absolutely air tight and would keep indefinitely."[41]

Venison.

Another version was made of dried buffalo meat, pulverized, and, with dried berries added, put in buffalo bags with hot marrow grease. The latter was the Indian-made pemmican familiar to voyageurs, explorers, and early frontiersmen for many decades. It could be eaten cold or served as a soup called "rubbaboo." While it may not have been the most appetizing of dishes, it was considered "the most nourishing food that has ever been prepared." Many settlers attempted to make pemmican, but "it took a half breed to do it right," according to the missionary. Perhaps it found a place in the cellars of early pioneers, but as more and tastier foods became available, pemmican passed into history along with the fur trader and the free-roaming Indians of Minnesota.[42]

By the late 1850s, elk herds had diminished in Minnesota, leaving as targets for the food-hunters' guns deer, fowl, such small game animals as squirrels and rabbits, and, in the northern parts of the state, moose. In the Grand Rapids region near the end of the century, hunters regularly provided moose meat to the local butcher shops, where "good cuts" of steak and roast sold for 10 cents a pound.[43]

Perhaps Minnesota housewives were satisfied with the traditional methods of preserving meats and fish and were not eager to put them up in glass or tin cans as they did fruits and vegetables. Instructions for canning meats are lacking in the household guides published before 1900, but in 1909 the author of *Household Discoveries* helpfully included a complete description of the process. "Meats to be canned," he wrote, "are first cut into suitable pieces, boiled until tender and packed in glass jars surrounded by boiling water. The meat jelly, or 'aspic,' in which they have been cooked, is then seasoned to taste and poured over them, boiling hot, until the jar is filled to the brim, and they are then sealed while hot." The aspic was said to preserve the meat and improve its flavor.[44]

Tin cans, too, could be used for cooked meats. With the cans filled, the "cover is then soldered in place, a small hole is punctured in it and the water surrounding the can is boiled until steam escapes from the aperture. The opening is then closed with solder." The book explained that as the can cooled a vacuum would be formed "by which the sides of the can are made slightly concave." If the concavity disappeared, it was a "sure indication that the contents were not properly preserved and have become putrid."

By hindsight, the outlines of the coming revolution that would help relegate these time-consuming procedures to footnotes in the history of food preservation could be perceived when the *Minnesota Pioneer* of December 18, 1851, published an announcement of considerable significance to St. Paul housewives. An icehouse was being constructed near the upper landing large enough to hold 900 tons of ice. The availability of a year-round supply of ice would dramatically lessen dependence on the vagaries of outdoor storerooms, cellars, and springhouses to preserve perishable foods.

The everyday benefits of "one of the greatest of summer luxuries" inspired editors and household guides to urge everyone to build icehouses. "Here in Minnesota, we are highly favored, as a general thing, with rivers and lakes near at hand," said the *Farmer and Gardener*, and consequently the "Luxury" of ice was readily available. Other publications pointed out that a costly structure was not necessary. The writers of *Buckeye Cookery* advised that "A cheap ice-house may be made by partitioning off a space about twelve feet square in the wood-shed, or even in the barn. The roof must be tight over it" and a coat of coal tar would protect the interior walls from constant moisture. A separate icehouse was considered even more desirable and in the 1880s could be constructed for as little as $25 to $50.[45]

"To Gather Ice for Home Use."

It was recommended that ice be harvested "from still places in running streams or from clear ponds," preferably on days when the temperature stood near zero, so the ice would immediately freeze dry and thus be easier to handle. It was generally agreed that "ice put up in sharp, cold weather, before it has been subjected to any thaw, will keep much better and be much more useful in the hot days of summer than if its packing had been delayed until late winter or early spring, and then the ice put up half melted and wet."[46]

As early as the 1880s the purity of St. Paul's ice supply became an issue when the plan to harvest it from the Mississippi River was blocked by an ordinance prohibiting the cutting of ice at any point on the stream below the Falls of St. Anthony. The ruling resulted from concern over contamination of the river by the Minneapolis sewage system. Smaller villages and farmers were perhaps less encumbered in their search for clean ice, and the harvesting of it was often accomplished as a community effort. A typical icecutting scene was briefly described in the diary kept by a farmer at Eden Prairie: "They manage to get out ice here in quick time[,] cut it in long cakes and hitch horses to it, which can pull out pieces 2 ft wide & 10 to 14 ft long." On a day when the temperature stood at 14 degrees below zero before sunrise, the ice was "about 20 inches thick and very fine; clear of snow and clear as chrystal."[47]

Before the ice blocks were packed into the icehouse, the floor was covered with a foot-thick layer of sawdust. A space was left between the ice and the walls to be insulated with additional well-packed sawdust. Any crevices between the layers of ice were filled with the same material. If sawdust in sufficient quantity was not available, chaff or finely cut straw was substituted. As the ice settled, more insulation was added, for the keeping quality of the ice depended on its minimal exposure to air.[48]

Stored ice sometimes became quite smelly, and a remedy was suggested by the *Minnesota Pioneer* of June 3, 1852, the first summer after St. Paul's icehouse opened: "Take old ice, no matter, if sour, a year old, and to every ten pounds of it, add one teaspoonful of saleratus, and it will be just as sweet and fresh as when first packed."

When the first block of ice was brought into a kitchen and put into a home-constructed or store-bought icebox, the 19th-century housewife witnessed a change of the first magnitude in her efforts to provide healthful food. She also experienced a work-easing convenience comparable to the replacement of a fireplace by a cookstove. The simple application of cold to prolong the quality of food and protect it from spoiling marked the first stage in a revolution in refrigeration that has led to home freezers in the 20th century. Ice was the helpful natural forerunner of the developing technology that has since rendered unnecessary many of the procedures, the labor, and the time that once went into the effort of keeping meat and fish on the pioneer table.

A MOTHER'S NEGLECT.

"Never mind, dear, I'll do the cooking; your mother should have taught you—your are not to blame."

CHAPTER SEVEN

Kitchens and Kitchenry

WHETHER RICH OR POOR, the primary concern of 19th-century housewives was food for their families. If her circumstances allowed, a woman could hire readily available servants and cooks to ease her work load and to help maintain a stylish home with a well-appointed kitchen. More likely, however, the Minnesota pioneer homemaker fought the food battle with a minimum of assistance from helpers and modern conveniences. She might not, in fact, even have had a kitchen in which to cook, for a separate room solely devoted to food preparation was not the prevailing standard in Minnesota homes during the early years of settlement. Nor did she usually have much in the way of kitchen utensils or cupboards in which to store them.

An early Duluth settler recalled, for example, that his family's "whole outfit comprised a feather bed and a lunch basket in which were a knife, fork and two small china dishes. . . . We built our bedsteads out of green tamarack poles . . . and made a table of two boards which were found floating in the Bay" of Lake Superior. For a southern Minnesota family who moved from rented rooms at Rochester to Marshall in 1873, the spartan conditions so often experienced by earlier arrivals still obtained. Their new house was a 10-foot-square "board shanty," which the housewife noted wryly "will be not very commodious." The somewhat larger 16-by-24-foot home of a Steele County family in 1856 had a room that served as kitchen, dining, and living quarters combined. In it was a "nice" table with drop leaves and compartmentalized drawers at each end.[1]

The ground floor of this family's house included a small pantry or "buttery," as it was sometimes called. These terms referred to a closetlike, ground-floor room, often without a door or windows, that was usually located near the cooking area. In it the housewife might mix her cakes, make starch from raw potatoes, cure beef and pork in brine, make soap, candles or yeast, churn butter, make cheese, prepare vegetables and other foods, or store staples that were not placed in the cellar.[2]

"In modern houses," said *Buckeye Cookery*, "the pantry is next in importance to the kitchen." Ideally, the storeroom was fitted with an abundance of shelves, boxes and drawers arranged to accommodate china, linens, and infrequently used utensils, along with preserves, dry groceries, pickles, bread, cake, bags of fruit, and bunches of dried herbs. In some of Minnesota's more grand mansions, such as the Alexander Ramsey house in St. Paul, large pantries also became the servants' dining area.

The placement of shelves and boxes "will suggest itself to any tidy person," commented Juliet Corson, "as it

affords the easiest access to their contents." Windows were considered best placed on a north wall to avoid heating the room by sunlight, and, cautioned *Buckeye Cookery*, they should have "wire gauze or other screen to keep out flies."

Household guides of the day advocated separate kitchens and pantries and proposed an assortment of guidelines to achieve "neat and cheerful" surroundings for food preparation. Some up-and-coming Minnesota settlers soon incorporated such rooms into their homes, although pantries were far more common than separate kitchens. A kitchen was added to Henry H. Sibley's limestone house in Mendota (the oldest remaining private dwelling in the state) only after the fur trader was married in the 1840s. Before that, cooking had been done in a stone fireplace located in the cellar. The new house Mr. and Mrs. John North built in 1850 in what is now Minneapolis was considered distinctive because it had not only a separate kitchen but also a pantry and a cistern. These features were also present in the large, elegant frame home constructed in 1855 at Taylors Falls for lumberman William H. C. Folsom, which included a kitchen, a pantry with a cistern *and* a pump, as well as a separate summer kitchen. This house also had an unusual feature for its day — a built-in storage wall for dishes located between the kitchen and the dining room and accessible from both rooms.[3]

The walls of kitchens in such homes were usually plastered and treated with "a good old-fashioned whitewash" which was reapplied once a year. One household guide

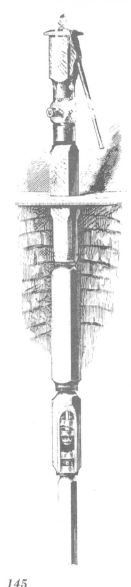

advised that the whitewash was less likely to rub off if it was mixed with a "weak solution of glue." The floor might be packed clay, a puncheon of split logs, "loosely laid" rough boards bleached white from many scrubbings with lye, or wide white pine boards smoothly finished and painted.[4]

In the early years floors could have been covered with an inexpensive homemade oilcloth like that recommended by an 1847 household guide. To make it, the householder was advised to "buy cheap tow cloth, and fit it to the size and shape of the kitchen. Then have it stretched, and nailed to the south side of the barn, and, with a brush, cover it with a coat of thin rye paste. When this is dry, put on a coat of yellow paint, and let it dry for a fortnight. It is safest to first try the paint, and see if it dries well, as some paint never will dry. Then put on a second coat, and at the end of another fortnight, a third coat. Then let it hang two months, and it will last, uninjured, for many years. The longer the paint is left to dry, the better. If varnished, it will last much longer."[5]

Floor care ideas changed with time, and three decades later another homemakers' encyclopedia favored unpainted hardwood kitchen floors rubbed with oil two or three times a year. Grease spots might then be "easily wiped up," but if they failed to respond to such simple treatment an application of soft soap or hot lye and a scouring with ashes might be necessary for removal.[6]

By 1880 the availability of commercially made linoleum was announced in the news columns of the *Minneapolis Tribune.* The paper said on October 16,

1880, that this "Remarkable" new product was "composed of cork, making a clean, warm, soft, very handsome and durable floor covering. Its claims to extraordinary durability have been thoroughly tested. It is printed in handsome designs, and sold by all carpet dealers."

Of the four principal features in today's kitchens — a stove, refrigerator, sink, and built-in cupboards — three were often missing from the mid-19th-century frontier home. Only a stove was usually, but not always, present, and even its aspect would not bring a nod of recognition from today's homemaker. It was a rare Minnesota home that had a sink, an icebox, or built-in cupboards in the 1850s. Such cupboards as existed were likely to be hand-crafted chests or merely open shelves. One household authority suggested that careful thought should be given to the value of investing in "a wide, roomy dresser" in which to store pots, kettles, and kitchen crockery to "bring order out of the natural chaos of the kitchen." [7]

"Clean a Small Section."

If the housewife did have a sink, it was usually located in the pantry. Like the cupboards, it was not attached to the wall nor did it necessarily have a drain. Rather it was often a chestlike piece of wooden furniture that in the 1850s had a top lined with zinc or copper and space below for a pail to catch the waste water. Another variation known as a dry sink had no drain hole at all and was intended only to hold a wash basin and a water pitcher.

Many homes without sinks or drains got along with buckets and washbasins for which water had to be carried both in and then out again. It was a fortunate housewife who had an inside pump, "one of the first mechani-

cal inventions used in the house," wrote a later social historian. "When it was connected with the cistern, a water barrel under the eaves was no longer needed." In rural areas beyond the reach of the municipal water and sewage systems developed after the Civil War, home water supplies were obtained by individual householders from private and public wells, springs, and other typhoid-carrying sources. In such homes, washstands, holding buckets and basins, served as both kitchen sink and wash-up area well into the 20th century.[8]

By the end of the 19th century a cast-iron or wrought-steel sink that stood on four legs could be part of a very up-to-date kitchen. One authority suggested that the cast-iron sink be painted or coated with white enamel and the steel sink be painted, galvanized, or coated with blue enamel.[9]

Domestic guides of the era had little to say about sinks or water supplies, although they stressed that general cleanliness was important in an era when typhoid fever was a widespread problem. For those housewives lucky enough to have drains, one guide recommended a "handful of washing-soda thrown upon the strainer over the drain-pipe" as a good practice to follow before "greasy water is poured down it after a meal is over." To control "unpleasant or unhealthy" odors, a pailful of copperas water or a mixture of water and chloride of lime heated and poured into drains would "keep them entirely free from dangerous emanations." The latter was to be put into them on Mondays and Thursdays during the summer, and only on Mondays during the winter.[10]

The center of warmth and cooking activity in frontier kitchen areas might be a fireplace, but during the period of Minnesota settlement it was much more likely to be a heavy cast-iron stove. These cumbersome objects were considered so important that in the early years they were often transported west in settlers' wagons. Mrs. John North, who arrived in Minnesota with her husband in 1849, traveled west from Syracuse, New York, by steamboat, rail, and stagecoach. When the Norths reached Galena, Illinois, they decided to buy some household furnishings before boarding a steamboat for the trip up the Mississippi River to St. Paul. For $23 they bought a kitchen table, chairs, a washtub, pails, a washboard, other household miscellany, and a cookstove with "four boiling places, beside two in the hearth that can be used in summer, without heating the other part of the stove much."[11]

Spider.

Along with the stove, the Norths received from the merchant "a tin boiler and tea kettle, — an iron kettle, . . . an iron pot, larger — a rather small spider [*frying pan*] — a dripping pan — a flatiron heater — a steamer — a round cake cutter — a large dipper — a tin reflector for baking on the stove hearth." In addition, the merchant supplied two baking tins, which Mrs. North described as "all the oven will hold at once."

Ann North found no fault with the stove, "But — oh! my cookery!" she wrote. She had no difficulty frying pork and cooking potatoes, but a cranberry pie was a different matter. She failed to sweeten it sufficiently before she put it in an overheated oven, where the crust baked to a "dark, handsome snuff" color and the juice from the cranberries bubbled out all over the oven. Her husband, an adaptable man who later founded the town of North-field and moved on to new frontiers in California, discovered the pie was palatable if he mixed up the crust and the fruit and poured molasses over them. Gradually Mrs. North gained experience in cooking and mastered the intricacies of the oven. Not long afterward, she wrote that she made "first rate" bread and pie crust.[12]

That cookstoves were regarded as highly desirable is indicated by an advertisement in the November 10, 1849, issue of the *Minnesota Chronicle and Register* published at St. Paul. Although no separate kitchen was listed, the paper declared that a 5-room house for sale at $600 was a great bargain because it included a large cookstove, a root house, a stable, and a pantry.

The pride of a Cannon Falls family was a cookstove with an elevated oven, which they bought in St. Paul about 1856 and used daily for 50 years thereafter. A less durable stove was among the possessions of a family living at Hastings in the 1850s. That "small sheet iron stove through the cracks of which the fire could be plainly seen," a house with a dirt floor, and sparse handmade furnishings were never forgotten by the woman who experienced them as a child.[13]

Even the rudest fireplace or a stove with cracks would have delighted a Fillmore County woman who spent her first winter in Minnesota cooking over a fire on a flat stone set on the floor of a one-room cabin. Smoke saturated the house, but the warmth of the fire, sustained somewhat by insulating the attic with cornstalks, helped to make the cabin somewhat more comfortable.[14]

By the 1850s such a bewildering array of stoves could be purchased from local dealers that prospective Minnesota settlers were advised to buy one after they arrived and save the cost of shipping. In 1853, for example, the firm of J. H. Byers in St. Paul offered "one of the Cheapest and most Economical Stoves Extant." In 1867 an advertisement in the *Minneapolis Daily Tribune* announced "The Celebrated Stove, Crusader," featuring improved fuel-saving and baking qualities and a draft system that supplied heat to the house during the winter. The paper included a list of "well-known citizens" who owned the Crusader.[15]

With an eye to stimulating business in Minnesota, the Cleveland Co-Operative Stove Company in 1881 introduced a highly ornamented, wood-burning monster described as "especially adapted to the wants of the trade in the North-West." Named "City of Saint Paul," the stove featured a movable grate in the firebox to bring the fire closer to the cooking surfaces for "quick heat" and a "Low swing Fender" designed to give "excellent convenience for Broiling." The oven door was lined with tin and "handsomely swelled and ornamented with Nickel-plated Centers and Handles." On the smallest of three models, the oven measured 21 by 22 inches; on the largest, 23 by 24 inches.[16]

The wholesale price of each of the three models in 1885 was $17, $17.20, and $20, respectively. For a little more money, the buyer could add three optional fea-

CITY OF SAINT PAUL
FOR WOOD

tures: an "Extension Top" that provided an "encased portable copper Reservoir" for heating water and a cast-iron "Warming Closet of the latest and most approved pattern," costing a little over $9; "an elegant elevated shelf," costing $2.40; or a specially designed "Light and Handsome Sub-Base" for $1.30 or $1.60 depending on the size of the stove. All in all, the manufacturer claimed, "In ornamentation, capacity, operation and general construction," the "City of Saint Paul" was "the finest stove at the price, ever offered in this section."[17]

The Cleveland company manufactured 23 other cookstoves in 1881, among them a wood-burner called the "Farmer's Friend." It was distinguished for its large size, its economy, and its capacity to accommodate lengths of wood up to 27 inches in one model and 29 inches in the other. By contrast only the largest model of the "City of Saint Paul" could accommodate 27-inch firewood. Wholesale prices for the "Farmer's Friend" in 1885 were $17.75 for the smaller model and $20.10 for the larger. A copper reservoir and cast-iron warming oven were also available for about $9. Wood, hard or soft coal, and coke were acceptable fuels to use in the company's largest and most versatile model, the "New Windsor Range." It provided six openings for surface cooking and a single damper control. Other models were named "Winona," "Double Eagle," "Bright Side," "Kennard," "Red Stocking," "Duchess," and "Prairie Flower."[18]

A model of the Charter Oak stove, made by the Excelsior Manufacturing Company in 1887 and "ACKNOWLEDGED THE KING OF ALL RANGES," featured a three-flue construction for better circulation and distribution of heat under the oven. "The chief merit of this arrangement," the company claimed, "lies in the fact that the *greatest amount of heat is first expended just where the oven is always the coldest, after which the least heat is applied where less is required.* By this plan a more equal temperature is secured in the oven than by any other known construction."[19]

The purchaser of a new cookstove also had to bear the expense of several additional items essential to its operation. She needed stove lifters to uncover the surface cooking openings, shovels and ash buckets to remove and carry out the ashes, and several lengths of stovepipe, as well as the mandrel stakes, groovers, and mallets to

Tea Kettle.

SAD HEATER.

install the pipe. With these tools, she (or her husband) could fold the edges of a length of pipe together over the stake and secure them to one another with the groover and mallet. Other accessory "stove furnishings" available from manufacturers included a supply of "Stove Fix," described as an "indestructible cement for replacing burned or broken fire backs and linings in all stoves," iron teakettles, round and square gridirons, Dutch ovens, ham boilers in three sizes, sugar kettles, sadiron heaters, and extra shelves.[20]

The joy felt by a housewife as she gazed upon her newly acquired cookstove was usually abruptly terminated by her first attempts to use it. Especially demanding of skill was the complex system of dampers and ventilators that controlled the oven heat. The speed with which it heated depended in part on the fuel burned. Cookbooks offered some information on the relative heat values of various woods, the most common fuel. Hickory and white ash were considered the most desirable, while pine was said to be low in fuel value. Such advice was of little help if the frontier cook had no choice. Usually she burned what happened to be available, whether it was wood, coal, corncobs, buffalo chips, hay, straw, or dried sunflowers. Another consideration was that the oven would not bake well if the stove was positioned where a cold draft from opened doors would affect its performance.[21]

Here, for example, are *Buckeye Cookery's* directions for baking cakes: "A good plan is to fill the stove with hard wood (ash is best for baking), let it burn until there is a good body of heat, and then turn damper so as to

154 *COOKING ON THE FRONTIER*

GRIDIRON.

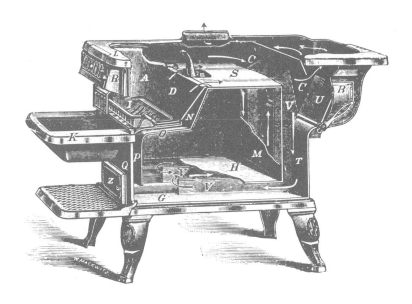

throw the heat to the bottom of oven for fully ten minutes
before the cake is put in. . . . Generally it is better to
close the hearth when the cake is put in, as this stops the
draft and makes a more regular heat. Keep adding wood
in small quantities, for if the heat becomes slack the cake
will be heavy. Great care must be taken, for some stoves
need to have the dampers changed every now and then,
but as a rule more heat is needed at the bottom of the
oven than at the top. . . . All systematic housekeepers
will hail the day when some enterprising Yankee or Buckeye girl shall invent a stove or range with a thermometer
attached to the oven, so that the heat may be regulated
accurately and intelligently."[22]

Another early authority tackled the problem of obstinate ovens this way: "Heating ovens must be regulated by experience and observation. There is difference in wood in giving out heat; there is great difference in the construction of ovens; and when an oven is extremely cold, either on account of the weather, or want of use, it must be heated more. . . . A smart fire for an hour and a half is a general rule for common-sized family ovens; provided brown bread and beans are to be baked. An hour is long enough to heat an oven for flour bread. Pies bear about as much heat as flour bread: pumpkin pies will bear more. . . . Some people wet an old broom two or three times, and turn it round near the top of the oven, till it dries; this prevents pies and cake from scorching on the top. When you go into a new house, heat your oven two or three times, to get it seasoned before you use it."[23]

If she paid any attention to the detailed suggestions in household guides for the everyday care of her stove — and it is doubtful that many women did — the housewife would have had no time to cook. The hectoring tone of most instructions is indicated by the following typical injunction of *Buckeye Cookery*: "It is the 'little foxes that spoil the vines' in the kitchen as well as elsewhere — the neglect of little things causes loss of time, patience and money." This volume then outlined a daily routine that adjured the homemaker to be sure to bring in an ample supply of dry kindling and wood; empty the ashes every morning, but "better still, clean your stove or range at night"; remember that removing ashes and cinders was "a very particular work, as the corners often secrete quite an amount of ashes that must be removed if you would have a perfectly clean stove"; and be sure to "Rap on the sides of the pipes, to dislodge the soot and ashes that collect there [and] sweep all out with a long-handled brush-broom."[24]

Even more comprehensive instructions on the care of the cookstove were set forth by Juliet Corson:

"(1.) Let down the grate and take up the cinders and ashes carefully to avoid all unnecessary dirt; put them at once into an ash-sifter fitted into the top of a pail or keg with handles, and closed with a tight fitting cover; take the pail out of doors, sift the cinders, put the ashes into the ash-can, and bring the cinders back to the kitchen [*to be reburned*?].

"(2.) Brush the soot and ashes out of all the flues and draught-holes of the stove, and then put the covers on, and brush all the dust off the outside. A careful cook will save all the wings of game and poultry to use for this purpose. If the stove is greasy wash it off with a piece of flannel dipped in hot water containing a little soda.

"(3.) Mix a little black-lead or stove polish with enough water to form a thin paste; apply this to the stove with a soft rag or brush; let it dry a little and then polish it with a stiff brush.

"(4.) If there are any steel fittings about the stove, polish them with emery paper; if they have rusted from neglect, rub some oil on them at night, and polish them with emery paper in the morning. A 'burnisher', composed of a net-work of fine steel rings, if used with strong hands, will make them look newly finished.

Our 45 Cent Shovel.

"(5.) If the fittings are brass, they should be cleaned with emery or finely powdered and sifted bath brick dust rubbed on with a piece of damp flannel, and then polished with dry dust and chamois skin.

"(6.) Brush up the hearthstone, wash it with a piece of flannel dipped in hot water containing a little soda, rinse, and wipe it dry with the flannel wrung out of clean hot water."[25]

All this sounded a good deal simpler than it was. But worse still was the major annual cleaning when the stovepipes also had to be taken down — a job that could be counted upon to get soot all over the kitchen and the woman herself. Testimony that this work was put off as long as possible appears in the diary of a Minnesota woman who wrote in annoyance: "had to clear out the stoves & pipe or not have any dinner."[26]

The large size of many cast-iron cookstoves and their complex exterior decorations of leaves, flowers, scrolls, and other ornate designs added to the work of cleaning. Unrealistically, one cookbook advertisement proclaimed all that was necessary was a 6-ounce, 10-cent package of Rising Sun Stove Polish, a product intended to avoid the multiple hazards of staining the hands, pitting the iron, and filling the house with a "poisonous and sickening odor when heated." One package "shook up with water will make several bottles of odorless liquid or paste polish, and the consumer pays for no expensive tin or glass package with every purchase." A homemade formula for stove polish called for pulverized resin dissolved in benzine and mixed with finely ground black lead. The mixture was supposed to be applied to the stove with a paint brush, rubbed until smooth, and then burnished "with a soft stove brush." Sheet-iron stoves could be treated with a mixture of only resin and benzine, applied with a soft cloth and rubbed to a shine.[27]

By the 1890s a markedly trim, easier to clean, steel frame stove that used gasoline for fuel was available. The distributor claimed erroneously that this dangerous new device, which was to cause severe and at times fatal burns to some users, was so simple "any child can operate it" and it "cannot explode." Specific precautions had to be observed: the "Stove should not be filled when there is a light or flame of any kind in the room, and gasoline should be kept in a perfectly air-tight can." Each stove was equipped with a cylindrical gasoline tank. A pipe brought the gasoline supply from the tank to the stove burners, which, it was claimed, produced a smoke-free, odorless, blue flame for cooking.[28]

Some models were available with surface burners only; others featured an oven, and ovens were also sold separately. In 1897 a series of five tin-lined ovens — in sizes ranging from 19 by 12½ by 13½ inches to 19 by 13 by 21 inches — retailed for as little as $1.40 to as much as $2.50 apiece. A description intended to promote sales maintained that "Anything done in them comes out sweet, clean and wholesome."

The Acme gasoline stove with a single burner sold for $2.63, while the four-burner "Acme Cabinet Stove" sold for $21 complete with an oven. A Minneapolis store offered a money-back guarantee if the customer was not satisfied with a four-burner "elegant Gasoline Stove" on sale for $8.98 but "worth $18."[29]

As early as 1880, Rochester residents were warned that "Property owners who are using gasoline stoves have been notified by the insurance companies that they have annulled their policies, as there is a clause that states that if that or other inflammable liquids are used a written consent must be granted by said companies to hold them liable." Seventeen years later, however, "deodorized" stove gasoline, described as "74 degrees" fire test, was still sold by the barrel through the 1897 Sears Roebuck mail order catalog. It was priced at 10 cents a gallon, but the firm did "not solicit" orders from Iowa because that state required a 175 degree fire test. Not until 1909 did an act of Congress declare all inflammable materials "non-mailable matter." After that the stoves gradually disappeared from the market.[30]

Economy and convenience were two claims made for the much safer kerosene-burning "Acme Central-Draft, Round-Wick, Oil Cook Stoves." They also threw off less heat in the kitchen in summer, and soon became popular hot-weather substitutes for wood-burning stoves. A $14 investment provided two 10-inch burners and one "powerful" 16-inch burner, and the stove was said to do "more and better cooking and baking than most ranges or gasoline stoves." Nickel-trimmed, it weighed approximately 80 pounds, was mounted on rollers, and, like others in the line, was extolled as the "embodiment of art and utility." It was available with or without an oven. Heat for the separate oven — which could be used with a gasoline stove as well — was supplied by the burner. A "Summer Queen" oil stove with two 3-inch burners sold for $1.15 in 1897. It could accommodate a $1.55 oven that was 11 inches wide, 12 inches deep, and 10 inches high.[31]

Provided the home had access to a city gas supply (which had been available for lighting purposes in St. Paul and St. Anthony since 1857), an additional option open to a Minnesota housewife in the 1890s was a new natural gas range. One offered for $18 by a mail order house in 1895 had four burners plus a baking and broiling oven. It was notable for the absence of elaborate ornamentation that often disguised the purely utilitarian function of many wood-, coal-, and coke-burning stoves of that period and the early 20th century as well.[32]

When the 19th-century housewife spoke of her "refrigerator," she did not mean the smooth, gleaming, electrically operated dependable appliance we know today. She meant an icebox. In 1852 Catherine Beecher, who was often far ahead of her time, published directions for the home manufacture of a simple, functional, and inexpensive cooling device. "Take a barrel and bore holes in the bottom," she wrote. "Lay some small sticks crossing, and set a half barrel within, with holes bored in the bottom. Nail list [supports] along the edge of each, and make a cover to lay on each, so that the cover resting on the list will make it very close. Then put ice into the inner one, and the water will filter through the holes in the bottom, and while the ice is preserved, it will make the inner half barrel a perfect refrigerator."[33]

Extravagant and enthusiastic claims were made for the commercially manufactured iceboxes available in the 1850s. An advertisement in the *Pioneer and Democrat* of 1856 described a new "improved refrigerator" that "answers all the purposes of a cellar, with none of the inconveniences of the latter." The Holmes Iron and Agricultural House of St. Paul promoted Schooley's Patent Refrigerator for use by families, hotels, and steamboats. It was "Warranted to keep Meat, Butter, Vegetables, etc., cold and pure. The contents, by a new and peculiar arrangement, are kept perfectly DRY, thus preventing the accumulation of mould. The quantity of ice consumed is quite small." [34]

Developments in commercially produced iceboxes centered on improved insulation and circulation of air. Some manufacturers also applied decorative touches to the exteriors of the more expensive models, in keeping with the custom of embellishing everyday products. The Minnesota Refrigerator Company in 1888 claimed that its "celebrated" wooden dry air refrigerators were free of condensation on the inside and used 70 per cent less ice than others of comparable size. These iceboxes with their shellacked interiors and exteriors were available in a choice of ash, oak, birch, or butternut cabinets trimmed in bronze or brass with "glass, panel, or plain front as desired." Special patented locks at the top, sides, and bottom supposedly prevented the doors from warping, and fitted roller casters facilitated moving the boxes. The five models listed as family size ranged in price from $60 for one measuring 3 feet 8 inches in width, 3 feet 9 inches in height, and 2 feet 6 inches in depth, to $150 for the

largest, which was 2 feet wider, taller, and deeper. In-between models sold for $75, $100, and $125.[35]

Other less expensive iceboxes of simpler construction were priced as low as $7 for one in softwood and $8 for the same cabinet in hardwood. A double-door "Glacier" icebox, constructed of hardwood and measuring 51 inches high, 39 inches wide, and 25 inches deep, sold for $30.

With each model the manufacturer provided a list of simple suggestions for efficient operation that included filling the ice chamber regularly and inspecting each block of ice for cleanliness, since any dirt or sawdust clinging to it was bound to clog the drainage pipe. The

KITCHENS 163

recommendations warned against wrapping ice in a blanket to retard its melting — the process indispensable to effective cooling of the box. Food was not to be stored in the ice chamber, doors were never to be left open or even ajar, the icebox was to be in a level position to avoid the risk of overflowing water, and, lastly, "Housekeepers should see that their Refrigerator is at all times kept neat and clean."

In addition to its stove and icebox, the 19th-century kitchen was sure to contain various utensils for cooking which were frequently hung on the walls. The kinds and numbers of utensils present in a frontier kitchen varied considerably from place to place within the period from the 1850s to the early 1900s. Handmade ones were not unusual. A "real nice rolling pin, and a pudding stick" as well as a butter bowl and ladle were among the useful pieces John North fashioned for his wife. The bayonet from a Minnesota man's Civil War rifle was turned into a bread knife after a blacksmith modified it to accommodate the "good wooden handle" the soldier made for it. On the other hand, a Swedish family who moved into a cabin at Watertown brought "solid silver knives, forks, and spoons. . . . Quantities of copper and brass utensils burnished until they were like mirrors hung in rows" on the cabin wall next to the silver.[36]

Hickory rods for beating eggs and other "requisite conveniences" — funnels, a wooden "beetle for mashing potatoes," skimmers, a meat cleaver, "sugar-nippers," iron skewers, scoops, graters, and "a long iron fork, to take out articles from boiling water" — were implements

the early settlers used every day. For her daily cooking the Minnesota housewife also needed a flour board, rolling pin, milk strainers, sieves, chopping block, preserving kettle, spiders and cooking pots, cake, pie, and bread pans, a variety of suitable storage vessels, a salt box, knives, long-handled spoons, and a colander.[37]

Those who had only a fireplace relied on iron pots that could be suspended on cranes or on crane hooks, Dutch ovens, a roasting spit, and tin reflectors to concentrate the heat. Deep frying pans that stood on legs above the flames or were suspended on a tripod were also essential. Frying pans varied in size, but one writer suggested that a pan used for fireplace cookery should be approximately 4 inches deep, 12 inches long, and 9 inches wide.[38]

Skillet and Lid.

If she had copper utensils, a prudent housewife regularly inspected the linings of saucepans, pots, and kettles for ruptures that would expose the copper to acids in food, thereby forming "a poisonous combination." To prevent such a tragedy and to save the otherwise durable copper pan, a new lining could be applied — a job often done by itinerant peddlers. The housewife with an eye to economy also preserved the quality of her tin-lined pots and pans by using wooden paddles and spoons to avoid excessive wear on the tin that resulted from direct contact with metal utensils.[39]

Buckeye Cookery objected to copper and brass for general use because of the extra care and attention necessary to keep them clean and to prevent "poisonous deposits" from developing. Tin cookware, while subject to the corrosive effects of oils, salts, and acids, was considered

safer and less troublesome if it was kept properly clean and carefully dried over heat to prevent rust. Iron pots and pans, when well maintained and completely dried after washing, were considered as good as porcelain or graniteware for cooking oysters, tomatoes, and other delicacies. Stainless steel did not become available until the 20th century, but aluminum was widely advertised before 1900.[40]

"Making do" applied to the utensils the housewife used just as it did to the food she prepared. A round glass bottle filled with lead shot to give it weight could be used as a rolling pin or to convert a large pan into a tube cake pan. A rolled-up piece of pasteboard could also be substituted for the tube, but it was more difficult to keep in place. A tin tube made to taper slightly at one end was useful for coring apples.[41]

Some cookbooks supplied instructions for the home manufacture of such useful items as a toaster large enough to accommodate six slices of bread. The edges of a sheet of tin were "turned up about half an inch and bound with wire, and perforations are cut about two inches apart in the shape of a V through the bottom, and the sharp points turned up so as to penetrate and hold the bread in place. A stiff wire handle is fastened firmly to the middle of the back, so that the toaster is kept at the right angle before the fire, and, if it toasts too rapidly at top or bottom, it may easily be inverted."

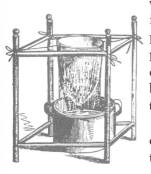

A jelly stand, helpful during preserving time, could be constructed from four upright, foot-high posts "joined at the top and bottom with rounds, as the legs of the chair are joined." The simple frame supported a jelly bag that was wired at the top and secured to the corner posts with cords. A pancake turner made from a flat piece of tin secured to a wood handle, mush sticks, and stirring paddles were also easily fabricated at home.

Wood Bowls.

Both luxuries and necessities could be readily purchased in Minnesota stores as early as 1849. Ann North bought "White and very pretty crockery" and some tinware in St. Paul that year. Such household necessities as a cocoa-shell dipper, wooden bowl, stone jug, pair of salt spoons, teakettle, bread knife, and tin dishpan were on a St. Paul housewife's shopping list in 1857.[42]

An advertisement in the *Minnesota Pioneer* of September 15, 1853, announced that "Richard Marvin, On Third Street, St. Paul, Is Now Engaged Exclusively As a Dealer In Glass, Glassware, Chinaware, Queensware And Crockery." Testifying to St. Paul's continuing growth, Marvin said "the trade of our town will now warrant an establishment devoted solely to this branch of business." His stock included earthenware, English and French china, "All the varieties of American cut, plain and pressed glassware," German and Bohemian glassware, "Britannia coffee and teapots, casters, pitchers, etc.," as well as "elegant japanned tea trays." The dealer assured his customers that all "goods are put up in the best manner, by careful and experienced packers, and may be transported any distance by wagon or otherwise, without risk or breakage."

CROCKERY.

The quality of store-bought articles varied along with the price. Housewives were told that the "very best

TINSMITH.

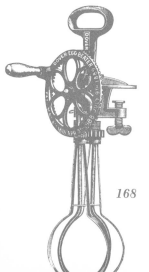

double plate tinware" was a lifetime investment while "the poor cheap kind" would not last for a year. They discovered it was better to spend an additional 25 cents to buy strong stoneware jars instead of the less expensive earthenware. When their purses permitted, they also added a few luxuries to their kitchen furnishings. A waffle iron, a custard kettle or double boiler, jelly molds, a spice cabinet, or a Dover rotary egg beater — already "Known in Every Village of the Civilized World" by 1880 — brought a new dimension to family meals.[43]

Many Minnesota housewives, however, continued to beat innumerable eggs into countless cakes and puddings without the help of a rotary egg beater. Perhaps some of them followed the advice in Miss Leslie's cookbook or merely performed the task in their own way. Miss Leslie recommended breaking the eggs into a shallow, broad, earthenware pan rather than a tin pan and favored using hickory rods instead of a tin wire utensil to beat them, since "the coldness of the metal retards their lightness."[44]

Her energy-conserving method was carefully outlined: "Beat with a short quick stroke, holding the egg rods in your right hand close to your side, and do not exert your elbow, or use your arm violently with a hard sweeping stroke; of this there is no necessity. If beaten in a proper manner, (moving your hand *only* at the wrist) the eggs will be light long before you are fatigued. But you must continue beating till after the froth has subsided, and the pan of eggs presents a smooth thick surface, like a nice boiled custard. White of egg is done if it stands stiff alone, and will not fall from the beater . . ."

A standard item in nearly every kitchen was a coffee grinder — a mechanism that often did double duty to produce home-ground flour. In the unlikely event a pioneer family arrived in Minnesota without a grinder, one could be purchased in St. Paul or St. Anthony stores by 1852. Various models were in use; some were wall mounted, others stood on the table, and still others were held in the lap while doing the grinding.[45]

Despite the fact that commercially ground coffee was available by the early 1860s, most homemakers continued to purchase whole beans well into the 20th century. The finest coffees, according to *Buckeye Cookery*, were Mocha and Java, and these along with such varieties as Rio, Maracaibo, St. Domingo, and Laguara were offered by Minnesota grocers as early as the 1850s. If purchased raw, as some household guides advocated, the beans had to be carefully roasted "to a dark rich brown," free from burned grains that would ruin the flavor.[46]

Such luxuries as the French biggin or dripolator, and even the "widely known" National coffeepot, were probably less frequently seen in Minnesota households during the early days than pots fashioned by the housewife herself. Some women simply boiled the coffee in an ordinary pan and poured it through a strainer when it was served. Others measured the depth of a container, cut a piece of flannel and stitched it into a sack that extended the full depth, allowing additional material at the top. A hem sewed around the open end admitted a circle of wire or a cord so that the top of the sack could be folded over the opening of the pot and the wire tightened or the cord tied to secure it in position. After the ground coffee was put into the sack and boiling water poured over it, the pot was covered, put over the fire, and simmered for fifteen minutes. A simpler method was to pour the ground coffee into a fragment of muslin or gauze, tie it up into an improvised bag, and put it in a pot of cold water. It was boiled for five minutes and the coffee was considered done.[47]

Egg coffee — still popular in many households of the state — was made by mixing the yolk and sufficient cold water to moisten the ground coffee, then adding it to hot water, boiling rapidly for five minutes, and simmering for fifteen. Some housewives used, instead of egg, a codfish skin that was washed, dried, and cut into one-inch pieces. Either served the purpose of clarifying the brew. A roll of cloth was sometimes stuffed into the nose or spout of the boiler to prevent the flavor from escaping.

Teapots and coffeepots could be cleaned periodically by filling them with a generous quantity of wood ashes and water, bringing the contents to a gradual boil, and letting the mixture stand until the water cooled. Then a scrubbing in hot water and soapsuds, followed by two or three scaldings, thoroughly cleansed the pots. The same method was applied to other cookware. When wood ashes were lacking, soda was substituted. Stains in enameled vessels that did not respond when wood ashes or soda were boiled in them had to be rubbed with sand or brick dust, then rinsed well and dried.[48]

The household guides and cookbooks of the 19th century repeated over and over the necessity for the housewife to maintain a well-ordered home, "eternal vigilance" to detail, devotion to the achievement of perfection, and a time for doing everything. "The woman who is satisfied only with the highest perfection in her work, drops the drudge and becomes the artist. There is no dignity in slighted work; but to the artist, no matter how humble his calling, belongs the honor which is inseparable from all man's struggles after perfection. . . . A dirty kitchen and bad cooking have driven many a husband and son, and many a daughter too, from a home that should have been a refuge from temptation. 'Bad dinners go hand in hand with total depravity; while a properly fed man is already half saved.'" That the image projected by these guides to 19th-century homemaking is no more to be trusted than the never-never land of sweetness and light conveyed by those of the 20th century is sharply apparent in the following quotation. Reality, it would seem, was quite different — then as now.[49]

A woman who settled on a farm in Minneapolis during the 1850s recalled the colorful Red River oxcarts that passed noisily by her house, although, she said, she never had time to watch them. "I was always holding a baby under one arm and drawing water from the well, so could not tell which way they went. I only saw them when they were straight in front of me. Women in those days never had time to look at anything but work."[50]

CHAPTER EIGHT

Minnesota Cookbooks of the 19th Century

WHEN A ST. ANTHONY HOUSEWIFE in the 1850s confided to a friend her recipe for molasses sponge cake, she was giving away a family jewel, and like many such gems it defied description.

"I take some molasses and saleratus and flour and shortening, and some milk," she said.

"How much?" her friend inquired.

"Oh, a middling good sized piece, and enough milk to make it the right thickness to bake good."[1]

If her friend was an experienced 19th-century cook, she would not expect any further information. For housewives in the 1850s, experience was the most reliable — and sometimes the only — guide to cooking available. Even as late as 1896 the introduction to a promotional cookbook given away by a Minneapolis druggist commented: "It is often said: 'Good cooks never measure.' Not so. They measure by judgement and experience." Today it is often said: "Anyone who can read, can cook."[2]

The marked difference in the attitudes expressed by these two statements can be explained by the revolution that took place in cooking and cookbooks during the latter decades of the 19th century. That revolution led by two influential eastern women — Mary Johnson Bailey Lincoln and Fannie M. Farmer — swept away vague quantities like "a middling good sized piece" and replaced them with standardized level measurements, codified recipes, and complete step-by-step directions. Mrs. Lincoln established the famous Boston Cooking School and Miss Farmer became its principal. The results of their work in standardizing recipes appeared in two landmark cookbooks published in 1887 and 1896 as well as in their later volumes on cookery.[3]

Until this revolution was completed, however, the bride who looked to 19th-century "domestic economy" volumes for guidance faced a formidable assignment. Cookbooks of any kind were not common in the United States during the first half of the century. The first cookbook published in the colonies was *The Compleat Housewife* by Eliza Smith, issued at Williamsburg, Virginia, in 1742. It was not, however, a native product, for it had been initially printed in England in 1727.[4]

Better known among America's 18th-century cookbooks was *American Cookery* by Amelia Simmons. Her work, first published in 1796, was reprinted 11 times thereafter until 1822. Seven years later *The Frugal Housewife* by Lydia Maria Child made its appearance in

Boston. That copies of this slender volume, as well as others discussed below, made their way westward is confirmed by their presence in the Minnesota Historical Society's collection. Thirty-two editions of Mrs. Child's work were published over a 21-year period, and in 1832 it was retitled *The American Frugal Housewife*. The last printing occurred in 1850, a time when other leaders in the field were becoming established.[5]

Among them was Eliza Leslie, whose cookbooks and reputation grew considerably after 1828 with the publication of *Seventy-Five Receipts, for Pastry, Cakes, and Sweetmeats*. Miss Leslie, who has been called by one modern authority, James Beard, "the best cook of her time," was quickly followed by such other eastern authors as Catherine Beecher, Mary F. Henderson, Juliet Corson, Maria Parloa, and Sarah T. Rorer, and Bertha F. Kramer of Chicago, whose pen name was "Aunt Babette." Interestingly, many of these women, like Mary Lincoln and Fannie Farmer at the end of the century, were identified with cooking schools. The advice they and others offered was not limited to recipes but embraced almost any activity associated with housekeeping as well as the care of the sick.[6]

Even if the young Minnesota housewife read the works of these authors, it is debatable whether she was edified or simply further confused. Some recipes offered a bewildering array of quantities defined in terms of teacups, coffee cups, tin cups, wine glasses, gills, drachms, drops, gallons, quarts, pints, fractions of pounds, large spoons, teaspoons, tablespoons, "well-heaped" spoons, pinches, pecks, and pieces. Utensils in pint, quart, and gallon sizes were the only standard measuring containers in existence at mid-century. A scale was particularly useful to weigh ingredients in such recipes as one for sponge cake that called for "Ten eggs, their weight in granulated sugar, half their weight in sifted flour. . . . "[7]

The inexperienced cook's problems were further compounded by the many skills she needed to master in order to keep house under the era's moral strictures of prudence and thrift. She was often told, after all, that "a woman can throw out with a spoon faster than a man can throw in with a shovel."[8]

Few 19th-century authors came to young women's aid with the evangelical zeal of Catherine Beecher. Her household guides tackled not only the problems of cooking but the whole catalog of domestic hazards unprepared brides encountered when they assumed the "arduous" duties of the housewife. In her work as a teacher, Miss Beecher fretted over her students' lack of training and information. While other authors offered some of the same rules and instructions as Miss Beecher, agreeing with her "habit of doing everything in the best manner," they did not bear down on the "defective domestic education" that caused the "deplorable sufferings" of young ladies. Nor did they articulate the trials that sapped the physical energy and taxed the minds of the untrained. The books Catherine Beecher wrote during the 1840s and 1850s, and coauthored with her sister, Harriet Beecher Stowe, in the 1860s, were aimed at providing remedies and offering solutions that would lead to

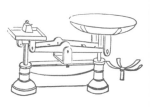

"habits of system and order" in everything, including cooking.[9]

Characteristically, Miss Beecher recognized the confusion inherent in the lack of standard measurements and attempted to deal with it. One of her many sensible suggestions was "to have a particular measure cup kept for the purpose, and after once weighing all those receipts that are given by weight, to *measure* the quantity by this cup, and then write the measures in your receipt book, and keep the cup only for this purpose."[10]

She also tried to furnish equivalents, but forthrightly admitted that they were inexact. Such rules as "A pint equals eight ounces" and "A quart of brown sugar or of Indian meal, equals a pound and two ounces of the same" were clear enough. But she warned her readers that "Spoons differ so much in size" that other rules were uncertain. For instance, how meaningful was the statement that "Four spoonfuls equal an ounce" if the cook had no idea which spoon to use? Even less definite was "One great spoonful of flour, loaf sugar, or of melted butter, equals a quarter of an ounce of same. It should be a little heaped." How the cook heaped melted butter was not explained.

The general lack of emphasis before the 1850s on the details of weights and measurements is reflected in the fact that Miss Beecher's equivalents appeared in the final chapter under the title "Miscellaneous Advice and Supplementary Receipts." A shift in emphasis is revealed by *Miss Leslie's New Cookery Book* (1857) and *Miss Parloa's New Cook Book* (1880), both of which carried tables of measurements in the front matter. Miss Leslie's full-page table furnished an assortment of data suggesting the common containers used at that time: "Four table-spoonfuls will generally fill a common-sized wine-glass," a "common-sized tumbler holds half a pint," and "Four wine-glasses will fill a half pint tumbler, or a large coffee cup." [11]

Eliza Leslie clearly earned a place among the outstanding pioneer 19th-century cookbook authors. A well-worn copy of her 600-page "complete manual of domestic cookery *in all its branches*" is in the Minnesota Historical Society's collection. Its author, who also wrote children's stories and contributed to women's magazines, became wealthy through the sale of her culinary works, which were distinctive in their emphasis on the use of American provender such as venison, buffalo, and game. Indian meal was basic to many of her recipes for breads, griddle cakes, muffins, and even cakes for dessert. Her "Very Plain Indian Dumplings," a combination of corn meal, salt, and boiling water, were "an excellent appendage to salt pork or bacon." More than any other individual cookbook of the period, her work foreshadowed the now-popular phrase, "traditional American food." [12]

With recurring enthusiasm Miss Leslie summoned her primary theme that implicit in the nation's plentiful food supply was the opportunity to improve nutrition, cooking practices, and the kitchen habits of America. Characteristically, she observed that in "America, where good things are abundant, there is no necessity of imbibing the flatulency of weak washy soups." Her recipe for "Squat-

MISS LESLIE'S

NEW

COOKERY

BOOK.

ter's Soup" underscored the point. When served with wild turkey or roasted buffalo hump, young sweet corn, and stewed grapes sweetened with maple sugar, it "will make a good backwoods dinner."[13]

For a company dinner, Miss Leslie furnished a recipe for soup made from four wild ducks, seasoned with salt, pepper, and minced sage, and simmered with the addition of onions and a quarter of a pound of butter rolled in flour. The cooked soup was then thickened with boiled or roasted chestnuts that had been peeled and mashed. Quite different but unquestionably appropriate for a gift to "friends going the overland journey to the Pacific" was her "Portable Soup," a forerunner of the bouillon cube. The soup required three days to prepare and was made "into a jelly, and then congealed into hard cakes, resembling glue." Further, her awareness of the American way of life inspired other recipes such as one for "Camp Catsup" that she claimed would keep for years if the bottles were well corked and stored in a dry place. The formula called for strong ale or porter mixed with white wine and minced shallots, seasoned with mace, nutmeg, and gingerroot, then boiled slowly and bottled with the addition of a teaspoon of salad oil.[14]

When the practical-minded author focused on meat cookery, she called attention not only to the abundance of meat in America but to its reasonable cost. Therefore it was unnecessary, she said, for anyone to prepare more than was essential for use at any one time. Only well-done meat was wholesome and digestible, she declared, and underdone meat "is now seldom seen but at those public tables, where they consider it an object to have as little meat as possible eaten on the first day, that more may be left for the second day, to be made into indescribable messes, with ridiculous French names, and passed off as French dishes, by the so-called French cook, who is frequently an Irishman."[15]

Some 20 years later, Mrs. Mary F. Henderson studied cooking in Europe as well as in America, and in her book, *Practical Cooking and Dinner Giving*, proved that she was favorably and irrevocably impressed by the French. "American women," she declared in 1876, were not "less able and apt than the women of France," but their cooking was "inferior" only because they seemed "possessed with the idea that it is not the fashion to know how to cook." Her six-page glossary included the French names for soups, fish, sauces, meats, poultry and game, sweetbreads, vegetables, food cooked in shells, macaroni, eggs, salads, fritters, patties, puddings, and desserts. Where appropriate, she scattered French words throughout the recipes. She also reflected the French love of salads, noting that it was "an accomplishment to know how to dress a salad well, which is especially prized by the fashionable world."[16]

She was not so completely French in her orientation, however, that she neglected to include a few recipes "For the Sick" and "Some Dishes For 'Baby.'" She also explained the intricacies of "How They Eat Oranges in Havana," and told how to arrange mixed fruits in a "raised dish," so the "general appearance should be fresh and *négligé*," yet without "danger of an avalanche."[17]

Maria Parloa and Juliet Corson, two other eastern authors represented in the Minnesota Historical Society's collection, were like-minded in their efforts to be explicit. In her 1879 book, Miss Corson adopted a then-revolutionary departure by heading each recipe with a tabulation of ingredients. It is probable that this innovation stemmed from a desire to meet the growing public interest in "cheap and good cookery," since she also listed the cost of each ingredient and added the total expenditure required for each recipe in the index.[18]

The book was divided into four sections: lessons for the young daughters of working people, referred to as "artisans"; instruction for the grown daughters and wives of workingmen who could afford "moderate expense"; courses for plain cooks, young housewives of moderate and comfortable circumstances, and domestics who sought employment in families "where the table is nice without being too expensive"; and, lastly, the "Ladies' Course" that provided "some of the elegancies of artistic cookery with those economical interests which it is the duty of every housewife to study."

Ten years later Miss Corson dropped the tabular style of presenting recipes as well as the food costs in her 1889 volume intended as "an every-day book for American housekeepers." She offered "the most acceptable etiquette of American hospitality," advice on marketing, carving, and table service, suggestions for children's diets and care of the sick, plus hundreds of recipes, some of considerable interest.[19]

For example, she told how to cook sliced venison with

currant jelly for three minutes in a chafing dish; how to dress a pig for roasting; and how to prepare "Stewed or Potted Pigeons." She described how to can tomatoes and dry corn. Her recipe for a simple "Salt Fish Dinner" advised the housewife to soak codfish overnight, simmer it the next day, and serve it with boiled potatoes and beets. An enriched "Pullet with Toulouse Ragoût" involved cooking young hens and serving them in a white sauce glorified with truffles, sweetbreads, cockscombs, mushrooms, and "chicken quenelles" (a dumpling of chopped or pounded chicken meat mixed with soft bread, seasoning, and raw egg yolk to bind it together).[20]

Good cooking, Miss Corson wrote, demanded "intelligent comprehension" of the fundamentals of food chemistry, economic values, and the "physiology of nutrition." Miss Parloa, however, felt it was "unwise to leave much to the cook's judgment." Thus Miss Parloa included such details as how long to stir, how long to simmer, and how a dish should be served and garnished. Anticipating the 20th-century development of designating pan sizes for baking cakes and quick breads, this prolific author specified the use of deep or shallow pans, "sheets," or loaf pans.[21]

Maria Parloa, like Miss Corson, interjected into her recipes such French terms as souffle, blanquette, chartreuse, chaud, froid, quenelles, and pâté. Also like her contemporary, she offered typical American recipes for fried chicken and pot pie, pumpkin soup, "Salt Fish with Dropped Eggs," and "Boiled Turkey with Celery."[22]

Both authors produced a number of cookbooks and

were recognized domestic authorities. Miss Corson conducted cooking classes throughout the United States and in Canada, and in 1884 she appeared at the University of Minnesota's agricultural college in St. Paul. A full report of the series of six lectures, liberally accented with her strong views on food and nutrition, was published by the university's board of regents.[23]

The 1,200 Minnesota women who attended the classes were given practical lessons on a broad range of cookery. They also learned that lentils, fresh or dried beans, and peas were more strength sustaining when they were prepared with fat meat, suet, or butter, and they heard Miss Corson lament the fact that Americans thought only meat provided nourishment. She declared that the nutritive value of some vegetables — "what the dressmakers would call 'trimmings'" — was indeed comparable to meat.

While some cookbook authors focused on nutritious foods at moderate costs, Bertha Kramer, the anonymous "Aunt Babette," wrote primarily for those women who needed to increase their own knowledge before successfully governing servants and managing a household. Many of the hundreds of recipes she included in *"Aunt Babette's" Cook Book* (1889) were German and Jewish, but she also offered classical American foods. She devoted a chapter to "Easter Dishes," intended for use during the Jewish celebration of Passover, and she also told how to roast a turkey, prepare fried chicken and sauerbraten, and how to smoke the breast of the "fattest goose you can find" for "Geraucherte Gansbrust."[24]

A COURSE OF LECTURES

ON THE

PRINCIPLES OF DOMESTIC ECONOMY
AND COOKERY,

BY MISS JULIET CORSON,
Superintendent of the New York School of Cookery.

She provided recipes for succotash, cranberry sauces and pudding, pumpkin pie, and strudels. Her "Brod Torte" (in three versions) was made of rye-bread crumbs, spices, eggs, almonds, and brandy and wine or lemon and orange juice, or both. Baked in a spring form, the torte was made "still finer" by cutting it in layers spread with jelly.[25]

She advised the "Dear Ladies" never to put yeast "on top of the ice" in an icebox and reminded them that while it was no disgrace not to be able to afford brandied fruit, they should not "try and put up fruit in whiskey or some other cheap stuff." She also provided instructions for making a "Family Medicine Case" for the treatment of common illnesses. The directions she gave in the recipes were often detailed, even though the measurements were not always explicit.[26]

Perhaps some of the "Dear Ladies" were among the "Plucky Housewives . . . who master their work instead of allowing it to master them." To such women was dedicated *Buckeye Cookery and Practical Housekeeping*, published in Minneapolis in 1877 and one of the earliest locally issued domestic guides in the Minnesota Historical Society's collection. The book originated with a group of women at Marysville, Ohio, who aimed to "pack between its covers the greatest possible amount of practical information of real value to all, and especially to the inexperienced." Later editions enlarged on and updated their efforts.[27]

Typical of the period's household encyclopedias, this orderly guide abounded with recipes (some contributed

and signed by Minnesota women), rules, procedures, directions, and suggestions. Its broad subject matter took cognizance of the fact that a woman not only had to cook, she had to know how to use gall soap to wash floors and bedsteads, dampened sawdust as a sweeping compound, cayenne pepper to discourage mice, rats, and vermin, lime for whitewashing, kerosene to keep stoves and iron utensils from rusting, and carbolic acid to disinfect sinks and drains.[28]

When a pause in work allowed the housewife time to consult the manual, she could learn how to care for herself and her babies, wash her silk dresses, make soap and starch, give a party, clean house, buy and cut up meat, make a mustard plaster, treat burns, feed the sick, clean sponges, and put on wallpaper. She also found advice on planning menus, the latest in etiquette, hanging pictures, and what to do about a leaking roof and a frozen water pump. All this information and more was intended to free her from "the whole train of horrors that result from bad housekeeping" and general inexperience. Best of all, however, the housewife could learn how to prepare everything from boiled eggs and salt-rising bread to roast goose and Yorkshire pudding.[29]

Beginning with the 1877 edition, the compilers attempted to provide precise information and included a "Table of Weights and Measures" to help unravel the numerous systems. The cook was told that "1 ounce contains 8 fluid drachms (¼ gill)" and "4 gills . . . make 1 pint," while "1 tea-cupful equals 8 fluid oz. or 2 gills." The volume also offered a "Cooks' Time-Table" of dubious helpfulness. It listed the "Mode of Preparation," the "Time of Cooking," and the "Time of Digestion."[30]

An improved table of weights and measures that demonstrated the increasing acceptance of the concept of accurate measurements appeared in the 1881 edition. The broadened subject matter included such additional specifics as "1 pint best brown sugar weighs 13 oz.," "Soft butter the size of an egg weighs 2 oz.," and "3 coffee-cups sifted flour (level) weigh 1 lb." Although the appearance of a *level* measurement of any kind represented a giant leap forward, the *Buckeye* authors found some problems still unsolvable. Like Miss Beecher three decades earlier, they, too, came to grief over the disparity in the sizes of spoons and cups.[31]

By the time Fannie Farmer's first edition of the *Boston Cooking-School Cook Book* was published in 1896, some utensils had been developed to eliminate the guesswork in measuring. Miss Farmer told her readers: "Tin measuring-cups, divided in quarters or thirds, holding one half-pint, and tea and table spoons of regulation sizes, — which may be bought at any store where kitchen furnishings are sold, — and a case knife, are essentials for correct measurement. Mixing-spoons, which are larger than tablespoons, should not be confounded with the latter."[32]

Even though it preceded Miss Farmer's book by 15 years, exact measurements for baking powder, spices, and extracts were used throughout *The Snow Flake Cook Book* (1881). Published in St. Paul by Charles Groff, who presented it to users of his "Celebrated Snow

Pure Aluminum Measures.

Flake Baking Powder," the book's recipes ran the gamut of cookery.[33]

Along with the breads, cakes, and pie fillings that were prepared with his products, the 100-page book included directions for cooking meats, fowl, fish, soups, salads, jams and jellies, and vegetables. There were, too, 11 different recipes for making coffee, which Groff wholesaled to local grocers. To make his book complete, he added a section of household advice appropriated from Catherine Beecher.[34]

Another unusual book was that published in 1885 by the St. Paul Roller Mill Company to promote its Orange Blossom Flour. In its 50 pages, *The Orange Blossom Cook Book* intermixed a history of flour, an unresolved romance, 21 recipes, and general baking instructions. The mill's manager introduced the book as the company's effort to offset the "deficiency" of instruction popular cookbooks provided on "every point about bread making." He promised, too, that later editions would follow, but if they did, they seem not to have survived, for only the first can be found in the Minnesota Historical Society's collection.[35]

The story, in which the guide to breadmaking was woven, revolved around Lucy Knight, a cultured young heiress from Minnesota who operated a cooking school in Florida. One of her students, Sophie Southgate, discovered that her health, ruined by the "course of study and course of diet" in a young ladies' seminary, was quickly restored when she ate breads made exclusively from Orange Blossom Flour. Romance developed when an urbane colonel, Frank Mayo, realized his considerable admiration for the "two earnest, warm hearted and truthful women." At the end of the first installment, the colonel faced the dilemma of choosing between them.

Digressions from the main story allowed for a recital of the gradual progress made in flour and milling. In her role as teacher, Lucy Knight brought in recipes and instructions on the art of breadmaking. Special emphasis was given to the excellence of the hard wheats grown in Minnesota, the enterprise of the millers in the state, and their leadership in the production of quality flour.

E. M. May & Son of Minneapolis had a distinctly different product to promote in 1887 — a catering service that consisted of a "full drilled corps" of servants, an array of table appointments, awnings, and special lights, and an assortment of prepared foods that can only be called lavish. From May's *Catalogue*, a hostess could order a haunch of venison, fillets of hare with truffles, a "Mounted Wild Goose," or a "Boar's head Roman fashion." Molded ice cream and sherbet were available in the dramatic shapes of a large deer ($5.00) or an elephant ($6.00) that would serve 12 guests. Edible, decorative pyramids made of fruit, macaroons, bonbons, or ice cream were offered too.[36]

The *Catalogue* also furnished numerous essays on such socially important subjects as table courtesies, leisurely dining, ballroom etiquette, how to choose wines, and establishing a well-ordered kitchen and dining room. Provided were tables of weights and measures and the digestability of food, menu suggestions, and a calendar of foods in season. Selected recipes explained how to prepare cream puffs, sparrow pie, champagne jelly, "Angels' cake," and canvasback ducks, among other dishes.

More than any other Minnesota cookbook, May's *Catalogue* reflected the elegance in living and dining that was available to at least some city residents during the 1880s. Its high style contrasts sharply with living conditions 40 years earlier when Ann North was glad enough to travel from her home in St. Anthony to St. Paul just to purchase crockery.

Simple fare, as opposed to elegant feasting, characterized a cookbook given away to advertise the Minneapolis drugstore of Thomas K. Gray in 1896. Ten thousand copies of *T. K. Gray's Cook Book* were produced at a cost of "several hundred dollars." Four more editions appeared biennially up to 1904, suggesting that the initial investment was justified.[37]

Alternating pages described an assortment of compounds and nostrums to cure, correct, and rehabilitate people and horses. Hair restoratives, paints, and chewing gum were other products advertised — all of which were available at Gray's store.

The recipe sections of Gray's cookbook displayed considerable imagination. One devoted to leftover food was entitled "Made-over Delicacies," while another was labeled "Picnic Dainties." Names for recipes such as "Minnehaha Cake" and "Prairie Tea Cake" suggest an attempt to identify the cookbook with the locale, although there was nothing that distinguished the basic ingredients from those of other cakes in that period.[38]

A more unusual give-away cookbook was presented to the customers of Blichfeldt & Halvorsen, Minneapolis grocers, in 1890. Instead of a small, locally produced volume, the store presented complimentary copies of *A Complete Library of Cookery*, published in 1890. With over 300 pages, the book comprised household management and recipe sections by Mrs. N. K. M. Lee, Eliza Leslie's "Seventy-Five Receipts, for Pastry, Cakes, and Sweetmeats," information on infants and invalids by S. P. Hedges, a Chicago physician, and "manuals" on soups, breads, and salads by Mrs. Emma P. Ewing, dean of the School of Cookery at Ames, Iowa.[39]

Mrs. Lee's contribution to the book was originally published in Boston in 1832 under the title *The Cook's Own Book; Being a Complete Culinary Encyclopedia: Arranged Alphabetically*. As it reappeared in 1890, the book contained more than 2,500 recipes along with general cooking instructions and useful information on marketing, kitchen utensils, how to carve meats, and dinner-table etiquette. In a separate section entitled "Confectionery," Mrs. Lee offered recipes for candies, 36 different ways to use almonds, "Curds and Whey," ice creams, "Pine Apple Chips," and other fruit-flavored foods. Although Mrs. Lee's recipes might have been considered old fashioned by the 1890s, they stood up well against those of more "modern" cookbook authors, and they undoubtedly were used with confidence by the recipients of the grocers' gift.

Even the Northern Steamship Company of St. Paul, a James J. Hill enterprise, used a cookbook to promote

business in 1899. Advertisements appearing on almost every page of *Our Chef's Best Receipts* hailed the merits of Hill's Great Northern and Duluth, Missabe & Northern railways, as well as hotels and merchants located in St. Paul and Duluth.[41]

The introduction boasted that its "best receipts are not to be found in any other book of receipts." While the chef was not identified, other persons who contributed to the collection were named. Credit was given, too, for the quoted lines describing the general content of each chapter. Thus Ralph Waldo Emerson's statement, "The amassed thought and experience of innumerable minds," keynoted a miscellaneous selection including a recipe for cheese fondue, a formula for cleaning wallpaper, recommendations for washing point lace, and the suggestion that "Common cooking molasses will remove grass stain from garments."

Recipes, however, far outnumbered the helpful hints in the cookbook. The form in which they were presented reflected the gradual drift toward a standard columnar listing of ingredients, but chancy directions for amounts — "Enough flour to roll" or "Sugar to suit taste" — continued to prevail.

The growing interest in standard measurements was also apparent in cookbooks compiled between 1874 and 1900 by the ladies of Minnesota churches as fund-raising projects to defray particular expenses of a congregation. In each book, the recipes are written in the distinctive styles of the individual donors and are completely unencumbered by consistency of form or by any one system of measurement. The women carefully named the ingredients, but they sometimes neglected the exact amounts, although terms such as teaspoon, cup, and pint were used frequently. Often the recipes were devoid of directions, and rare is the contributor who furnished comments on cooking and baking times. References to pan sizes were, of course, generally lacking as well.

These slender volumes have a charm of style and the ambiance of a potluck supper to which each contributor donated her specialty. The informality of the recipes, expressed in the comfortable language of the kitchen, add to their personal quality. The recipes reflect the imagination and tastes of Minnesota cooks and indicate a surprising consensus on the popularity of certain foods — doughnuts and coleslaw, for example. They also reveal some unexpected omissions in the preferences of that time, for none contains a recipe for Minnesota wild rice.

Drawn from personal collections kept in boxes, drawers, or memories, the recipes are a rich and reliable sample of the selection and availability of food as well as the manner in which it was prepared. Including as they do directions for soups, meat, fish, fowl, breads, desserts, and fixings, these contributions from churchwomen have become an archive documenting the foods 19th-century Minnesota housewives set on their tables.

The earliest church-sponsored cookbook in the collection of the Minnesota Historical Society was published in 1874 by the Parish Aid Society of Ascension Church at Stillwater. The book, entitled *Family Friend*, apparently met a welcome reception, for it was reissued in 1893 and again in 1906. Perhaps the readers appreciated especially its recipe index, its complete selection of dishes (desserts in particular), and its "Lenten Soups" without meat.[42]

A book of "Valuable Recipes" published about 1877 by the ladies of Westminster Presbyterian Church in Minneapolis is particularly notable for its casual style. Among its contributors was a woman whose penchant for rhyme resulted in this description of how to broil steak:

BROILERS.

> *Pound well* your meat until the fibres break;
> Be sure that next you have, to broil the steak,
> Good coals in plenty; not it a moment leave,
> But *turn it* over, *this* way and then *that*;
> The lean should be quite rare, not so the fat.
> The platter, now and then, the juice receive,
> Put on your butter, place it in your meat,
> *Salt, pepper*, turn it over, serve and eat.[43]

The book also offered sometimes vague instructions for curing hams and making beer, along with formulas for preparing cough medicine, a prescription for cholera, and a cure for wrinkles that called for a contented mind and glycerine added to the morning wash water.

A personal quality in recipe writing also characterized *The Tried and True Cook Book*, published in 1881 by the ladies' society of the First Baptist Church in St. Paul. Like other Minnesota housewives of the 1880s, the contributors cooked parsnip stew and made squash and cranberry pies; they made batter for Indian meal muffins at night and baked them for breakfast the next day. For "Sunday Pudding," tapioca was "put to soak on Friday night" and baked into a pudding on Saturday to be ready on the Sabbath. These women also offered recipes for a lotion for chilblains and a hair restorative.[44]

In 1892 the Dayton Avenue Presbyterian Church in St. Paul hosted a cooking school conducted by Mrs. Willet M. Hays, and in answer to requests for a printed version of the domestic science teacher's lessons, the women of the church published *A Cook Book*. In the tradition of Catherine Beecher, Mrs. Hays described cooking as "the most useful, elevating, dignified and important of all occupations lying at the very foundation of our peace, prosperity and happiness."[45]

Along with a complete selection of recipes, the book recorded Mrs. Hays's views on the principles of cooking, and the need for nutritional awareness and the practice of economy. The simple system of "ordering wisely, cooking properly and wasting nothing," said Mrs. Hays, could keep food costs to $1.50 a week for each person in any city in the country.

Such counsel on general cooking principles did not appear in the 40-page *Christmas Cook Book* published in December, 1899, by the Ladies' Aid Society of the Methodist Episcopal Church in Buffalo, Minnesota. Instead the book was limited to signed recipes comprising a medley of individual specialties grouped under general headings. Using the ingredients normally found in every kitchen, 177 recipes told how to make such dishes as "Grandma's Pumpkin Butter," raisin-dotted "Minnehaha Frosting," "Dried Apple Cake," and even a "Pork Cake" made of salt pork, molasses, spices, eggs, soda, currants, raisins, and "enough flour to make as a

pound cake." The only recipe directly associated with the book's title was a "Christmas Pudding" that required 12 hours of boiling![46]

Dessert recipes were also plentiful in *The "Central" Cook Book*, a collection of over 300 signed recipes published by the women of the Central Presbyterian Church of St. Paul in 1900. The book is the most recently published example of church-sponsored cookbooks selected from the Minnesota Historical Society's collection. Among its dessert receipts is this unusual one for "Scripture Cake": "1 cup butter (Judges 5:25); 3 cups sugar (Jer. 6:20); 2 cups figs (I. Sam. 30:12); 1 cup almonds (Gen. 43:11); 1 tablespoon honey (Ex. 16:21); spice to taste (I. Kings 10:10); 3½ cups flour (I. Kings 4:22); 2 cups raisins (I. Sam. 30:12); 1 cup water (Gen. 24:17); 6 eggs (Isa. 10:14); pinch salt (Rev. 2:13). Follow Solomon's advice for making good boys and you will have a good cake (Pro. 23:13)."[47]

As the century came to a close, Minnesota housewives had an increasing number of locally issued cookbooks available to them. One destined to have a long life was published by the *Northwestern Farmer*, a journal headquartered in St. Paul. On October 15, 1893, the newspaper invited its women readers to contribute recipes for a book to be called *The Country Kitchen*. "The demand among farmer's wives is for a simple common sense recipe book special adapted to their particular use," the newspaper explained. "The trouble with most, if not all cook books is that they are not practical every day affairs, but are fit to be consulted only on special occasions, when something extra is to be served. They [*the recipes*] are too elaborate and expensive, and take much care and time to prepare." [48]

The 133-page book, with "Every Recipe Contributed by A Farmer's Wife or Daughter," appeared in 1894 and sold for 50 cents a copy. Contributors from many midwestern states and Canada were identified by name and place of residence. Twenty printings and nine revised editions followed, the latest issued in 1973. As the editors promised in 1893, the contents cover "every department found in the most elaborately prepared cook books." [49]

Among other Minnesota-produced cookbooks issued before 1900 are *A Choice Collection of Tested Recipes*, collected by a committee of 14 women and published by the *Register*, an Austin newspaper, about 1883; *Tested Recipes*, contributed by the ladies of St. Mark's Protestant Episcopal Church of Minneapolis and published in 1891; *Washburn, Crosby Co.'s New Cook Book*, published in 1894 and given to customers of the Minneapolis flour-milling company; *The Duluth Home Cook Book*, compiled by ladies of Duluth and other cities and published in 1895 for the benefit of the Children's Home and Hospital in Duluth; and *Marshall Ladies' Choicest and Best*, with recipes collected in 1898 by the women of St. Cecelia Guild in that southwestern Minnesota town.

The combined record offered by over 30 cookbooks used by Minnesotans in the 19th century is notable for what it does not include as well as for what it does. A summary of some general observations may help bring into sharper focus the total picture of cooking and housekeeping in Minnesota from 1850 to 1900.

1. The authors and compilers of most of the 19th-century volumes, including the church-sponsored cookbooks, added to their comprehensive collections of recipes information about other household concerns. These commentaries ranged over such tasks as laundering and dyeing clothes, home remedies and care of the sick, and how to remove stains on everything from marble table tops to a cookstove. Their goal was to instruct in the complete role of the American housewife, whose duties went far beyond cooking alone. While specialized cookbooks focusing on one type of dish — frozen desserts, sandwiches, or chafing dish recipes, for example — were published in the East in the late 1800s, they do not appear among books issued in Minnesota in the 19th century.

2. In using most cookbooks published before 1900, housewives depended largely on experience, for the recipes generally lacked precise measurements and step-by-step directions. Although some authors listed ingredients in columnar form, that system was not standardized until the late 1890s.

3. Although the principal item in pre-Civil War American diets was meat (especially beef), the food available from 1850 to 1900 was unexpectedly varied, considering the transportation and distribution systems of that time. There were some surprises in the lists of foods Minnesotans ate at mid-century, too; chief among them was oysters.

According to one account, the first fresh oysters were brought to Minnesota by Governor Alexander Ramsey, a former Pennsylvanian, "in kegs from Chicago, in February, 1850." So great an appetite for oysters prevailed in the Ramsey household that the bill for a month's supply in January, 1880, totaled over $23, paid at the rate of 40 cents a quart. That the Ramseys were not alone in this preference is manifest by the astonishing number of oyster recipes appearing in Minnesota cookbooks throughout the 19th century.[50]

Another surprisingly long-lived food choice was salted codfish, which was sent upriver by steamboat to Minnesota in the 1850s and shipped by rail after the late 1860s. An early pioneer recalled that while en route to Houston County his family depended for food on "the biggest slab of codfish I ever saw." Another settler found his favorite food in short supply in southern Minnesota and, when he "got to hankering for codfish," he determined to return to the East where he would not have to do without it. He apparently was among a minority, for codfish seems to have been a staple food in many Minnesota homes at least until 1900.[51]

4. The quantities of food prepared by 19th-century cooks were consistently larger than those suggested by recipes in today's cookbooks. This undoubtedly reflects the fact that families had more children then, and that two or more generations often resided in the same household.

5. Lack of refrigeration was the major factor that made necessary much of the work in food preservation that seems so remote to modern housewives. Attempts to preserve meats, vegetables, and fruit resulted in the widespread use of methods that are definitely considered unsafe today. While pickling is still a common practice, present-day cookbooks contain only a fraction of the

pickle recipes of their predecessors, and the range of foods accorded that treatment is much narrower.

6. A wide variety of vegetables was consumed by Minnesotans in the late 19th century, but only a few were eaten raw in salads. The exception was the popular cabbage made into coleslaw, which is a reminder that the versatile vegetable could be available throughout much of the year when properly stored. Only late in the century did recipes for lettuce or other raw vegetable salads appear; they were not numerous even then, nor were fruit salads.

Much more to Minnesotans' liking were salads made of potatoes, meat, fish, poultry, and eggs. Apparently Sarah Rorer's Minneapolis audience took no heed when she suggested in 1894 that "Meat salads are appropriate for lunch and supper, but are too heavy for a course dinner." Many of her listeners may have nodded approvingly, however, when she added that she "would as soon think of going without her bath as her salad at dinner."[52]

Next to potatoes, corn was the vegetable used in the most varied guises. It was served on or off the cob, with other foods, as pudding, patties, fritters, soup, mock oysters, and hominy. To make the latter, housewives separated the outer skin from shelled corn by scalding it in a bath of hot lye followed by three careful washings in clear water. Hominy was produced commercially in St. Paul as early as 1855.[53]

7. Without a doubt, desserts made up the largest single category of recipes contributed to Minnesota church-sponsored cookbooks. Cakes led the field, followed

closely by puddings, pies, and gelatin concoctions. The number of pudding recipes seems disproportionately large when compared to today's cookbooks. Their titles reflected the dominant ingredient: crackers, tapioca, apples, blueberries, corn meal, rice, prunes, and, of course, bread crumbs.[54]

8. Scarcities of some commodities, the unsatisfactory condition of supplies, and frugality prompted imaginative uses of leftovers, and many cookbooks gave recipes for such dishes.

It is clear from the letters and reminiscences of Minnesota housewives that eggs, sugar, coffee, and tea were among the items frequently in short supply. The complaint of one woman who contemplated "a big day's work" of "baking & sauce making pickling &c &c — & only half sugar enough to do with" could have been chanted by a chorus of women about other shortages as well. Thus molasses and sorghum — the words were used interchangeably — sweetened cakes, cookies, breads, muffins, and griddle cakes. (Honey, however, was seldom used in baking, even though it was usually present in the home.) Maple sugar, prepared by the settlers or purchased from Indians, was a favored item frequently substituted for commercial sugar. Some enterprising young boys at Faribault mixed a dark maple sugar with "scrapings from the brown sugar barrel" to sell to their neighbors. For many years a popular community get-together was a "sugaring-off" party where "maple sugar, hot or cold or in any manner wished" was the featured refreshment.[55]

Some household guides recommended preferred kinds of coffee beans, but when they were not available, Minnesota cooks resorted to brews made of browned potatoes, beets, barley, toasted corn meal, and parched rye. And when commercial teas were not in stock, "prairie tea" and currant tea made acceptable drinks; sassafras and ginseng teas were drunk as well.[56]

9. The skills of innovative as well as traditional cookery were brought to Minnesota by housewives who had learned them in other areas of the country. Yet few regional foods appear in the Minnesota cookbooks, and those recipes that can be identified as regional came in largest numbers from New England and the Middle Atlantic states, with a scattered few from the South and some for chili sauce representing the Southwest.

Notably lacking from the local 19th-century cookbooks are ethnic recipes. That they were used and had not been lost is evidenced by the profusion of treasured ethnic recipes found in *100 Years of Good Cooking*, a 20th-century compilation of Minnesota family recipes first published on the occasion of the centennial of Minnesota statehood in 1958. Yet cookbooks published in Minnesota as late as the 1890s reflect only a few of the nationality groups known to reside in the state. A sampling of church-sponsored cooking guides reveals a rather large number of recipes that owed some debt to French cooking (at least in name); a lesser number were clearly English or Scottish in origin; still fewer were characteristically German; and only a sprinkling represented Italian and Scandinavian foods.[57]

There are several possible explanations for the lack of ethnic recipes. Immigrants in America tended to associate primarily with people of similar nationality, limiting their social contacts with other cultural groups. Some newcomers, on the other hand, were motivated to become Americanized as quickly as possible, which would further inhibit them from exhibiting their distinctive culinary traditions. Compared with today, there was little public display of ethnic pride, and too often nationality minorities were on the receiving end of a widespread prejudice on the part of the majority. In Minnesota the need for cookbooks with recipes for national dishes was not strongly felt, since cooking was taught in the home. It is, in fact, only in recent decades that a concerted effort has been made in this country to collect and publish recipes that reflect the national origins of many Americans.[58]

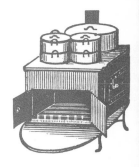

In this context, the ethnic recipes in *"Aunt Babette's" Cook Book* seem quite extraordinary for their time. A volume of similar interest, and one widely used in Minnesota, is *The Settlement Cook Book*, compiled by Mrs. Simon Kander in Milwaukee, Wisconsin. First published in 1901, the book of Jewish and American recipes has been regularly reprinted and revised to the present time.[59]

10. The 19th-century cookbooks in the collection of the Minnesota Historical Society tend to support the broad concept expressed in *The Tried and True Cook Book:* "A knowledge of cooking has long been considered one of the most important elements of a house-keeper's educa-

tion, and no other department furnishes her so large an opportunity as this for exhibition of her taste and refinement, as well as of her skill." [60]

As this quotation suggests, these volumes — often overlooked by social historians — furnish valuable clues to the home life of yesteryear. They not only offer a record of foods served and preferred, they also etch in bold outlines the role of women as well as the manners and morals of a far different age. Their emphasis on prudence, frugality, thrift, virtuous hard work, and numerous — but solely domestic — responsibilities of the housewife echoes an era remote from today's values, laborsaving devices, and changing attitudes toward women. These fragile documents, suffering from use and abuse, clearly point up the contrasts in the greatly altered position of women in the 19th and 20th centuries.

What remains unchanged, however, is an interest in good food. The sampler of recipes from the 19th century in the following chapter testifies to the American woman's high level of cooking skills and her ability to use the ingredients at hand. When she ladled brilliant red cranberries between butter-rich dough, or served her homemade tart-sweet wild plum catsup or currant jelly with a dinner of prairie chicken, Saratoga potatoes, and thin slices of homebaked bread and butter, she was indeed making imaginative use of her available food supplies. [61]

Cookery as practiced by Minnesota housewives in the 19th century represents a special legacy. It is instructive for its insights into the past and rewarding for the opportunity it gives to expand the vision of one generation looking back on another.

CHAPTER NINE

Selected Recipes

THE FOLLOWING 19th-century recipes are drawn from cookbooks or manuscripts collections in the Minnesota Historical Society and from selected other cookbooks published in the state. They were chosen for two reasons: first, they are typical examples of the cookery of a century ago; and second, they will add variety and interest to 20th-century menus.

All the recipes in this section are safe to use, and the modern cook need have no worries about trying them. Some of those printed here have been tested and adapted to today's smaller households. These appear with an asterisk (*) in front of them. Others are printed as they appeared in the old cookbooks as a challenge to the modern cook who wishes to match skills against the women of an earlier era. In recipes requiring baking powder, the double-acting type should be used in amounts listed for tested recipes and in smaller amounts than is indicated in untested recipes.

The varieties of soup turned out in Minnesota kitchens included simple blends of vegetables and seasonings in hearty, appetite-satisfying combinations as well as elegant mixtures that might be served from a graceful, highly prized tureen. It was understood, then as now, that food not consumed at one meal would be turned to account for another. Most cookbooks in the Minnesota collection spelled out how to make "stock." The following simple recipe is typical:

SOUP STOCK

"Twenty-five cents worth shank of beef, boil all day, set away to cool, take off the grease, boil that grease in water, skim and save for dripping; 1 quart of stock will make about 2 quarts of soup." ASCENSION CHURCH, *Family Friend*, 9.

BROWN SOUP

"Carrot, onion and tomato, boil in water several hours; put on the stock, when boiling put in the vegetables with about a pint of water, half as much as the stock, two tablespoonfuls of browned flour wet with cold water, mash smooth and put in a little allspice, ground mace and cloves, pepper and salt; brown in an iron spoon tablespoonful of brown sugar, put it in and let it soak off the spoon, 2 hard boiled eggs chopped up in tureen, a few thin slices of lemon, then pour the soup on them. Wine improves this. You can also use macaroni." ASCENSION CHURCH, *Family Friend*, 9.

TO GET UP A SOUP IN HASTE

"Chop some cold cooked meat fine, and put a pint into a stew pan with some gravy. Season with pepper and salt and a little butter if the gravy is not rich, add a little flour moistened with cold water, and 3 pints boiling water. Boil moderately half an hour. Strain over some rice or nicely toasted bread and serve. Uncooked meat may be used by using 1 quart cold water to a pound of chopped meat, and letting it stand one-half hour before boiling. Celery root may be grated in as seasoning, or a bunch of parsley thrown in." ASCENSION CHURCH, *Family Friend*, 6.

*WINTER HOTCH-POTCH

1 lb. lamb neck	¾ lb. split peas
3 qts. water	6 ribs celery, diced small
4 carrots, sliced	1 onion, diced small
4 turnips, sliced	1 tbsp. salt
1 whole carrot	⅛ tsp. pepper
1 whole turnip	

Soak the peas overnight. Add the peas, half the sliced carrots and turnips, and a whole one of each to the water and let boil two hours, then take out the whole carrot and turnip; bruise and return them; put in the meat, and the rest of the carrot and turnip, the pepper and salt, and boil slowly three-quarters of an hour; a short time before serving, add the onion and celery. Serves 10 to 12. LEE, *Complete Library*, 245.

MULLIGATAWNY SOUP

"Cut up a chicken; put it into a soup-kettle, with a little sliced onion, carrot, celery, parsley, and three or four cloves. Cover it with four quarts of water. Add any pieces of veal, with the bones, you may have; of course, a knuckle of veal would be the proper thing. When the pieces of chicken are nearly done, take them out, and trim them neatly, to serve with the soup. Let the veal continue to simmer for three hours.

"Now fry an onion, a small carrot, and a stick of celery sliced, in a little butter. When they are a light brown, throw in a table-spoonful of flour; stir it on the fire one or two minutes; then add a good tea-spoonful of curry powder, and the chicken and veal broth. Place this on the fire to simmer the usual way for an hour. Half an hour before dinner, strain the soup, skim off all the fat, return it to the fire with the pieces of chicken, and two or three table-spoonfuls of boiled rice. This will give time enough to cook the chickens thoroughly." HENDERSON, *Practical Cooking*, 92.

CODFISH CHOWDER

"Fry several small pieces of salt pork in a deep vessel; remove part of them and put into the vessel a layer of the fish cut into small pieces. Add a little pepper, then a piece or two of the fried pork, then a layer of sliced raw potatoes; season with a little pepper and salt; then a layer of Boston crackers, split. Repeat until as large as desired. Lastly, cover with crackers, then add water till you can see it at the side of vessel. Cook one hour, then remove the cover, add a cup of cream; scald a short time." MAY & SON, *Catalogue*, 47.

OYSTER SOUP

"Pour one can standard oysters into a colander to drain; pour a cup water over oysters, stirring oysters with spoon. Set liquor on stove to boil and skim thoroughly. Put 1 quart milk into double boiler to heat; roll oyster crackers very fine; thicken the hot milk with it; add a tablespoon of butter and salt. Put the oysters into hot salted liquor and cook until edges begin to schrimp. Remove both dishes from stove and pour contents together and serve." CENTRAL PRESBYTERIAN CHURCH, *Cook Book*, 6.

A SWEDISH FISH SOUP

"Take one dozen small panfish, skin and bone them. Boil the heads and bones in two quarts of water with a tablespoonful of salt and a handful of dried mushrooms. Egg and crumb the pieces of fish, and fry in boiling lard, letting them drain on brown paper. Pare and chop fine a red beet, two onions and half a dozen leeks, and a parsley root. Cut fine, also half a small white cabbage. Cook these separately in salted water for half an hour. Strain the fish broth upon them, put the fried fish in the tureen and pour broth and vegetables upon them. Small dumplings [*see p. 240, below*] are often added, and sometimes part of the fish is minced fine and mixed with them." WASHBURN, CROSBY CO., *New Cook Book*, 9.

POTATO SOUP

"One-half dozen of medium sized potatoes, pare and put on to boil in a quart of cold water. When half done drain and cover with a pint of fresh boiling water, add a sprig of parsley, a stalk of celery, a slice of onion, let boil until potatoes are done, put 3 pints of new milk on to boil. Press potatoes through a sieve, rub a tablespoonful of flour and butter together, and stir into the boiling milk, pour over potatoes and stir until smooth, season with salt and pepper and serve very hot." ASCENSION CHURCH, *Family Friend*, 8.

a, Soup Pot; b, Colander; c, Meat Cleaver; d, Meat Board with Handle to Hang By; e, Meat Saw.

GREEN CORN SOUP

"Two quarts of milk, ten ears of corn scraped down, season highly." WESTMINSTER PRESBYTERIAN CHURCH, [*Valuable Recipes*], 6.

*LENTIL SOUP

1 cup lentils	1 cup canned tomatoes
8 cups water	Salt and pepper to taste
1 whole onion	1 ring of wurst or
1 cup coarsely cut celery	½ lb. wieners

Combine first six ingredients and cook slowly for 3 hours in a *covered* pot. Add the meat, cut into bite-sized pieces, ½ hour before serving. The soup can be cooked with a ham bone, or the broth from a ham or smoked tongue may also be used instead of water. Serves 8 amply. BERTHA L. HEILBRON COLLECTION.

SELECTED RECIPES 207

CHERRY SOUP

"This delicious soup is to be eaten cold, it is a summer soup. Use large, dark red or black cherries, a quart is sufficient. Take a bottle of claret, or any other red wine, and twice as much water as you have wine; half a cup of pearl sago, a few slices of lemon and some cinnamon bark or stick cinnamon, cook about one-half hour, cherries and all. If you find that the soup is too thick add more wine and water, sweeten to suit the taste, a cupful of sugar is the most I ever use.

"Strawberry, blueberry and raspberry soups may be prepared according to above receipt." *"Aunt Babette's" Cook Book,* 26.

NORWEGIAN SOUP

"One large cup sago, one pound raisins, one pound currants, one pound best prunes, one tablespoon vinegar, pinch salt and several cinnamon sticks. Water to make like thick sauce; cook several hours; sugar to taste. Thin at the last with one pint good red wine; take out cinnamon sticks; keep thinned with water." ST. CECILIA GUILD, *Marshall Ladies' Choicest and Best,* 9.

BREADS

A wide variety of breads, as different as appetites and the contents of the cupboard allowed, were placed on frontier tables. These ranged from yeast breads to the sweetened doughs of coffeecakes and doughnuts, which were often served for breakfast in the 19th century. Some bread recipes were simple and quick to prepare; others were involved and time-consuming. Their names often indicate a family treasure or a locally evolved recipe, such as "Grandmother's Graham Bread" or "St. Paul Poor Man's Bread." For recipes in addition to the representative sample of Minnesota breads that follows, and for a discussion of yeasts, see chapter 2.

VIENNA BREAD

"Sift in a tin pan four pounds of flour, bank up against the sides, pour in one quart of warm milk and water, mix into it enough flour to form a thin batter. Then quickly and lightly add one pint of milk, in which is dissolved one ounce of salt, one oz. compressed yeast — leave the remainder of the flour against the sides of the pan, cover the pan with a cloth, set in a place free from draught, for three-quarters of an hour. Then mix; the rest of the flour, with the dough, will leave the bottom and sides of the pan; let it stand two and one-half hours, finally divide the mass into one-pound pieces, to be cut in turn, into twelve parts each; rise one half-hour, bake ten minutes in a hot oven." DAYTON AVENUE PRESBYTERIAN CHURCH, *Cook Book*, 20.

GRANDMOTHER'S GRAHAM BREAD

"3 cups Graham flour; ¾ cup molasses; 1 pint sour milk; 2 teaspoons soda. Mix sour milk and soda, then add molasses. Stir well and add flour sifted. Bake in slow oven." CENTRAL PRESBYTERIAN CHURCH, *Cook Book*, 27.

RYE AND INDIAN BREAD

"One large cup sago, one pound raisins, one pound currants, [corn] meal, scalded (by placing in a pan and pouring just enough *boiling* water over it, stirring constantly with a spoon, to merely wet it, but not enough to make it into a batter), one-half tea-cup molasses, two teaspoons salt, one of soda, one tea-cup yeast; make as stiff as can be stirred with a spoon, mixing with warm water, and let rise all night; then put in a large pan, smooth the top with the hand dipped in cold water, let it stand a short time, and bake five or six hours. If put in the oven late in the day, let it remain all night. Graham may be used instead of rye, and baked as above. In the olden time it was placed in kettle, allowed to rise, then placed on the hearth before the fire, with coals on top of lid, and baked." *Buckeye Cookery*, 30.

*JOHNNYCAKE

2 cups corn meal
2 cups sour milk
3 eggs

2 tbsp. butter (melted)
2 tbsp. sugar
1 tsp. baking powder
1 tsp. salt (optional)

Combine dry ingredients; combine milk, slightly beaten eggs, melted butter. Add dry ingredients to milk mixture. Stir, but do not beat. Bake in three 9-inch pie pans at 425 degrees for 30 minutes. WESTMINSTER PRESBYTERIAN CHURCH, [*Valuable Recipes*], 35.

*ST. PAUL POOR MAN'S BROWN BREAD

"1 heaping cup each of corn, rye and graham flour; sift together as closely as possible and beat together thoroughly with 2 cups New Orleans molasses; 2 cups sweet milk; 1 cup sour milk; 1 dessertspoon [2 teaspoons] soda dissolved in a little sour milk; 1 teaspoon salt; pour into a tin form [⅔ full] with cover; place in a kettle of cold water and boil four hours [as for steamed pudding]." CENTRAL PRESBYTERIAN CHURCH, *Cook Book*, 26.

SODA BISCUIT

"Put one quart of flour, before sifting, into sieve, with one teaspoon soda and two of cream tartar (or three of baking powder), one of salt, and one table-spoon white sugar; mix all thoroughly with the flour, run through sieve, rub in one level table-spoon of lard or butter (or half and half), wet with half pint sweet milk, roll on board about an inch thick, cut with biscuit cutter, and bake in a quick oven fifteen minutes. If you have not milk, use a little more butter, and wet with water. Handle as little and make as rapidly as possible." *Buckeye Cookery*, 38.

*GRAHAM GEMS

1 cup sweet milk	¼ tsp. salt
1 egg	3 tsp. baking powder
1 tbsp. sugar	1¼ cups graham flour

Beat egg in milk; add sugar, salt, and baking powder; stir in unsifted graham flour. Bake in greased muffin tins at 400 degrees for 15 minutes. Yield: 1 doz. medium-size muffins. FIRST BAPTIST CHURCH, *Tried and True*, 50.

OATMEAL MUFFINS

"One large coffee cup freshly cooked oat meal, one tablespoon butter, one tablespoon sugar, one teaspoon salt, mix well together, add one-fourth to one-half yeast cake dissolved in as little water as possible, and enough flour to mould very stiff. Rise till light, drop in warm gem [or muffin] pans, rise again until soft. Bake in a quick oven about twenty minutes." WASHBURN, CROSBY CO., *New Cook Book*, 60.

INDIAN BANNOCKS

"One pint corn meal, one quart milk; boil one pint of the milk and scald the meal thoroughly with it; three eggs. Thin the batter with cold milk; add three tablespoonfuls melted butter and two teaspoonfuls salt. Bake in shallow tins." WESTMINSTER PRESBYTERIAN CHURCH, [*Valuable Recipes*], 34.

*CORN LUNN

¾ cup butter	1½ cups sifted flour
¾ cup sugar	3 tsp. baking powder
4 eggs	1 tsp. salt
1½ cups corn meal	1 cup sweet milk

Cream the butter and sugar together. Add the eggs, one at a time, and beat well after each addition. Resift the flour with the baking powder and salt. Add the sifted ingredients and the corn meal to the batter alternately with the milk. Beat the batter only enough to blend the ingredients. Pour the batter into a greased 9 × 13 pan. Bake in a preheated oven for 30 minutes at 425 degrees. Serve hot. FIRST BAPTIST CHURCH, *Tried and True*, 47.

A "VERY GOOD" GINGERBREAD

"4 Cups of Flour (sifted). 2 eggs. 1 Tablespoon full of cloves also one of cinnimon [*sic*]. 2 Cups of Molassess [*sic*]. 1 Cup of Butter. 1 Table spoon full of Soda dissolved in a cup of warm water." ANNA RAMSEY'S BOOK OF RECEIPTS, 1865.

TEACAKE

"One quart flour, one cup sour milk, one tea-spoon soda, one-half pound lard, one-half pound chopped raisins or currants; roll two inches thick and bake in a quick oven; split open, butter, and eat while hot." *Buckeye Cookery*, 39.

CORN GRIDDLECAKES

"One pint corn meal, one teaspoon salt, one of soda. Pour on boiling water until a little thinner than mush. Let it stand until cool. Add yolks of three eggs, one-half cup of flour, into which two teaspoons cream tartar are mixed. Stir in as much sweet milk as will make batter suitable to bake, beat whites, and add just before baking." FIRST BAPTIST CHURCH, *Tried and True*, 48.

BUCKWHEAT CAKES

"One quart buckwheat flour, four tablespoonfuls yeast, one teaspoonful salt, one handful Indian [corn] meal, two tablespoonfuls molasses — not syrup — warm water enough to make a thin batter. Beat very well and set to rise in a warm place over night. If the batter is the least sour in the morning, stir in a very little soda dissolved in hot water." WESTMINSTER PRESBYTERIAN CHURCH, [*Valuable Recipes*], 33.

RAISED DOUGHNUTS

"1½ cups milk; 1½ cups sugar; 1 cup butter; 1 cup yeast; 1 [grated] nutmeg; 9 eggs; 1 small teaspoon soda; flour to make it the consistency of bread; let raise twenty-four hours; mold into round biscuit; raise again three or four hours, or until light; fry in hot lard and when done, roll in powdered sugar." CENTRAL PRESBYTERIAN CHURCH, *Cook Book*, 85.

SODA DOUGHNUTS

"One quart of flour, three teaspoons baking powder, half teaspoon salt, one egg, one tablespoon cream or piece of butter or lard, size of half egg; mix with sweet milk; soft." DAYTON AVENUE PRESBYTERIAN CHURCH, *Cook Book*, 32.

DROP CAKE

"One pint of milk, two eggs, one cup of molasses, two cups corn meal, three of rye flour; drop in hot lard and fry like doughnuts." DAYTON AVENUE PRESBYTERIAN CHURCH, *Cook Book*, 28.

*COFFEE FRUIT CAKE

½ cup butter	1 tsp. cream of tartar
1 cup sugar	½ tsp. soda
2 eggs	½ cup currants
1½ cups sifted flour	½ cup citron
¼ cup milk	1 cup raisins
¼ cup cold coffee	1 tsp. cinnamon
	½ tsp. ground cloves

Cream butter and sugar; add eggs one at a time. Beat well. Dissolve soda in milk; add cream of tartar to sifted flour. Add flour to butter mixture alternately with milk and coffee. Add spices and beat until well blended. Stir in the fruit. Pour batter into a greased and floured 9-inch square pan; bake at 375 degrees for 35 minutes. *"Aunt Babette's" Cook Book*, 269.

FISH AND SEAFOOD

If the recipes in the cookbooks of the Minnesota collection are representative, the denizen of the deep which most frequently graced the state's tables in the 19th century must have been the oyster! Although salted cod, salmon (sometimes fresh but usually canned), lobster, clams, crab, and shrimp were among the other seafoods used, oyster recipes overwhelmingly outnumber those for any other fish or crustacean. In none of the books does a recipe for the Scandinavian favorite, *lutefisk,* appear, but then as now numerous freshwater fish, including trout, whitefish, pike, pickerel, herring, bass, and smelt, were prepared.

"In preparing fish, half the cooks will spoil them by not using proper judgment," advised Mrs. Willet Hays in 1892. "First see that you have a fish with a good bright eye (if frozen, the frost should always be taken out in cold water, or your fish will be soft and fall to pieces.)" She recommended steaming fish in preference to boiling, and suggested that smelt, herring, ciscoes, and perch be fried, while whitefish be broiled or boiled.[1]

CURRIED OYSTERS

"Put the liquor drained from a quart of oysters into a saucepan, add a half-cup of butter, two table-spoons flour, and one of curry powder, well mixed; let boil, add oysters, and a little salt; boil up once and serve." *Buckeye Cookery,* 298.

LITTLE PIGS IN BLANKETS

"Season large oysters with salt and pepper. Cut fat English bacon in very thin slices. Wrap an oyster in each slice and fasten on with a toothpick. Heat a frying pan and put in the 'Little Pigs'; cook just long enough to crisp the bacon, about 10 minutes; place on slices of toast, that have been cut into small pieces, and serve immediately. Do not remove the toothpicks. The pan must be very hot before any of the 'pigs' are put in, and then much care must be taken that they do not burn." ASCENSION CHURCH, *Family Friend,* 14.

SCALLOPED OYSTERS

"Take deep dish; roll some crackers, not too fine; make a layer of crumbs, then oysters; season with salt and pepper, and a very little mace; put small lumps of butter in every layer until the dish is filled. Do *not* use the liquor of the oyster, but use a pint of water and milk mixed instead." WESTMINSTER PRESBYTERIAN CHURCH, [*Valuable Recipes*], 8.

CODFISH BALLS

"Pare potatoes; cut in quarters and measure 1 pint. Let stand in cold water for several hours. Wash the raw salt fish; pick it in half inch pieces and measure 1 cup. Put the potatoes and fish in a stew pan; cover with boiling water and cook until the potatoes are tender; then drain off water; add 1 teaspoon butter; ¼ salt-spoon of pepper and 3 grains cayenne. Mash and beat them till very light. When slightly cool, add 1 egg well beaten. Stir well; add more salt if needed. Shape in a tablespoon without smoothing much; slip them off into a basket and fry in smoking hot fat 1 minute; then drain on soft paper. It is best to beat and mash with a wire masher." CENTRAL PRESBYTERIAN CHURCH, *Cook Book*, 10.

CREAM CODFISH OR MOCK OYSTER STEW

"Small piece of salt cod, which has been soaked in cold water over night, and cooked until soft (which should be done by simmering slowly, not boiling.) Shred it first and mix well with a tablespoonful of dry flour. Put it in the chafing dish with 2 tablespoonfuls of butter, a dozen oyster crackers split; pour over the mixture 2 cups of hot milk or cream, season with pepper and stir constantly 5 or 10 minutes." ASCENSION CHURCH, *Family Friend*, 13.

SALMON LOAF

"1 can salmon, 3 eggs, 1 cup sweet milk, 5 rolled crackers, salt and pepper to suit the taste. Put in basin and steam 1½ hours. Cut in slices when cold." METHODIST EPISCOPAL CHURCH, *Christmas Cook Book*, 2.

TO BAKE A TEN-POUND MUSKELLUNGE
Stuffing

"One pound bread soaked in cold water and pressed dry, one pound fresh boiled fish chopped fine, one-half teaspoon powdered marjoram, one-half teaspoon powdered thyme, salt and pepper. Mix thoroughly and stuff fish. Put the fish in a covered baking pan with strips of salt pork in under it and over it. Bake three hours."

Sauce for Same

"Fry one slice of ham, brown four tablespoons of flour in butter and thicken one quart of soup stock. Pour the thickened stock on ham, add a small onion with a few cloves, boil ten minutes, strain and add one can of mushrooms and two tablespoons beef extract, two tablespoons sherry, two tablespoons claret, one-half lemon. Add the wine and lemon just as you take it from the stove." *Duluth Home Cook Book*, 22.

BAKED PIKE

"Take two or three white potatoes, boil, then mash them, with two tablespoons of butter, a small onion cut fine, black pepper and salt to taste. Salt the fish, put in a baking pan and stuff with the potato dressing; sprinkle a little flour over it. Put in the pan with the fish, two tablespoons of butter, two dessertspoons of salad oil, a dozen tomatoes sliced, or half a can, and a teacup of water. Bake in a moderate oven until done; when done, slice over it three hard boiled eggs. Stir into the gravy a tablespoon of tomato catsup, and one of Worcestershire sauce. Pour over the fish and serve." DAYTON AVENUE PRESBYTERIAN CHURCH, *Cook Book*, 38.

PLANKED WHITEFISH

"Split fish down the back, season and place skin down on hardwood plank two inches thick; pile coarse salt all around about an inch thick, place in oven; when done scrape off salt and garnish with parsley; serve on board." ASCENSION CHURCH, *Family Friend*, 13.

BROOK TROUT

"These delicate fish are always fried. Wash and drain in a colander; split nearly to the tail; flour them nicely, salt and put in fryingpan, hot but not burning; the fat of fried salt pork is preferable to lard, as you need the salt to prevent their sticking. Do not turn them until sufficiently brown. Fry crisp if you wish. They are nice fried and served with slices of fat salt pork. Do not cut off their heads." *Duluth Home Cook Book*, 19.

ROLLED FISH

Fish Kettle

"Take only the flesh of strawberry bass (Croppies) [*sic*]; cut in strips which when rolled will be about one and one-half inches high and about one and one-half inches across. Tie carefully with twine, and endeavor to have all the rolls uniform in size. Boil in equal parts of milk and water (very salt) until done — about ten minutes; care being necessary that they do not fall in pieces. Remove the strings and arrange on a platter."

Oyster Sauce. "One pint of cream; butter the size of an egg; flour to thicken; let boil and add three-fourths of a pint oysters with the liquor, and two tablespoonfuls sherry wine. Let boil and serve." ST. MARK'S PARISH, *Tested Recipes*, 53.

FROG LEGS

"The green marsh frogs furnish the best hams, as they are more tender and have less of the strong muddy flavor. They are generally liked fried. Pare off the feet and truss them by inserting the stump along the shin of the other leg. Put them with salt, pepper and lemon juice to steep for an hour, then drain and roll in flour, then in beaten egg and in fine bread crumbs. Fry to a light brown in hot fat. Serve with fried parsley." WASHBURN, CROSBY CO., *New Cook Book*, 30.

MEATS, POULTRY, AND GAME

Like their 20th-century descendants, the pioneers seem to have preferred beef to other meats, although pork, veal, liver, heart, tongue, brains, and sweetbreads were also popular. If one is to judge by the locally published cookbooks, there was also a chicken in nearly every pot. The versatile bird easily dominated the poultry pages of Minnesota cookbooks, and turkey, goose, and duck recipes are relatively rare. Game and wild-fowl recipes are also notable by their scarcity, especially in church-sponsored cookbooks. While the recipes that follow are only a sampling of the good meat dishes of 19th-century Minnesota, the methods of preparing meats were similar to those of today. Boiling, however, seems to have been more frequently used then than it is now, while sautéing seems to have been less popular than it is today.[2]

Meats

BEEF A LA MODE

"In a piece of rump cut deep incisions; put in pieces of pork cut into dice, previously rolled in pepper, salt, cloves and nutmeg. Into an iron stew pan place pieces of pork, slices of onion, slices of lemon, one or two carrots and a few small bay leaves; lay the meat on and put over it a piece of bread crust as large as a saucer, ½ pint of wine and a little vinegar, and afterwards an equal quantity of beef broth; cover closely and cook until tender; then take it out, rub the gravy through a sieve, skim off the fat, add some sour cream, return to the stew pan and cook 10 minutes. Can be served hot or cold." ASCENSION CHURCH, *Family Friend*, 20.

*BEEF ALABRAISE

4 lbs. rump roast	½ tsp. thyme
Salt pork, cut into	½ cup port wine
¼-inch squares	¼ cup vinegar
1 onion, chopped	¼ cup salad oil
1 tsp. parsley	Salt and pepper
2 cloves garlic, diced	

Roll the salt pork squares in the onion, garlic, and spices before carefully larding the roast, forcing the salt pork into the meat so that it is beneath the surface. Add the remaining seasoning to the wine, vinegar, and oil to prepare a marinade. Steep the beef in the marinade overnight. Turn the meat several times while it is in the marinade. Roast uncovered in a 325-degree oven, basting with the marinade that is poured into the roasting pan, for about 1¾ hours. Serves 8. LEE, *Complete Library*, 12.

MACARONI BEEF

"One pound of maccaroni [*sic*] to four pounds of beef — lard the beef well with pork — salt and pepper to taste; one onion in the pan; baste frequently. For the gravy — half a cup of tomato catsup, two tablespoons of Harvey sauce [*see p. 222, below*], wine-glass of sherry wine. Thicken the gravy with corn starch; when ready to serve, take out the onion. Cook the maccaroni in boiling water until tender. When ready to send to the table, lay the maccaroni around the beef, and pour the gravy over it." DAYTON AVENUE PRESBYTERIAN CHURCH, *Cook Book*, 72.

BEEF OLIVES

"One and one half pounds of beef, cut very thin. Trim off the edges and fat; then cut in strips three inches wide and four long; season well with salt and pepper. Chop fine the trimmings and the fat. Add three table-spoons of powdered cracker, one teaspoon of sage and savory mixed, one-fourth of a teaspoon of pepper, and two teaspoons of salt. Mix very thoroughly and spread on the strips of beef. Roll them up and tie with twine. When all are done, roll in flour. Fry brown a quarter of a pound of pork. Take it out of the pan, and put the olives in. Fry brown, and put in a small stewpan that can be tightly covered. In the fat remaining in the pan put one tablespoon of flour, and stir until perfectly smooth and brown; then pour in, gradually, nearly a pint and a half of boiling water. Stir for two or three minutes, season to taste with salt and pepper, and pour over the olives. Cover the stewpan, and let simmer two hours. Take up at the end of this time and cut the strings with a sharp knife. Place the olives in a row on a dish, and pour the gravy over them." WASHBURN, CROSBY CO., *New Cook Book*, 14.

VEAL LOAF

Veal.

"Chop fine 3 pounds of leg or loin of veal and ¾ pound of salt pork. Mix. Roll 1 dozen crackers. Put 2 eggs and half the crackers in the meat, season with pepper and a little salt, if needed. Mix all together and make into a solid form. Spread the rest of the crackers smoothly over the outside. Bake one hour and eat cold." METHODIST EPISCOPAL CHURCH, *Christmas Cook Book*, 2.

FRICANDEAU OF VEAL

"Cut a thick, handsome slice from a fillet of veal; trim it neatly round and lard it thickly with fat bacon. Cut 1 carrot, 1 turnip, 1 head of celery into slices and put them into a stewpan with a bunch of savory heads, 2 blades of mace, 5 allspice and 2 bay leaves, with some slices of bacon at the top. Lay the Fricandeau over the bacon with the larded side uppermost; dust a little salt over it, and pour round it a pint of good gravy or broth. Place it over the fire and let it boil, then let it simmer very gently for two hours and a half over a slow fire, basting it frequently with the gravy. Take out the Fricandeau when done; skim off the fat; strain the gravy and boil it quickly to a strong glare [*glaze*]; cover the Fricandeau with it and serve up very hot upon puree of green peas. Be careful that the gravy does not touch the Fricandeau, but that it only covers the bacon and other ingredients at the bottom of the dish." CENTRAL PRESBYTE-RIAN CHURCH, *Cook Book*, 11.

SPRING LAMB, MINT SAUCE

"Rub the saddle of lamb with salt and butter, and while roasting baste frequently with the gravy and salted water. Cook ten minutes to a pound. The sauce is made from young leaves of mint chopped fine, adding two tablespoons of powdered sugar to three tablespoons of mint; after mixing add six tablespoons of white wine vinegar or cider, pouring it slowly over the mint. In order to extract all the flavor of the mint the sauce should be made in advance of dinner-time." WASHBURN, CROSBY CO., *New Cook Book*, 14.

TOAD-IN-THE-HOLE

"Mix one pint flour and one egg with milk enough [about 1½ cups] to make a batter (like that for batter-cakes), and a little salt; grease dish well with butter, put in lamb chops, add a little water with pepper and salt, pour batter over it, and bake for one hour." *Buckeye Cookery*, 199.

ROAST PORK

"A small loin of pork, three table-spoons bread-crumbs, one onion, half a tea-spoon chopped sage, half tea-spoon salt, half tea-spoon pepper, one ounce chopped suet, one table-spoon drippings. Separate each joint of the loin with the chopper, and then make an incision with a knife into the thick part of the pork in which to put the stuffing. Prepare the stuffing by mixing the bread-crumbs together with the onion, which must have previously been finely chopped. Add to this the sage, pepper, salt and suet, and when all is thoroughly mixed, press the mixture snugly into the incision already made in the pork, and sew together the edges of the meat with needle and thread, to confine the stuffing. Grease well a sheet of kitchen paper, with drippings, place the loin into this, securing it with a wrapping of twine. Put to bake in a dry baking-pan, in a brisk oven, basting immediately and constantly as the grease draws out, and roast a length of time, allowing twenty minutes to the pound and twenty minutes longer. Serve with apple-sauce or apple-fritters." *Buckeye Cookery*, 204.

a, Ham Boiler; b, Fish Kettle with Removable Tray.

HAM BOILED IN SHERRY WINE

"Soak a nice ham over night. Put it on to boil in the morning in six or eight quarts of water adding a few cloves and a large handful of bay [leaves] and one pint of sherry wine. As the water boils away, add a little hot water, keeping about as much until it is done. Boil six hours, or until the ham is very tender; then take off and skin, and rub it over with bread or cracker crumbs, and brown it in the oven." DAYTON AVENUE PRESBYTERIAN CHURCH, *Cook Book*, 78.

HARVEY SAUCE

"Chop twelve anchovies, bones and all, very small, with one ounce of cayenne pepper, six spoonfuls of soy, six ditto of good walnut pickle, three heads of garlic, chopped not very small, a quarter of an ounce of cochineal, two heads of shallots, chopped not very small, one gallon of vinegar; let it stand fourteen days, stir it well, twice or thrice every day; then pass it through a jelly-bag, and repeat this till it is perfectly clear; then bottle it, and tie a bladder over the cork." LEE, *Complete Library*, 186.

WINE SAUCE FOR MEATS

¾ lb. butter
5 tbsp. sugar

1½ pt. jelly
1 tsp. allspice
1 qt. wine

"Stir over the fire until thick." *Our Chef's Best Receipts*, 26.

BREAKFAST BACON

"Slice the bacon very thin, cut off the rind and hard part before slicing. Fill a shallow pan with cold sweet potatoes sliced. Cover the potatoes with the bacon and bake until the pork is crisp." WASHBURN, CROSBY CO., *New Cook Book*, 18.

LARDED LIVER

"Lard a calf's liver with bacon or ham, season with salt and pepper, tie a cord around the liver to keep in shape, put in a kettle with one quart of cold water, a quarter of a pound of bacon, one onion chopped fine, and one tea-spoon sweet marjoram; let simmer slowly for two hours, pour off gravy into gravy-dish, and brown liver in kettle. Serve with the gravy." *Buckeye Cookery*, 199.

*SWEET-SOUR SAUCE FOR BOILED TONGUE

5 gingersnaps
½ cup brown sugar

4 tbsp. vinegar
1 cup hot water

Crush gingersnaps, and mix with other ingredients. Cook until smooth. Then add 1 sliced lemon; ¼ cup raisins; sliced almonds. Serve over tongue that has been boiled and sliced. Makes 1½ cups. BERTHA L. HEILBRON COLLECTION.

SWEETBREADS WITH MUSHROOMS

"Parboil sweetbreads, allowing eight to a can of mushrooms. Cut them half an inch square and stew until tender. Slice the mushrooms and stew in the liquor for an hour. Then add to the sweetbreads a coffeecup of cream and a tablespoon of butter, also salt and pepper." FIRST BAPTIST CHURCH, *Tried and True*, 39.

Poultry
SMOTHERED CHICKEN

"Take medium sized chickens, clean and wash, and split down the back. Lay flat in a baking pan, put a few thin slices of salt pork over them, adding a little water. Set in the oven and invert another pan over them, so as to cover tightly. Roast at a steady, but moderate heat, about half an hour; then baste with the water in which the fowls are cooking occasionally until done. Just before they are ready to be taken out, remove the cover and let them brown. Thicken the gravy left in the pan with browned flour, adding a little water if necessary, season with pepper, salt and parsley." FIRST BAPTIST CHURCH, *Tried and True*, 21.

"FRITOT" OF CHICKEN

"Cut up [and bone] a young chicken (raw.) Put it in a bowl with salt, pepper, two spoons of olive oil, juice of a lemon; let it stand for an hour; add two raw eggs, two spoons of flour; mix all well together. Fry in lard, not too hot, for ten or twelve minutes. Serve with cream or tomato sauce." DAYTON AVENUE PRESBYTERIAN CHURCH, *Cook Book*, 78.

*CHUTNEY CHICKEN
Prepare a day ahead of serving

2 frying chickens, quartered	1 tbsp. flour
1 1-lb. can of tomatoes	½ cup chutney
1 tsp. minced salt pork (optional)	1 tsp. salt
3 tbsp. butter	¼ tsp. pepper
2 tsp. minced onion	

Cook the chicken. It may be sautéed (if young) in a little hot fat, or it may be roasted or boiled as for fricassee. Put the canned tomatoes into a blender and spin to a pulp, or force the tomatoes through a food mill or sieve. Sauté the minced pork in a stew pan. Add butter and minced onions, cooking until golden. Add flour and stir well. Pour the tomato pulp into the pan, season with salt and pepper. Stir the sauce until it is smooth. Mix the chutney into the sauce, then add the cooked chicken. Allow the whole to simmer slowly for 15 to 20 minutes. Transfer to a bowl and refrigerate overnight to blend flavors. Reheat to serve. Serves 8. HENDERSON, *Practical Cooking*, 177.

CHICKEN PUDDING

"Dress and cut one chicken into small pieces, put it into a saucepan or kettle with a little water, season with salt and pepper, let boil until it begins to grow tender, then take out and put into a three-quart pudding dish; have ready one quart green corn grated or cut fine, to which add three eggs beaten light and one pint sweet milk; season with salt and pepper, and pour this mixture over the chicken, dredge thickly with flour, lay on bits of butter and bake until done." *Buckeye Cookery*, 279.

BOILED TURKEY

"Wash the turkey thoroughly and rub salt through it; fill it with a dressing of bread and butter, moistened with milk and seasoned with sage, salt and pepper, and mixed with a pint of raw oysters; tie the legs and wings close to the body, place in salted boiling water with the breast downward, skim often, boil about two hours, but not till the skin breaks; serve with oyster-sauce [*see p. 217, above*]." *Buckeye Cookery*, 282.

Game and Wild Fowl

ROAST HAUNCH OF VENISON

"Wash in warm water and dry well with a cloth, butter a sheet of white paper and put over the fat, lay in a deep baking-dish with a very little boiling water, cover with a close-fitting lid or with a coarse paste [*pastry dough*] one-half inch thick. If the latter is used, a thickness or two of coarse paper should be laid over the paste. Cook in a moderately hot oven for from three to four hours, according to the size of the haunch, and about twenty minutes before it is done quicken the fire, remove the paste and paper or dish-cover, dredge the joint with flour and baste well with butter until it is nicely frothed and of a delicate brown color; garnish the knuckle-bone with a frill of white paper, and serve with a gravy made from its own dripping, having first removed the fat. Have the dishes on which the venison is served and the plates very hot. Always serve with currant jelly." *Buckeye Cookery*, 171.

SQUIRRELS

"The large grey and fox squirrels are the best for eating, and may be cooked in any way suitable for rabbits, but they are in greatest request for

BRUNSWICK STEW

2 large squirrels	1 qt. tomatoes
1 pt. lima or butter-beans	6 potatoes
6 ears corn	½ lb. fat salt pork
½ tsp. pepper	½ lb. butter
½ saltspoon cayenne	1 tbsp. salt
2 tsp. white pepper	1 onion
	1 gal. water

"Boil together salt and water, add the onion, herbs, [beans,] corn cut from the cob, diced pork, pepper and let come to a boil, cut the squirrels in joints and wash them clean, add to the stew as soon as it boils. Cut the potatoes in slices and parboil them, put them into the stew with the tomatoes and sugar about an hour before it is done. Ten minutes before taking from the fire add the butter cut in bits and rolled in flour, taste to adjust the seasoning and serve in soup plates." Washburn, Crosby Co., *New Cook Book*, 26.

RABBITS

"Rabbits, which are in the best condition in midwinter, may be fricasseed like chicken in white or brown sauce. To make a pie, first stew till tender, and make like chicken-pie. To roast, stuff with a dressing made of bread-crumbs, chopped salt pork, thyme, onion, and pepper and salt, sew up, rub over with a little butter, or pin on it a few slices of salt pork, add a little water in the pan, and baste often. Serve with mashed potatoes and currant jelly." *Buckeye Cookery*, 173.

OPOSSUM, COON, etc.

"Opossum, raccoons and other small animals are good if you think so, and are cooked like rabbits." Washburn, Crosby Co., *New Cook Book*, 26.

ROAST QUAIL OR PRAIRIE CHICKEN

"Tie a piece of salt pork over the breast of each bird, place them in a pan and put them in the oven; bake as quickly as possible, basting frequently with melted butter. Pigeons are very nice cooked in same matter." First Baptist Church, *Tried and True*, 23.

ROAST WILD DUCK

"Before roasting, parboil with a carrot peeled and put inside. This absorbs the *fishy* taste. If you have no carrot at hand, an onion will do, but unless you mean to use onion in the stuffing, a carrot is preferable. When parboiled throw away the carrot; lay [duck] in fresh water for one-half hour; stuff with bread crumbs, seasoned with salt, pepper and sage, with or without onions. Roast till brown and tender. Baste frequently with butter and water, and then with dripping. Add to the gravy, when taken up, one tablespoonful of currant jelly, and a pinch of cayenne. Thicken with brown flour." St. Mark's Parish, *Tested Recipes*, 50.

DRESSING FOR FOWLS

"Crumb as much bread as is needed to stuff the fowl. Into it rub thoroughly as much butter as will make it moist. Season with sage, pepper and salt. Add chopped oysters if oyster dressing is required. The steam and juice of the fowl furnish all the moisture necessary, and no dyspeptic need fear to eat his fill of this dressing which is light as a feather." *Duluth Home Cook Book*, 99.

VEGETABLES

The time suggested for cooking vegetables in many 19th-century Minnesota cookbooks was often several hours, and the cook was usually admonished to add lots of water. Eliza Leslie, ever ahead of her time, urged the use of only enough liquid to cover the food when cooking, as "There is generally, in our country, too much water allowed to the vegetables." Potato recipes far outnumber those for other vegetables in the Minnesota collection; corn recipes are second, and tomatoes seem to have been the third most-used vegetable. In 1857 Miss Leslie advised "long cooking" for tomatoes "otherwise they will have a raw taste, that to most persons is unpleasant." By the 1870s, however, raw tomatoes were recommended as a relish. Scarcely a vegetable now in common use fails to appear in the

Minnesota volumes. Today's cook may find among the recipes that follow some long-forgotten "new" ways to prepare a family favorite.[3]

FRIED ASPARAGUS

"Blanch the asparagus a couple of minutes, and then drain it; dip each piece in batter and fry it in hot fat. When done, sprinkle with salt and serve hot. This is nice and easy to prepare." *Buckeye Cookery*, 325.

SWEET AND SOUR GREEN BEANS

2 cups cooked green beans ½ cup vinegar
½ cup brown sugar   2 tsp. flour

"Mix sugar and flour in saucepan and slowly add vinegar; heat to boiling, stirring all the while. Add hot beans, salt to taste, and add a tablespoon of butter." BERTHA L. HEILBRON COLLECTION.

BOSTON BAKED BEANS

"Soak beans over night. In the morning parboil until the beans begin to peel. Pour off the water and remove the beans to an earthen bean-baker or jar, placing a piece of pork in the bottom of the jar. Add a teaspoon of mustard, 2 tablespoons of molasses, a little pepper, the salt to be governed by the pork. Fill the jar with boiling water and bake four hours." METHODIST EPISCOPAL CHURCH, *Christmas Cook Book*, 6.

BEET GREENS NICELY SERVED

"Boil greens ½ hour; drain and season with salt, pepper and butter. Serve on buttered toast 1½ inches square with poached eggs on top of the greens." METHODIST EPISCOPAL CHURCH, *Christmas Cook Book*, 4.

*RED CABBAGE

Cut fine 1 medium cabbage; mix in 1 tsp. salt; cut up a sour apple with it; heat 1 tbsp. goose oil or butter in stainless steel kettle; add cabbage and apple; cut up onion very fine and throw it in the cabbage; stew slowly, covered up; add a little hot water after it boils about 5 minutes; when tender put in 2 tbsp. vinegar, a few cloves, 4 tbsp. brown sugar, and a little cinnamon; taste, if necessary add more sugar. Serves 8. *"Aunt Babette's" Cook Book*, 125.

CORN OYSTERS

"To one quart grated corn, add three eggs, three or four grated crackers; beat it well and season with pepper and salt to taste. Take half butter, and half lard, to try [*fry*], drop with a spoon; when corn is very juicy will require more crackers." WESTMINSTER PRESBYTERIAN CHURCH, [*Valuable Recipes*], 35.

CORN PUDDING

"8 ears of corn; split the rows, cut and then scrape from the cob; fill baking dish half full of sweet milk, thicken with ½ teacupful of flour, 3 eggs well beaten, lump of butter the size of an egg, pepper and salt to taste; bake in moderate oven ¾ of an hour." ASCENSION CHURCH, *Family Friend*, 37.

EGGPLANT STUFFED

EAR OF CORN.

"Cut sufficient from one end of the plant to be able to scrape out the inside, leaving the hull perfect. Put what was taken from inside into sauce pan with ½ cup of minced ham; cover with water and boil until tender, then drain off the water; add ½ cup of dried bread crumbs, 1 large tablespoonful butter, half of a small onion chopped, saltspoonful of salt, half as much pepper. Stuff the hull with this mixture and bake about 20 minutes." ASCENSION CHURCH, *Family Friend*, 37.

HOMINY

"Soak one cup over night in cold water. In the morning drain and put to cook in three cups of boiling salted water and boil gently till soft; it ought to take about three hours. Fine hominy can be cooked in one hour if soaked in warm water, changing it once or twice for warmer. Boil in the last water." WASHBURN, CROSBY CO., *New Cook Book*, 52.

WILTED LETTUCE

"Place in a vegetable dish lettuce that has been very carefully picked and washed each leaf by itself, to remove all insects. Cut across the dish four or five times, and sprinkle with salt. Fry a small piece of fat ham until brown, cut it in small pieces; when very hot add cup of good vinegar, and pour it boiling hot over the lettuce; mix it well with a fork, and garnish with slices of hard-boiled eggs. Be certain to have the fat so hot that when vinegar is poured in, it will boil immediately. Add half a cup or a cup of vinegar according to strength of vinegar and quantity of lettuce." *Buckeye Cookery*, 333.

ONION SOUFFLÉ

1 cup white sauce	½ cup bread crumbs
1 cup finely chopped cold cooked onions	⅔ cup milk
	¼ teaspoon pepper
½ teaspoon salt	3 eggs

"Soak crumbs in the milk, add the white sauce, onions, pepper and salt, yolks of the eggs well beaten. Add whites of eggs last. Turn into buttered pudding dish, and bake slowly 45 minutes." *Our Chef's Best Receipts*, 115.

PARSNIP STEW

"Place a half dozen slices of sweet salt pork in an iron vessel, and let them fry until slightly brown. Having scraped, washed, and sliced three good sized parsnips, put them in with the pork and above them a dozen peeled potatoes, cut once in two if large. Pour over a little boiling water and cover tightly, so that the cooking may be done in part by the steam. The whole should be stirred occasionally with care not to mash it, yet to brown it as evenly as possible. A little boiling water may be added from time to time. When ready to serve it should be rather moist, yet with no liquid in the vessel." FIRST BAPTIST CHURCH, *Tried and True*, 43.

FRIED POTATOES

"The potatoes must be raw, large, unblemished, and of a good round shape. First take off a thin paring of the skin. Then pare the whole potato round and round, (not too thin,) till you have gone through it all, and nothing is left unpared but a little lump in the centre. Then put these continuous rings of potato into a frying-pan, in which is boiling plenty of fresh butter, or butter and lard mixed. Fry them brown and tender, and arrange them handsomely in a dish for breakfast." LESLIE, *New Cookery Book*, 348.

*HOUSEKEEPER'S POTATOES

4 cups boiled potatoes, diced   1 tsp. butter
2 cups chicken or beef stock   1 tsp. lemon juice
1 tsp. parsley   Salt and pepper to taste

"Season the potatoes with salt and pepper and add the stock. Cover and simmer 12 minutes. Add lemon juice, parsley, and butter; simmer two minutes longer." Serves 6 to 8. PARLOA, *New Cook Book*, 31.

SARATOGA POTATOES

"Slice potatoes very thin, wash in four waters, dry in a towel and fry in very hot lard. Take them out with a skimmer, drain, and sprinkle with salt." FIRST BAPTIST CHURCH, *Tried and True*, 41.

A PRETTY WAY TO SERVE POTATOES

"Steam, mash and season with butter and salt, sweet potatoes; make into small, round balls. Have ready white potatoes, also mashed and seasoned, with the white of an egg beaten stiff, and added. With the hands mold the white potato around the sweet potato balls, then roll in beaten egg, and then in fine, sifted dried bread crumbs, and brown a delicate color in a frying basket in deep fat. Serve hot in the midst of parsley leaves." CENTRAL PRESBYTERIAN CHURCH, *Cook Book*, 107.

FRENCH FRIED SWEET POTATOES

"Prepare and fry the same as the white potatoes. Or, they can first be boiled half an hour, and then pared, cut, and fried as directed. The latter is the better way, as they are liable to be a little hard if fried when raw." PARLOA, *New Cook Book*, 31.

SALSIFY OR VEGETABLE OYSTERS

"Parboil after scraping off the outside, cut in slices, dip it into a beaten egg and fine breadcrumbs, and fry in lard. Or, slice crosswise five or six good-sized plants, cook till tender in water enough to cover, then add a pint or more of rich milk mixed with one table-spoon flour, season with butter, pepper and salt, let boil up and pour over slices of toasted bread; or add three pints milk, or half milk and water, season and serve with crackers like oyster soup." *Buckeye Cookery*, 342.

STUFFED TOMATOES

"Select 6 large firm tomatoes, cut small piece from stem end, so as to scoop out the pulp, preserving the shape of the tomatoes; ½ cup minced ham or breakfast bacon, 3 tablespoonfuls cracker crumbs, 1 even tablespoonful butter, 1 egg well beaten, and the inside of the tomatoes, pepper and salt; stuff the hulls and bind together; bake about 20 minutes." ASCENSION CHURCH, *Family Friend*, 38.

SALADS AND SALAD DRESSINGS

For "a *good* salad, four persons are required," wrote Eliza Leslie in 1857, "a spendthrift for oil; a miser for vinegar; a man of judgment for salt; and a madman for stirring the dressing." While Miss Leslie included only two salad recipes in her cookbook, it was clear by the 1870s that salads were gaining in popularity. By 1900 they were well established on the menu.[4]

Cabbage (as coleslaw), potatoes, and chicken were the most often used salad ingredients in the Minnesota cookbooks. Other meats, seafoods, and eggs were also prominent ingredients of 19th-century salads. In that era, recipes using raw fruits and vegetables were rare; with the exception of cabbage, salads were usually composed of cooked foods. In 1880 Miss Parloa suggested that "small round radishes may be arranged in the dish with a lettuce salad." By the end of the century, cucumber, tomato, celery, onion, and lettuce were also being used raw.

SIDNEY SMITH'S WINTER SALAD

vegetable chopper

"Two large potatoes, passed through kitchen sieve,
Unwonted softness to the salad give;
Of mordant mustard add a single spoon —
Distrust the condiment which bites too soon;
But deem it not, though made of herbs, a fault
To add a double quantity of salt;
Three times the spoon with oil of Lucca crown,
And once with vinegar procured from town.
True flavor needs it, and your poet begs
The pounded yellow of two well-boiled eggs.
Let onion atoms lurk within the bowl,
And, half-suspected, animate the whole;
And lastly, on the favored compound toss
A magic tea-spoon of anchovy sauce.
Then, though green turtle fail, though venison's tough,
Though ham and turkey are not boiled enough,

Serenely full, the epicure shall say,
'Fate can not harm me — I have dined to-day.'" *Buckeye Cookery*, 288.

CABBAGE SALAD

"Take ¼ medium sized head cabbage, remove the heart, place it in the chopping bowl and add 2 good sized apples, peeled, quartered and cored, and 1 small onion, about the size of a black walnut. Slice the onion quite fine, as you put it in. Then chop all together very fine. When done, add ½ teaspoon salt; 1 teacup sugar; ⅔ cup good vinegar; ⅓ cup water; stir all together thoroughly. The onion can be omitted if desirable." CENTRAL PRESBYTERIAN CHURCH, *Cook Book*, 20.

OLD-FASHIONED SLAW

"Piece of butter the size of an egg, half teacup of vinegar, one of sweet cream, yelks [*sic*] of two eggs, heaped tablespoonful of sugar. Put the butter and vinegar in a skillet and heat; mix egg, cream and sugar together, and stir slowly into the heated vinegar. Have the cabbage chopped or cut and sprinkle with salt and pepper; put it into the mixture and let it scald for a minute or two. If the vinegar is very strong, do not take full quantity, or weaken a little." WESTMINSTER PRESBYTERIAN CHURCH, [*Valuable Recipes*], 22.

POTATO SALAD

"Boil four good sized potatoes in their jackets, peel, cut in dice, put into a colander and marinate with French dressing in which has been grated a few drops of onion. When cold moisten slightly with mayonnaise which has had 1 teaspoonful of minced cucumber pickles and one of minced capers mixed with it.

"Put a layer in the salad bowl, a thin layer of sliced and salted cucumbers, a spoonful or two of mayonnaise on this, then more potatoes, etc., until all are used, putting potatoes last, and mayonnaise liberally on top. Garnish with pitted olives, cold boiled beets cut in any shape desired, hard boiled eggs or capers.

"It is hardly possible to put too many good things into potato salad." *Our Chef's Best Receipts*, 29.

HOT POTATO SALAD

"Four eggs, ½ cup sugar, ½ cup thick cream, ½ cup butter, ½ teaspoon black pepper, 2 tablespoons salt, ½ teaspoon mustard, 1½ cup of vinegar, pinch of cayenne pepper. Place the vinegar, butter, sugar on the stove and when heated to the boiling point add the eggs and cream, well beaten. Stir constantly and boil 1 minute. Cook your potatoes thoroughly and chop while hot adding 1 small onion to a quart of potatoes. Pour over sufficient dressing to moisten thoroughly." METHODIST EPISCOPAL CHURCH, *Christmas Cook Book*, 6.

SWEET POTATO SALAD

"Boil three large sweet potatoes, cut into ½ inch squares; cut into very small pieces 2 stalks of celery, season with salt and pepper, and pour over a French dressing made as follows: 3 teaspoonfuls salad oil, 2 teaspoonfuls vinegar, 1 teaspoonful onion juice, 1 teaspoonful salt, 1 teaspoonful pepper. Let the salad stand on ice awhile. Garnish with pickles, olives and parsley." ASCENSION CHURCH, *Family Friend*, 45.

CHICKEN SALAD

"One chicken chopped fine, three-fourths the quantity chopped celery, two hard boiled eggs, one teaspoon each of salt, pepper and made mustard, three teaspoons salad oil or melted butter and two of white sugar, one cup vinegar. Rub yolks of eggs to a smooth paste with the oil or butter, mix with the other ingredients and pour over the chicken and celery, stirring well with a silver fork. Garnish with the whites of eggs cut into rings.

In the winter, when celery cannot be obtained, chopped cabbage with a little celery seed makes an excellent substitute." FIRST BAPTIST CHURCH, *Tried and True*, 25.

EXCELLENT MEAT SALAD

"Chop any kind of meat in chopping bowl. Add a little cabbage, celery, small quantity of onion, a few cucumber pickles. Chop all together and pour over it the following dressing:

"Boil 1 quart of vinegar. Mix together 1 cook's spoonful flour and butter, teaspoon mustard, teaspoon salt, ½ teaspoon pepper, ¼ teaspoon curry powder, yelks [*sic*] of 3 eggs, 1 cup sugar. Mix well and add the boiling vinegar and boil 5 minutes, stirring meanwhile." METHODIST EPISCOPAL CHURCH, *Christmas Cook Book*, 6.

OYSTER SALAD

"Put three dozen large oysters in a stewpan with a blade of mace, salt, pepper, and a piece of butter, bring to a boil and leave in the liquor until cool. Chop fine some choice celery about the same quantity as the bulk of oysters, mix all together with one pint of salad dressing, and put in a bowl; set on the ice until ready to serve, and garnish with lemon and cut vegetables." MAY & SON, *Catalogue*, 46.

HERRING SALAD

"Four pounds of roasted veal; boil five large beats [*sic*], let them get cold; boil six good sized potatoes, allow them to get cold. One dozen German herrings; put them in cold water for twelve hours. These ingredients to be prepared the day before.

"Cut veal into small pieces; do not hash it; same with beats, potatoes and herrings. Mix well, having sliced up a hard apple and one small onion, to be put in the salad; season to taste with salt and pepper, serve with oil and vinegar; decorate with hard boiled eggs, beats and potatoes." DAYTON AVENUE PRESBYTERIAN CHURCH, *Cook Book*, 100.

CELERY SALAD

"½ teaspoonful mustard, ½ cup vinegar, 1 level tablespoonful sugar, 3 eggs, little cayenne pepper, 1 tablespoonful butter; boil together, add ½ cup sour cream, beat with egg beater and when cold pour over celery." Ascension Church, *Family Friend*, 45.

SUMMER SALAD

"Take 5 large ripe tomatoes; cut off a slice on top of each and carefully remove seeds, being careful not to break the walls. Fill the tomato shells with cucumbers prepared as for the table [*pared and sliced*] cut up fine, and finely cut celery. Set each tomato on a crisp lettuce leaf or several small leaves around it, and serve with the salad dressing [of your choice] . . . or fill tomato shells with cold slaw and chopped celery." Central Presbyterian Church, *Cook Book*, 21.

FRUIT SALAD

"One pineapple, 3 large oranges, 3 bananas, ½ lb. white grapes, juice of 1 lemon, 1 cupful sugar; peel oranges and take off white skin; cut the grapes in halves and remove the seeds; put ⅓ of the pineapple, peeled and sliced, into a dish; slice one of the oranges into it, removing the seeds, then a banana sliced, ⅓ of the grapes; sprinkle powdered sugar over all. Repeat this and then pour over lemon juice." Ascension Church, *Family Friend*, 46.

SALAD DRESSING

"Yelks [*sic*] of 2 eggs, pinch of cayenne pepper, one table-spoon mustard, 1 tablespoon salt, 1 tablespoon cornstarch, 2 tablespoons sugar. Mix to a smooth paste, then add alternately, 1 cup vinegar and 1½ cups of cream. Boil until thick like custard." Methodist Episcopal Church, *Christmas Cook Book*, 6.

CREAM DRESSING FOR COLESLAW

"Two table-spoons whipped sweet cream, two of sugar, and four of vinegar; beat well and pour over cabbage, previously cut very fine and seasoned with salt." *Buckeye Cookery*, 293.

OIL DRESSING [MAYONNAISE]

"One egg-yolk, add oil drop by drop, beating rapidly. When stiff, add a little lemon juice, then more oil, then lemon juice, and so on till you have the desired quantity. Season a little more highly than cooked dressing. Lemon-juice is better than vinegar, as, unless the vinegar is pure it is liable to curdle the dressing. Have every ingredient, the dish and the beater as cold [as] possible. DAYTON AVENUE PRESBYTERIAN CHURCH, *Cook Book*, 96.

SALAD DRESSING WITH POTATO

"Peel one large potato, boil, mash until all lumps are out, and add the yolk of a raw egg, stir all well together and season with a teaspoon of mustard and a little salt; add about half a gill [¼ cup] of olive-oil and vinegar, putting in only a drop or two at a time, and stirring constantly, as the success of the dressing depends on its smoothness. This dressing is very nice with celery or cabbage chopped fine, and seasoned with a little salt and vinegar." *Buckeye Cookery*, 294.

*MRS. S. T. RORER'S FRUIT SALAD DRESSING

4 tbsp. sugar	½ cup sherry
½ tsp. cinnamon	2 tbsp. Madeira

"Mix sugar and cinnamon together, add the wine and stir constantly until sugar is dissolved." *Our Chef's Best Receipts*, 28.

SALAD DRESSING WITHOUT OIL

4 eggs

½ cup of vinegar

2 tbsp. cream

1 tbsp. sugar

¼ tsp. salt

½ tsp. mustard

2 well-beaten eggs

"Add the sugar, salt and mustard, then the vinegar and the cream. Stir, in double boiler, until it is the consistency of cream. Use cold." GRAY, *Cook Book*, 41.

ACCOMPANIMENTS AND MADE-OVER DELICACIES

Minnesota cooks often added dumplings, forcemeat balls, and noodles to soups and stews to give that little something extra to meals, and they were wise, too, in the use of leftovers in making flavorful, economical dishes. Both accompaniments and made-over delicacies embellished many otherwise plain foods and helped satisfy appetites sharpened by hard work and cold weather.

DUMPLINGS

"One-half cup flour sifted with two teaspoonfuls of baking powder; one egg, beaten lightly; add enough milk to stir flour into a stiff batter. After thickening the gravy, drop in the batter a spoonful at a time. Cover tightly; cook fifteen minutes." *Duluth Home Cook Book*, 38.

TO ENRICH SOUP

"When stock is drawn off, season with celery salt. A little vermicelli boiled in it for fifteen minutes will give it more body — or some of the fancy letters, stars, triangles, etc., that are made particularly for soups can be used, or eggballs can be made by mixing raw egg with just enough wheat flour or corn starch to make it into round balls, then drop them into the soup and boil for ten minutes. A little milk, a tea-spoon to one egg, is an improvement; also a sprinkle of salt. These balls are sometimes called 'noodles.' If a richer soup is needed, take slices of raw veal and a little salt pork, and chop very fine with a slice of wheat bread. Season highly with pepper, salt, tomato catsup, and chopped lemon peel, moisten with two well-beaten eggs, and roll into balls as large as a walnut, with floured hands. Fry the balls in butter to a dark brown, and let them cool; turn into the soup and boil about ten minutes. Cut a lemon into very thin bits, slice two hard-boiled eggs, put them into the tureen; add a glass of claret or port wine to them and turn in soup; it is a very 'dainty dish.'" *Buckeye Cookery*, 308.

HASH

"Chop the cold cooked meat rather fine; use half as much meat as of boiled potatoes. To a quart of the meat and potatoes add two slices of dry bread, all chopped fine, a little butter, salt and pepper, and milk or water enough to make it moist. Put into a pudding dish well buttered, and bake. It should be stirred once or twice during the baking and come out light and delicious." FIRST BAPTIST CHURCH, *Tried and True*, 39.

CHICKEN CUTLETS

"Mince some cold chicken, add some chopped boiled ham, also onions and parsley chopped with salt and pepper to taste; add a little bread crumbs, if handy; put over the fire until it boils, putting in your chicken and other ingredients. Simmer very slowly, then add one egg, beaten, for every cup of mince. Stir all over the fire until it thickens; put away to cool; shape according to fancy. Strew with bread crumbs and fry on both sides." DAYTON AVENUE PRESBYTERIAN CHURCH, *Cook Book*, 82.

CURRY SAUCE FOR COLD MEAT

"2 tablespoonfuls of butter, 1 good sized onion minced fine, 8 or 10 pepper corns, blade of mace, 2 or 3 bay leaves; stir until the onion becomes nicely browned, then add 2 tablespoonfuls of flour, 1 tablespoonful curry powder, dessert spoonful vinegar, salt, 3 gills [1½ cups] boiling water, with tablespoonful fluid beef or same quantity good stock; let all simmer 5 or 10 minutes, stirring constantly; strain and stir in any kind of cold meat cut in thin slices." ASCENSION CHURCH, *Family Friend*, 27.

MINCING KNIVES.

CHICKEN CROQUETTES

"2 cups of chicken cut very fine, ⅓ cup of chicken broth, 1 small cup bread crumbs, a little mace, celery seed or celery salt, 4 tablespoonfuls of oil, 1 hard boiled egg, red pepper and salt, ¾ lemon; grate ½ rind; mix with raw egg and roll in cracker crumbs. Fry brown in boiling lard." ASCENSION CHURCH, *Family Friend*, 22.

CHICKEN QUENELLES

"Mix together half a cupful each of the soft part of bread and of finely chopped or pounded chicken-meat cooked; season the mixture highly with salt and cayenne, and moisten it with enough raw yolk of egg to bind it so that little olive-shaped pieces can be moulded between two small spoons; either roll the *quenelles* in egg and cracker-dust, and fry them, or poach them until they float in boiling broth or water, and then use them." CORSON, *Practical American Cookery*, 305.

RICE BALLS

"To 1 cup of steamed rice worked up fine and smooth, take 1 teaspoonful of melted butter, 1 egg, ½ cup sweet milk, ½ cup English currants, pinch of salt and a little nutmeg. Fill poacher cups with mixture, steam 20 minutes. Serve with maple syrup or sweetened cream." METHODIST EPISCOPAL CHURCH, *Christmas Cook Book*, 24.

FRIED APPLES FOR BREAKFAST

"Sour apples should be selected: Pippins, Northern Spies, etc. First fry some thin slices of pork, then the slices (without peeling them) of apples in the same hot fat." HENDERSON, *Practical Cooking*, 204.

BREAKFAST POTATOES

"Cut cold boiled potatoes into round or square pieces and dip them in beaten egg, put them on well-buttered pie plates and set them in the oven till well browned, and send to table hot." MAY & SON, *Catalogue*, 127.

BREAKFAST STEW

"Cut three-fourths of a pound of cold roast beef into small pieces, heat slowly with half a pint cold water, one table-spoon Chili-sauce, a tea-spoon salt, and half a tea-spoon pepper. Rub two table-spoons flour with some butter and a little of the hot gravy, add to the beef, let cook until the flour is done, and then serve with bits of dry toast. Slices of onions may be first cooked and the meat added to them, with or without Chili-sauce." *Buckeye Cookery*, 364.

STUFFED PEPPERS

"Cut off the tops of the peppers and remove the seeds. Making a dressing of chicken, ham or tongue; a whole onion; chop very fine; moisten to a paste with cream; season with salt and pepper. Fill them and over the top sprinkle cracker crumbs; place a piece of butter an inch square on each. Bake in a pan till brown. Eat cold." DAYTON AVENUE PRESBYTERIAN CHURCH, *Cook Book*, 80.

*GINGERED PEARS

3 lbs. pears	Juice and thin-sliced
2½ cups sugar	rind of 2 lemons
	Gingerroot sliced thin, to taste

Pare and quarter pears; put in a kettle in layers, alternating with a sprinkling of ginger, sugar, lemon juice, and rind. Simmer 3 hours. Peaches may be used instead of pears. CENTRAL PRESBYTERIAN CHURCH, *Cook Book*, 110.

"FRITADILLA"

"Soak one half pound of bread crumbs in a pint of cold water. Take the same quantity of any kind of roast or boiled meat, with a little fat. Chop it and then dry your bread in a cloth. Put into a stew-pan two ounces of butter, one tablespoonful of chopped onions; fry two minutes; add the bread; stir till rather dry, then add the meat and season with salt and pepper. Stir till very hot and then add two eggs. Roll into balls or cakes and fry brown; a nice lunch or breakfast relish." WESTMINSTER PRESBYTERIAN CHURCH, [*Valuable Recipes*], 12.

FISH PIE

"Take any cooked fish very carefully picked from the bone and mix it with white egg sauce, or drawn butter, thickened well and seasoned to fancy; put a layer of finely mashed potatoes at the bottom of a porcelain baking dish, then add all the fish, and over this another layer of potatoes. Smooth top over neatly and bake in moderate oven twenty minutes. If preferred the potatoes can be spread in the dish, the fish placed high in the centre of it, covered over with the potatoes; any delicate fish from the dinner of the day before can be used for this purpose." DAYTON AVENUE PRESBYTERIAN CHURCH, *Cook Book*, 40.

DESSERTS

The record of a St. Anthony housewife in the 1850s who, following a New England custom, made 21 pies each week — one for every meal — gives some idea of the importance early settlers attached to desserts. Locally published cookbooks were dominated by recipes for such sweets, and by far the most numerous were those for cakes. Puddings usually resembled Juliet Corson's description of "plain dishes cooked with simple and few materials," but they were often dressed up with highly flavored sauces. Pie fillings were created from store-bought and wild fruits, and such vegetables as squash and potatoes. In times of shortage, women intent on making desserts substituted molasses or homegrown cane syrup for sugar, potatoes or pumpkin soaked in vinegar for mincemeat, dried wild grapes for raisins, and green tomatoes or Japan apple-pie melon for apples. Cookie recipes resemble those still used today with such familiar names as "Hermits" and "Rocks." Fruit-flavored ice creams, sherbets, and molded gelatins had become very popular by the end of the century.[5]

Cakes

*PRAIRIE TEACAKE

1 egg	2 cups cake flour, sifted
1 cup sugar	2 tsp. baking powder
½ cup butter	Flavor to suit taste
1 cup sweet milk	

Cream butter and sugar; beat well. Add egg to butter mixture, blend. Sift flour with baking powder; add to butter mixture alternately with milk. Blend well. Bake in greased and floured 7 × 11 pan at 350 degrees for 35 to 40 minutes. Frost as soon as taken from oven and eat while warm. GRAY, *Cook Book*, 97.

FARMER'S FRUIT CAKE

"Soak three cups of dried apples over night in warm water. In the morning chop and then simmer two hours in two cups of molasses. Add two eggs, one cup of sugar, one cup of butter, one cup of sweet milk, one and one-half teaspoonful of soda, one teaspoonful each of ground cloves, cinnamon and nutmeg; five cups of flour. Bake in a quick oven." FIRST BAPTIST CHURCH, *Tried and True*, 76.

ALTAR GUILD FRUIT CAKE

"Four pounds raisins, 4 pounds currants, 1 pound flour, 2 pounds citron, 1 pound butter, 1 pound brown sugar, 12 eggs, 2 wine glasses brandy, 1 wine glass of wine, 1 coffee cup molasses, 1 teaspoonful soda dissolved in water; juice of 2 oranges, 1 tablespoonful cinnamon, cloves and allspice; 2 nutmegs, 1 glass currant jelly, 1 pound almonds. Bake 4 hours in a slow oven." ASCENSION CHURCH, *Family Friend*, 76.

*NUT CAKE

½ cup butter	1½ tsp. baking powder
1 cup sugar	2¼ cups sifted cake flour
2 eggs	1 cup chopped raisins
½ cup milk	1 cup chopped walnuts

Cream butter until light; add sugar gradually and beat well; beat in eggs one at a time; add milk alternately with flour and baking powder, sifted together, beating well after each addition; stir in raisins and nuts. Bake in 9 × 13 pan in 350-degree oven for 35 minutes. PARLOA, *New Cook Book*, 44.

*COFFEE SPICE CAKE

1 cup butter	1 square chocolate, melted
1 cup brown sugar	1 tsp. soda
1 cup molasses	3 cups flour
1½ cups raisins	1 cup strong coffee
1½ cups currants	1 tsp. each cinnamon, cloves,
2 eggs	allspice, and nutmeg

Cream butter and brown sugar, add molasses, beat in eggs one at a time, add chocolate. Add spices to sifted (or presifted) flour and soda. Alternate adding dry ingredients and coffee, mixing well after each addition. Stir in currants and raisins. Grease and flour the bottom of a 9 × 13-inch baking pan. Bake at 350 degrees 50 to 55 minutes. Use a powdered sugar frosting of sugar, cream, butter, sherry, etc. BERTHA L. HEILBRON COLLECTION.

MINNEHAHA CAKE

"One and ½ cups sugar, ⅔ cup water, stir till the sugar is nearly dissolved; 2 tablespoonfuls of melted butter, yolks of 5 eggs, whites of 3 eggs, (reserve 2 whites for frosting), add 2 cups flour and beat thoroughly, then stir in lightly ½ cup flour with 2½ teaspoonfuls baking powder.

"Frosting. 1 coffee cup sugar, ¼ cup water. Let boil till stringy. Do not stir or move while boiling. When partly cool, add the well-beaten whites of 2 eggs. Stone and chop fine 1 cup raisins, and add vanilla." ASCENSION CHURCH, *Family Friend*, 89.

*DATE CAKE

¾ cup sugar	2 cups flour
¾ cup butter	2 egg yolks
½ cup milk	¼ cup dates
½ tsp. almond flavoring	1 tsp. baking powder

Cream butter, add sugar and beat well. Add egg yolks, blend well. Alternately add flour, baking powder, and milk. Add almond flavoring to the batter, stir in chopped dates. Spread batter into two 8 × 8-inch pans; bake in a 350-degree oven 35 to 40 minutes. CENTRAL PRESBYTERIAN CHURCH, *Cook Book*, 78.

SPONGE CAKE

"Beat the yolks of 3 fresh eggs with a fork until very light; add 1 cup of sugar and beat well; add a little grated lemon peel and a spoonful of the juice, also ¼ of a cup of boiling water. Then add whites of the eggs beaten to a stiff froth, and lastly 1 cup flour. Mix quickly and bake in a moderate oven. Double this receipt for two loaves. All the beating and mixing should be done with a fork." CENTRAL PRESBYTERIAN CHURCH, *Cook Book*, 68.

*MADEIRA CAKE

1¼ cups butter	1½ cups flour
1 cup sugar	1 tsp. baking powder
3 large eggs	2 oz. Madeira wine

Cream the butter until light, gradually add sugar, beating to a light, white cream; add eggs, one at a time, beating well after each addition. Sift the baking powder with the flour and add the dry mixture to the butter mixture alternately with the wine. Blend to a smooth batter that is moderately stiff. Transfer the batter to a well-greased bundt pan. Bake in a 350-degree oven for 55 minutes. GROFF, *Snow Flake Cook Book*, 14.

MARSHMALLOW CAKE

"One and ½ cups white sugar, 1 cup butter, cream together; whites of 4 eggs well beaten, 1 cup sweet milk, 2 teaspoonfuls baking powder, 1 teaspoonful vanilla or lemon, 2½ cups sifted flour. Bake in three layers.

"Filling. Put 2 cups granulated sugar and ½ cup boiling water in a farina kettle and let boil. Have the whites of 2 eggs beaten till stiff. Put 15 or 16 marshmallows in to heat in a slow oven till soft and puffy, but not brown; when the syrup threads when poured from spoon, pour it over the eggs and beat well; add the marshmallows and beat till quite smooth, and when cool place between the layers." ASCENSION CHURCH, *Family Friend*, 84.

MARBLE CAKE

"White Part. One cup of sugar, one-half a cup of butter, one-half cup sweet milk, whites of four eggs, two and a half cups flour, two heaping teaspoons baking powder, or one teaspoon cream tartar and one-half teaspoon soda. Stir butter and sugar.

"Dark Part. One cup brown sugar, one-half cup molasses, one-half cup sour milk, two and one-half cups flour, one level teaspoon soda dissolved in the milk and molasses, yolks of four eggs, and one-half cup butter to be rubbed well together with the sugar. Add one-half teaspoon [each] cinnamon, allspice and cloves. Put dark part in pan first and then alternate." FIRST BAPTIST CHURCH, *Tried and True*, 68.

ANGEL FOOD LAYER CAKE

"1¾ cups sugar sifted 5 times; 1 cup flour sifted 5 times; whites of 9 or 10 eggs; ½ teaspoon cream tartar. When eggs are half beaten add cream of tartar, finish beating them; add sugar gradually and then flour.

"For Filling. Heat ½ pint of milk; stir in yolks of 4 or 5 eggs beaten with ½ cup sugar and tablespoon of cornstarch. When cold, flavor with vanilla and add blanched almonds or walnuts put between layers. Frost with boiled frosting [*see p. 251, below*]." CENTRAL PRESBYTERIAN CHURCH, *Cook Book*, 79.

*INDIAN POUND CAKE

½ cup butter
1 cup powdered sugar
4 medium eggs
1 cup sifted corn meal
½ cup sifted flour

1 tsp. baking powder
¼ tsp. nutmeg
½ tsp. cinnamon
¼ cup mixed wine and brandy

Cream butter and sugar until very light. Add eggs, one at a time, beating well after each addition. At low mixer speed, add sifted corn meal, flour, baking powder, and spices. Continue to mix until all ingredients are well blended. Add wine and brandy and thoroughly blend into the batter. Pour batter into a greased, wax paper-lined 4 × 8 loaf pan. Bake in a preheated 350-degree oven 55 to 60 minutes. Allow to cool 10 minutes. Turn out on cake rack and peel off wax paper. LESLIE, "Seventy-Five Receipts," 22, in LEE, *Complete Library*.

ENTIRE CHOCOLATE CAKE

"½ cup Baker's chocolate; 1 cup sugar; ½ cup milk; yolk 1 egg. Boil together until it thickens, then cool and stir into the following ingredients: 1 cup sugar; small ½ cup butter; 2 eggs; 1 cup sweet milk; 2½ cups flour (or more); 2 teaspoons baking powder; flavor with vanilla and add a little spice if desired.

"Filling. Boil 2 cups granulated sugar with ½ cup water. Stir this slowly into the stiff beaten whites of 2 eggs, and add about ⅔ cup of grated chocolate and 1 teaspoon vanilla." CENTRAL PRESBYTERIAN CHURCH, *Cook Book*, 70.

*DRIED APPLE CAKE

1½ cups dried apples, chopped
1 cup molasses
¼ cup butter
1 large egg
¼ cup sugar

¼ cup milk
2 cups flour
1 tsp. baking soda
¼ tsp. cinnamon
¼ tsp. cloves

Simmer the chopped dried apples in molasses for 15 minutes. Allow to cool. Cream butter, add sugar, and beat until light. Add egg and beat well. Sift the baking soda and spices together with the flour; add alternately with the milk to the butter mixture. The batter will be very stiff. Gradually add the cooled molasses and apple mixture, beating on low speed until all the ingredients are thoroughly blended. Pour the batter into a 9 × 9 greased pan and bake in a preheated oven at 350 degrees for 10 minutes. Reduce the heat to 325 degrees and bake 35 to 40 minutes longer. METHODIST EPISCOPAL CHURCH, *Christmas Cook Book*, 20.

BOILED FROSTING

"Two tablespoons of water poured onto one cup of white sugar; boil to a syrup; beat white of one egg light, while you beat let the syrup hot be dropped on spoonful by spoonful, flavor with anything you choose, boil until it ropes." FIRST BAPTIST CHURCH, *Tried and True*, 74.

MAPLE ICING

"2½ cups brown sugar; ⅔ cup cream; lump butter size of walnut; boil until sugary, and beat until cool; flavor with vanilla." CENTRAL PRESBYTERIAN CHURCH, *Cook Book*, 60.

MISS A. R.'S ICING

"Ten teaspoonfuls of powdered sugar to the white of one egg. Beat five minutes for every teaspoonful sugar." WESTMINSTER PRESBYTERIAN CHURCH, [*Valuable Recipes*], 54.

CARAMEL FROSTING

"One cupful of brown sugar, one square of Baker's chocolate, scraped fine; one table-spoonful of water. Simmer gently twenty minutes, being careful not to let it burn. Spread on the cake while hot." PARLOA, *New Cook Book*, 46.

Cookies

*SUGAR COOKIES

2 eggs
2 cups brown sugar, firmly packed
1 cup melted butter

2½ cups sifted flour
3 tsp. baking powder
1 tsp. nutmeg

Sift baking powder and nutmeg with the flour. Set aside. Beat eggs, add brown sugar, and beat until creamy. Add the cooled melted butter and beat until the ingredients are well blended. Add dry ingredients slowly to the egg mixture and continue beating until the dough is well mixed. Form the dough into two rolls, two inches in diameter. Wrap well in waxed paper or plastic wrap and chill for 12 to 24 hours. Slice thin and bake on a greased cookie sheet at 400 degrees for 8 to 10 minutes. The dough and the baked cookies freeze well. Yield: about 6 doz. METHODIST EPISCOPAL CHURCH, *Christmas Cook Book*, 21.

*ROCK COOKIES

1 cup butter
1½ cups sugar
3 eggs
2½ cups flour
1 tsp. cinnamon

½ tsp. allspice
1 tsp. soda
1 cup dates, pitted and
  chopped fine
1½ cups walnuts, chopped

"Cream butter and sugar. Add other ingredients. Drop with teaspoon onto unbuttered tins. Bake at 350 degrees for 15 minutes." Yield: 5 doz. FRANCES HEILBRON COLLECTION.

*HERMITS

"2 eggs; 2 cups sugar; ½ cup molasses; 1 teaspoon soda dissolved in 3 teaspoons hot water; 1 cup shortening (½ cup lard and ½ cup butter); 1 cup seeded raisins chopped fine and flavored; a teaspoon ground cinnamon; ½ teaspoon cloves; a little nutmeg; flour enough to roll very soft [3½ cups]; after dissolving

soda in hot water, put it in the molasses and stir till it foams."
Yield: about 6½ doz. CENTRAL PRESBYTERIAN CHURCH, *Cook Book*, 99.

MOLASSES COOKIES

"1 cup of molasses, 1 cup of sugar, 2 eggs, 2 tablespoons vinegar, 1 teaspoon cinnamon, 1 teaspoon ginger, 3 cups of flour."
METHODIST EPISCOPAL CHURCH, *Christmas Cook Book*, 22.

*ALMOND SQUARES

1 cup sugar	½ tsp. cinnamon
2 eggs	⅛ tsp. nutmeg
½ cup flour	½ cup chopped almonds
½ tsp. baking powder	

Stir eggs, sugar, and spices together. Add flour and baking powder, stir quickly. Add almonds to mixture and pour into a greased 8 × 8 pan. Bake at 350 degrees 45–50 minutes. After baking mark in squares and let cool. CENTRAL PRESBYTERIAN CHURCH, *Cook Book*, 109.

*COCONUT DROPS

2 egg whites (medium size eggs)
½ cup sugar   1½ cup shredded or flaked coconut

Beat egg white until stiff, gradually add sugar. Fold in coconut. Drop cookies from a teaspoon onto greased teflon cookie sheet. Bake at 300 degrees for 30 minutes. Yield: 2½ doz. ASCENSION CHURCH, *Family Friend*, 88.

PEANUT MACAROONS

"1 cup chopped peanuts; 1 cup powdered sugar; 1 tablespoon flour and the whites 2 eggs [beaten stiff]; the mixture is dropped on a buttered paper and baked to a light brown in a moderate oven. A quart of shelled peanuts will yield the necessary cup of chopped nuts." CENTRAL PRESBYTERIAN CHURCH, *Cook Book*, 103.

HARD BOILED EGG COOKIES

"One lb. flour, ½ lb. pulverized sugar, ½ lb. butter, yolks of 8 hard boiled eggs grated, 1 raw egg, grated rind of 1 lemon, mix butter, sugar, [rind], and eggs, and add the flour gradually. Roll quite thin, cut in fancy shapes, glaze the top with egg and bake in moderate oven." ASCENSION CHURCH, *Family Friend*, 92.

LEMON COOKIES

"Stir to a cream a ½ cup butter; 1 cup sugar; the grated peel 1 lemon and the juice of 2; beat thoroughly and add the whipped yolks 3 eggs; after this add the beaten whites and 3 cups flour, or enough to make a dough that can be rolled out, and 2 teaspoons baking powder; make the sheet about one-eighth of an inch in thickness, and cut into cakes." CENTRAL PRESBYTERIAN CHURCH, *Cook Book*, 88.

OATMEAL COOKIES

"Mix together 4 cups white flour into which you have sifted 1 teaspoon soda and 3 cups of oatmeal, 2 cups of sugar, 1 cup melted butter, 2 teaspoons salt. Moisten the mass with cold water to make a very stiff dough. Roll as thin as possible and cut in round cakes." METHODIST EPISCOPAL CHURCH, *Christmas Cook Book*, 21.

NUT OR FRUIT COOKIES

"1½ cups brown sugar; ½ cup butter; 3 cups flour; ½ cup warm water; 3 eggs; 1 tablespoon cinnamon; 1 teaspoon soda; 1 pound English walnuts chopped; 1½ cups raisins." CENTRAL PRESBYTERIAN CHURCH, *Cook Book*, 89.

JERSEY LILIES

½ cup butter	1 cup powdered sugar
½ cup milk	2 cups flour

"Cream butter and sugar, add milk and flour. Spread very

thin on a baking pan, mark in squares, and bake about 5 minutes. Put on back of stove and roll each square into a cornucopia, one end very tight, the other with the corner turned over like a lily, filling it with whipped cream." *Our Chef's Best Receipts*, 76.

PIES

APPLE CUSTARD PIE FILLING

"Peel sour apples and stew until soft, then rub through a colander. Beat 3 eggs for each pie, ⅓ cup butter, ½ cup sugar. Flavor with nutmeg." METHODIST EPISCOPAL CHURCH, *Christmas Cook Book*, 25.

BLUEBERRY PIE

"Fill the crust even full of blueberries, sift a little flour over the fruit, 4 tablespoonfuls sugar; cover with crust." ASCENSION CHURCH, *Family Friend*, 53.

*CRANBERRY PIE

2¼ cups cranberries, chopped   1 tbsp. butter
½ cup sugar   1 tsp. cornstarch

Combine all ingredients with ⅓ cup water and cook 20 minutes. Cool and pour into 8-inch baked pie shell. May be topped with meringue. FIRST BAPTIST CHURCH, *Tried and True*, 55.

*MINCEMEAT

6 oz. beef   4 oz. candied orange peel,
3 apples, chopped   cut fine
½ tsp. each cinnamon, cloves,   4 oz. candied citron, cut fine
   nutmeg   ½ cup apple cider
¼ cup raisins   1 tbsp. butter

"Season the meat well with butter, pepper, and salt. Place all ingredients except butter in a saucepan and cook until done. Brandy added to the above ingredients adds greatly to the flavor and piquancy of the mince meat, unless one's temperance principles should interfere. Add the butter to the pie while preparing for the oven, and when taken from the oven fill up with hot liquor, prepared of one-half pint French brandy, one-half pint water, one-half pound sugar, one teaspoon cinnamon, and one fourth teaspoon cloves. [This addition may be omitted or limited to ½ cup.] This is warranted to keep through any weather — if locked up. Bake the pie at 450 degrees for 10 minutes, then reduce heat to 350 degrees and bake 30 minutes longer." WESTMINSTER PRESBYTERIAN CHURCH, [*Valuable Recipes*], 36.

MOCK MINCE PIES

"Take three Boston or six butter crackers rolled, two eggs, one-half cup of butter, one cup of hot water, one cup of sugar, one cup of molasses, one-half pound of chopped raisins, one-half cup of vinegar, one teaspoonful cinnamon, one nutmeg, a little cloves and salt. Mix and bake as you would the ordinary mince pie. They are delicious." FIRST BAPTIST CHURCH, *Tried and True*, 54.

PLUM PIE

"Simmer the plums in a little sugar and water until they are tender, then take out the plums and add more sugar to the juice and boil it until there is just enough for the pies; turn it over the plums and let it cool. Line the plates with paste, fill them with plums, cover them with a puff paste, and bake them half an hour." FIRST BAPTIST CHURCH, *Tried and True*, 54.

PORK APPLE PIE

"You cut the pork so thin you can almost see through it. Cover the bottom of a pie tin with it, then cut the apples up on top of this. Put two thin crusts one on top of the other over this, then when cooked, turn upside down in a dish and serve with hard sauce. This recipe is over a hundred years old but nothing can beat it." MORRIS, ED., *Old Rail Fence Corners (1914)*, 133.

*PUMPKIN PIE

"Boil the pumpkin until it is somewhat darkened and put through a colander. Use 1½ cups of the pumpkin to a pie, ½ cup sugar, 3 eggs, pinch of salt, ½ teaspoon of ginger [and/]or cinnamon." Bake in an 8-inch pie shell. METHODIST EPISCOPAL CHURCH, *Christmas Cook Book*, 25.

RAISIN PIE

"Chop fine 1 cup raisins and squeeze into them the juice of 1 lemon. Add 1 cup boiling water, 1 tablespoon butter, 1 tablespoon corn starch, 1 cup of sugar. Bake with two crusts." METHODIST EPISCOPAL CHURCH, *Christmas Cook Book*, 25.

RASPBERRY OR STRAWBERRY PIE

"Paste, three cupfuls raspberries [or strawberries], one cupful sugar.

"Line a pie plate with the paste, prick over with a fork to prevent shrinking and blistering; cut a top-crust out a little larger than the other, prick also and bake; put the fruit and sugar in the pie plate, and cover with top crust; if the fruit is ripe they will thus steam tender; if not, just return to the oven until hot through." GROFF, *Snow Flake Cook Book*, 46, 47.

EARLY VIRGINIA

RHUBARB PIE

1 cup chopped pieplant	1 egg, well beaten
1 cup sugar	A little salt
1 tsp. butter	Shake of flour

"Beat the egg, add the sugar, then the salt and chopped pieplant. Pour into a plate lined with paste, add the butter broken in small pieces, and lastly a dust of flour." *Our Chef's Best Receipts*, 58.

BOSTON TOMATO

"Nine pounds of [ripe] tomatoes peeled, stewed, and sifted through a cullender [*sic*]. If it is desired to remove the seeds pass the pulp through a sieve; by allowing it to stand for a time it will settle so that considerable clear liquid can be poured off, thus expediting the cooking process. Add four pounds of sugar, one pint of vinegar, one teaspoonful each of cinnamon and mace. Care must be given that it does not burn; it may be stewed down very rich so as to keep well in an unsealed vessel, or stewed for a shorter time and sealed in glass fruit jars. It makes most delicious pies or tarts, baked with an undercrust only; and their deliciousness is increased by pouring over sweet cream when about to be eaten." FIRST BAPTIST CHURCH, *Tried and True*, 65.

SQUASH PIE

"One-half pound of butter, one-half pound of sugar, five eggs, one cup of milk. Boil and mash the squash as dry as possible. Cream the butter and sugar, beat the eggs very light, add squash enough to make it the consistency of mush. Sweet potatoes, common potatoes, or pumpkin, can be used for thickening this pie." FIRST BAPTIST CHURCH, *Tried and True*, 55.

*PASTE FOR FAMILY PIES

2 cups flour	½ cup butter
1 tsp. baking powder	4½ tbsp. cold water

Mix flour and baking powder, cut in butter, add water. Refrigerate dough for several hours. Makes double crust for 8-inch pie. GROFF, *Snow Flake Cook Book*, 45.

PUFF PASTE

"One lb. flour, ¼ lb. lard, ¾ lb. butter; cut the butter in four pieces. Rub the lard and one piece of butter well into the flour, then mix with cold water. Roll out very thin and lay on in small pieces the second piece of butter, sift flour over it, fold up, roll out. Repeat process, using the third then the fourth pieces of butter. It is better and easier to roll out if it is allowed to rest 15 or 20 minutes between each time it is rolled out, letting it stand in a cool place. Pie crust should always be made in a cool place. The crust can be rolled up and kept several days in a cool place, before baking." ASCENSION CHURCH, *Family Friend*, 52.

Puddings

BREAD PUDDING

2 cups milk
4 tbsp. sugar
Yolks of 4 eggs
White of 1 [egg]

Rind of 1 lemon
Little squares of
　　bread, buttered

"Bake, and when done beat remaining whites with little sugar and the juice of lemon. Serve hot or cold." *Our Chef's Best Receipts*, 62.

STEAMED CRANBERRY PUDDING

"One cup sugar, one-half cup butter, one-half cup milk, two eggs, two and one-half cups flour, two cups whole cranberries, two teaspoons Royal Baking Powder, three teaspoons cream tartar, one-half teaspoon soda. Steam three hours.

"Sauce: One-half cup butter, beat to a cream, one cup sugar, one-half cup milk, flavor and place in double boiler until thoroughly heated. Nice for any steamed pudding." *Duluth Home Cook Book*, 52.

BLUEBERRY OR WHORTLEBERRY PUDDING

"2 quarts whortleberries or blueberries; 1 pint New Orleans molasses; 2 teaspoons soda stirred in the molasses, and a pinch salt; 1 quart flour; steam three hours. Eat with hot sauce [*see p. 263*]. One-half of this recipe is enough for six people. Very nice." CENTRAL PRESBYTERIAN CHURCH, *Cook Book*, 52.

PEACH PUDDING

"Two-thirds can of fruit, ½ cup butter, 2 eggs, 1 cup sweet milk, 2 scant cups flour, 2 teaspoonfuls baking powder; put the peaches, with a little of the juice, in a round tin mold, drop the batter over the top in spoonfuls and set in a steamer over boiling water; boil one hour.

"Sauce for Peach Pudding: A scant half cup of butter rubbed to a cream, with 1 cup of pulverized sugar and the yolk of 1 egg beaten and ¼ cup of wine stirred at the last. This sauce should be soft but not liquid." ASCENSION CHURCH, *Family Friend*, 59.

COTTAGE PUDDING

"One cup sugar, one cup milk, butter size of an egg, three eggs, reserving whites of two for frosting, one pint flour, one teaspoonful cream of tartar, two of soda. When baked frost at once with cup sugar added to the [beaten] whites.

"Sauce: One cup sugar, one-half cup butter beaten to a cream, add one egg, and flavor with lemon or vanilla. [Heat while beating.]" FIRST BAPTIST CHURCH, *Tried and True*, 60.

EMERGENCY PUDDING

"3 cups flour; 1 cup corn meal; butter the size of small egg; scant cup New Orleans molasses; ½ thimble full each cinnamon and allspice; ¾ cup currants; 1 cup sugar; 2 eggs; milk or cream to make as stiff as for cake; bake in moderate oven one hour. Serve with cream sauce." CENTRAL PRESBYTERIAN CHURCH, *Cook Book*, 51.

BOILED INDIAN PUDDING

"One-fourth pound suet. Chop very fine and mix with 1 quart of Indian [corn] meal, 1 quart milk, boiled with a little cinnamon. Strain it into the meal while hot, add ½ pint of molasses. Let this cool, then mix 6 well-beaten eggs into it, and boil 4 hours. Leave room in pudding bag for the pudding to swell. Eat with syrup and butter." *Our Chef's Best Receipts*, 74.

RICE PUDDING

"Two quarts milk, one cup rice, four tablespoonfuls of sugar, a little salt, cinnamon. Bake till rice is well done." FIRST BAPTIST CHURCH, *Tried and True*, 60.

BREAD DOUGH PUDDING

"Take some bread dough as it is ready for its final kneading and work in butter as for biscuit; take small pieces and roll thin, with one line a small pudding dish or tin pan; put in a layer of some tart fruit, as pickled plums, canned or dried cherries, then another crust, then fruit, until the dish is half full, with a crust at the top. Let it rise until very light, then steam, the time depending upon the size of course. Eat warm, with any pudding sauce." FIRST BAPTIST CHURCH, *Tried and True*, 56.

BLACK PUDDING

"½ pint molasses; 1 large cup butter; 1¼ cups sugar; 1¼ cups sour milk; ½ teaspoon soda; 3 eggs; 2½ cups flour; 1 teaspoon cinnamon; ½ teaspoon cloves; a little nutmeg; 2 cups chopped raisins; steam one hour; then bake twenty minutes. A splendid 'ever ready' dessert; will keep weeks. Rewarm as you want to use.

"Sauce for Same. 4 tablespoons sugar; 2 tablespoons butter; 1 tablespoon flour; rub well together and stir in boiling water; flavor to taste. This is sauce enough for six persons." CENTRAL PRESBYTERIAN CHURCH, *Cook Book*, 47.

CHRISTMAS PUDDING

"1 cup bread crumbs, 1 cup flour, 1 cup suet, 1 cup raisins, 1 cup currants, 1 cup of citron and lemon peel mixed, 2 eggs, 1 cup milk, 1 cup sugar, spices to suit. Boil in a bowl 12 hours." METHODIST EPISCOPAL CHURCH, *Christmas Cook Book*, 24.

QUEEN OF PUDDINGS

"One pint bread crumbs, one pint milk, one cup sugar, the yolks of four eggs, the grated rind of a lemon, a piece of butter the size of an egg. Bake until done, but not watery. Whip the whites of the eggs stiff. Beat in a teacupful of sugar in which has been stirred the juice of the lemon. Spread over the pudding a layer of jelly or fruit. Pour over the whites of the eggs and replace in the oven. Bake lightly and serve with cold cream." FIRST BAPTIST CHURCH, *Tried and True*, 60.

TAPIOCA CREAM

"Soak over night 2 tablespoons of tapioca in milk. Heat to boiling point 1 quart of milk. Beat well together the yolks of 3 eggs, ½ teacup of sugar, 1 teaspoon of lemon or vanilla, pinch of salt and the soaked tapioca. Stir this into the boiling milk; turn into a dish and immediately spread over the top the beaten whites of the eggs. Serve cold." METHODIST EPISCOPAL CHURCH, *Christmas Cook Book*, 22.

VINEGAR SAUCE

"One cup boiling water, 1 cup sugar, 1 tablespoonful flour, 1 tablespoonful vinegar, a little nutmeg. Mix the flour in a little cold water, stir into the boiling water and sugar, a little salt. Boil 20 minutes." ASCENSION CHURCH, *Family Friend*, 61.

FOAM SAUCE
(A rich sauce for plum pudding.)

½ cup butter
1½ cups sugar
2 eggs

2 tbsp. brandy
1½ cups boiling water

"Beat butter and sugar to a cream, add well-beaten eggs. Just before sending it to the table pour on the [brandy and] boiling water." *Our Chef's Best Receipts*, 75.

LEMON DRESSING

"Juice and grated rind 1 lemon; 1 cup sugar; ½ tablespoon flour or corn starch, wet with a little cold water; beaten yolks 3 eggs; 1 tablespoon butter, all stirred into 2 cups boiling water. This is enough dressing for two puddings, but will keep several days." CENTRAL PRESBYTERIAN CHURCH, *Cook Book*, 64.

Frozen Dainties and Creams

VANILLA ICE CREAM

"The foundation given in this rule is suitable for all kinds of ice cream. One generous pint of milk, one cupful of sugar, half a cupful of flour, *scant*; two eggs, one quart of cream, one tablespoonful of vanilla extract, and, when the cream is added, another teacupful of sugar. Let the milk come to a boil. Beat the first cupful of sugar, the flour and eggs together, and stir into the boiling milk. Cook twenty minutes, stirring often. Set away to cool, and when cool add the sugar, seasoning, and cream, and freeze." PARLOA, *New Cook Book*, 39.

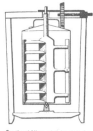

Sectional View, showing Interior of all our Freezers.

TUTTI FRUTTI ICE CREAM

"Two quarts rich cream, 1 pound pulverized sugar, 4 whole eggs; mix well together, place on the fire; stir constantly and bring to boiling point; remove and stir until cold; flavor with 1 tablespoonful vanilla; place in freezer and when half frozen, mix into it 1 pound preserved fruits, peaches, apricots, cherries, pineapples, etc.; all of these fruits are to be cut up in small pieces and mixed well with the frozen cream." Ascension Church, *Family Friend*, 104.

MAPLE ICE CREAM

"To a cup of rich maple syrup, add beaten yolks 4 eggs, stirring; cook in granite[ware] dish until it boils; strain through fine sieve; then cool; beat 1 pint cream; add to it stiffly beaten whites of 4 eggs; whip syrup until light; mix all together; then freeze." Central Presbyterian Church, *Cook Book*, 59.

RASPBERRY SHERBET

"Two quarts raspberries, 1 cup sugar, 1½ pints water, juice of 1 large lemon, 1 tablespoonful gelatine. Mash the berries and sugar together and let them stand 2 hours. Soak gelatine in cold water to cover; add 1 pint of the water to the berries and strain; dissolve the gelatine in ½ pint of boiling water; add this to the strained mixture and freeze." Ascension Church, *Family Friend*, 106.

FROZEN CRANBERRIES

"2 quarts cranberries; 6 cups sugar; 1½ quarts water; 4 large lemons; 2 oranges; stew cranberries as for sauce and run through colander; boil sugar and water together three minutes; then add to the berries; then add the grated rind and juice of the oranges, and then juice of the lemons; let stand until cool and then freeze. This is nice served with cold turkey." Central Presbyterian Church, *Cook Book*, 59.

THREE OF A KIND

"3 lemons (juice); 3 eggs (whites); 3 bananas (grated); 3 oranges (juice); 3 cups sugar; 3 cups water; mix all together and freeze." CENTRAL PRESBYTERIAN CHURCH, *Cook Book*, 62.

SPANISH CREAM

"One and one-half pints milk, one-half ounce gelatine; boil in a kettle of water; stir in yolks of four eggs, beaten with four tablespoons sugar; strain and boil again till thick as boiled custard. Beat whites of eggs stiff and stir in rapidly as soon as taken from fire. Flavor with lemon or vanilla. Pour into moulds and cool gradually; then put on ice." FIRST BAPTIST CHURCH, *Tried and True*, 79.

MOONSHINE

"This dessert combines a pretty appearance with palatable flavor, and is a convenient substitute for ice-cream. Beat the whites of six eggs in a broad plate to a very stiff froth, then add gradually six table-spoons powdered sugar (to make it thicker use more sugar up to a pint), beating for not less than thirty minutes, and then beat in about one heaping table-spoon of preserved peaches cut in tiny bits (or some use one cup jelly), and set on ice until thoroughly chilled. In serving, pour in each saucer some rich cream sweetened and flavored with vanilla, and on the cream place a liberal portion of the moonshine. This quantity is enough for seven or eight persons." *Buckeye Cookery*, 111.

a, *Round Fluted Mold*; b, *French Bread Pan*; c, *Melon Mold*; d, *Pudding Mold*; e, *Shell Mold for Jelly*; f, *Deep Fluted Mold*; g, *Individual Shell Mold for Jelly or Cream*; h, *Individual Jelly Mold*.

STRAWBERRY JELLY, SPONGE, AND CREAM

"One-third box gelatine in ⅓ cup cold water; let it stand 1 hour; ⅓ cup boiling water, 1 cup sugar, 1 cup strawberry juice.

"When the jelly is half thickened, beat light and add the whites of 3 eggs and a pinch of salt.

"To the strawberry sponge, add 1 cup cream after it has been whipped." ASCENSION CHURCH, *Family Friend*, 102.

GINGER CREAM

½ box gelatine	4 eggs, the yolks
½ cup cold water	½ cup sugar
1 pint milk	1 teaspoon salt

"Soak the gelatine in the cold water for 20 minutes. Boil the milk and add the well-beaten yolks, sugar and salt. Cook until it thickens like custard. Add the gelatine, strain into a pan, and set on ice. Add

1 tablespoon wine	¼ or ½ cup [candied] ginger,
1 tablespoon brandy	cut in small pieces
¼ cup ginger syrup	

"When thick add 1 pint cream, whipped. Pour into a mould." *Our Chef's Best Receipts*, 67.

BEVERAGES

Minnesotans quenched their thirst with all manner of drinks, from tangy or sweet mixtures of fruit and sugar (raspberry shrub was typical and popular) to bracing alcoholic punches and other potables. One early settler's recipe for wine was simple in the extreme: "Grape, currant, rhubarb and gooseberry wine: Mash home grown fruit with a home made potato masher, squeeze it through a coarse cloth, add sugar and place in warm spot to ferment. Draw off in kegs and allow to stand at least two years." When apples became available, pioneers made soft and hard cider — and sometimes vinegar if the bung was unintentionally left out of the cider keg.[6]

VIENNA COFFEE

"The peculiar flavor noticeable in the beverage commonly called Vienna coffee is obtained thus: Flavor the cream strongly with vanilla; whip dry and stiff. Drop a tablespoon of the cream on each cup of coffee just before serving. This coffee should be filtered, not boiled." GRAY, *Cook Book*, 55.

SPICED CHOCOLATE

1 quart milk	1 stick cinnamon
2 squares of chocolate	A little grated nutmeg

"Grate chocolate, boil the milk, reserving a little cool to moisten chocolate, which must be mixed, perfectly smooth to a paste. When milk boils put in and boil cinnamon, then stir in the chocolate and let boil quickly, pour into a pitcher, and grate in nutmeg. It is nice to add rich cream." GRAY, *Cook Book*, 53.

RASPBERRY SHRUB

"Place red raspberries in a stone jar, cover them with good cider vinegar, let stand over night; next morning strain, and to one pint of juice add one pint of sugar, boil ten minutes, and bottle while hot. [Serve in ice water.]" *Buckeye Cookery*, 144.

STRAWBERRY SYRUP

"Stir 5 ounces of tartaric acid in 2 quarts of water, and pour over 12 pounds of berries, using a large stone jar. Let stand 24 hours with a plate on top to keep the berries under water. Strain through a flannel bag, and to each pint of juice add a pint and a half of granulated sugar, and stir until the sugar is dissolved. Bottle and cork, but do not seal, and do not fill your bottles quite full. Allow 2 or 3 tablespoonfuls of the syrup to a glass of water or crushed ice when using." ASCENSION CHURCH, *Family Friend*, 140.

GINGER POP

"Three-quarters of a pound white sugar, three-quarters ounce ginger root, three quarters of an ounce of cream tartar, bruise the root, juice and grated rind of one lemon, one gallon of water, one tablespoon fresh yeast, essence of wintergreen or sassafras, or half of each, if you prefer. Put all in jar excepting yeast and essence, and pour the water over boiling-hot; cover, let stand until it is luke-warm. Then add yeast and essence, let stand in a cool place twenty-four hours, then strain and bottle. It will be ready for use in three days." *Duluth Home Cook Book,* 132.

BEER

"Four gallons of water, ½ pint of brewers' yeast, 3 quarts of sugar, 1 tablespoonful of sassafras. (Steep the sassafras in hot water.) Bottle air tight. Ready for use in two or three weeks." MAY & SON, *Catalogue,* 47.

DANDELION BEER

"One pail of dandelion water, three pints molasses, two handfuls strong hops, two tablespoons brewers' yeast, a few blackberry leaves will improve it; splendid." DAYTON AVENUE PRESBYTERIAN CHURCH, *Cook Book,* 155.

SODA BEER

"Two pounds white sugar, whites of two eggs, two ounces tartaric acid, two table-spoons flour, two quarts water and juice of one lemon; boil two or three minutes, and flavor to taste. When wanted for use, take a half tea-spoon soda, dissolve in half a glass of water, pour into it about two table-spoons of the acid, and it will foam to the top of the glass." *Buckeye Cookery,* 144.

PUNCH

"Pare very thin the yellow rind of twelve large lemons. Put two pounds of sugar in a large bowl; squeeze over it the juice of the lemons and add one quart best rum and one-half pint of brandy; cover this mixture and let stand two or three hours; add one-half pint of wine (Sherry or Madeira). Half an hour before punch is to be served, boil the yellow rind of the lemons in one quart of water, throwing in six teaspoonfuls of the best green tea, just before taking from the fire. Strain this liquor into the punch and add two quarts of boiling water." St. Mark's Parish, *Tested Recipes*, 101.

CURRANT WINE

"To every gallon of currant juice add two gallons of soft water; then add four pounds of brown sugar to each gallon of the mixture. Place in a keg and let stand to ferment about ten days, keeping the keg full, that it may run over as it ferments; when through working put in a pint of whisky; allow to remain a month, then bottle." *Duluth Home Cook Book*, 177.

*PINEAPPLE BRANDY

"Pare a large, ripe pineapple, saving the rind to make pineapple cider, and slice it about a quarter of an inch thick; then weigh it, and use an equal weight of powdered sugar; put the fruit and sugar in layers in a large glass jar, with sugar at the bottom and top; pour into the jar enough of the best brandy to stand an inch above the pineapple; then close the jar perfectly air-tight, and keep it in a cool, dry, dark closet for a month or longer.

"Use the fruit for the table; and the brandy, mixed with soda-water or seltzer, for a drink in hot weather." Henderson, *Practical Cooking*, 578.

BLACKBERRY CORDIAL

"To 1 quart of blackberry juice, add 1 pound of granulated or cut loaf sugar, 1 tablespoonful of mace, 1 of cloves, 1 of cinnamon; boil all together 10 minutes. When cold add 1 pint of French brandy to each quart of syrup, bottle and seal." Ascension Church, *Family Friend*, 141.

ODDMENTS

"Miscellaneous" was a random category that appeared in many 19th-century cookbooks. Sometimes it included household advice — how to remove ink spots, care for invalids, keep lamp chimneys from breaking, and build a homemade water filter, for example. It also contained recipes like those printed here that did not fit into established groupings.

BREAD OMELET

"1 cup of boiling milk with 1 tablespoonful of butter melted in it; pour this on 1 cup of bread crumbs, add salt and pepper and the yolks of 6 eggs well beaten. Mix thoroughly. Slowly add 6 whites cut to a stiff froth, mix lightly and fry with hot butter. This will make two; when almost done turn together in shape of half moon." ASCENSION CHURCH, *Family Friend*, 71.

POTPOURRI

"Brown a pint of stale bread dice, in a spider. Grate a half cupful of nuts. Grate a half cupful of dried cheese. Mix.

"Place a layer of the bread in the bottom of a baking dish; then a layer of the mixture, alternating until the dish is nearly full. Pour over this a third of a cup of milk. Bake at once in a moderate oven." GRAY, *Cook Book*, 25.

ROASTED CHEESE

"One-fourth pound of cheese, 2 tablespoonfuls butter, yolks of 2 eggs, 1 level teaspoonful mustard, ¼ teaspoonful salt, a little cayenne pepper. Grate stale cheese or cut soft cheese in small pieces. Mix butter, eggs, etc., together until smooth, spread on toast or buttered crackers and brown in oven. Sufficient for 6 people." ASCENSION CHURCH, *Family Friend*, 139.

EGG GEMS

"Mix together any kind of cold meat (chopped fine) with equal quantity of bread crumbs; use pepper, salt, and a bit of butter, and a little milk; fill some buttered gem pans with the mixture, then carefully break an egg on the top of each. Season with pepper and salt, and sprinkle some cracker crumbs on top. Bake eight minutes. A little grated cheese may be added to the cracker if desired." GROFF, *Snow Flake Cook Book*, 38.

SPAGHETTI AND CHEESE

"Cook 1 pound spaghetti in 3 quarts boiling salted water about 45 minutes, or until tender; drain through colander and set colander in oven in pan to dry paste somewhat; boil 1 can tomatoes down until it only makes 1 pint; season with salt and pepper and a scant teaspoonful sugar (if you like it). Prepare 3 ounces melted butter and an equal amount of grated cheese. Put into hot dish alternate layers of spaghetti, tomatoes and cheese, pouring over each layer some of the melted butter; then mix all with a fork, sprinkle a little cheese over top and serve as a separate course or with dinner vegetables, as preferred. *Italian method.*" ASCENSION CHURCH, *Family Friend*, 39.

BAKED BEAN SANDWICHES

"Rub cold baked beans through a sieve, add salt and pepper to taste and mix with mayonnaise to a smooth paste. Add finely chopped celery leaves or a little celery salt and spread between brown bread." *Our Chef's Best Receipts*, 43.

FRENCH SANDWICHES

"Chop four pounds of ham or tongue very fine, also four good sized pickles. Add two tablespoonfuls melted butter and three teaspoonfuls of made mustard. Mix all well together. Spread on thin slices of buttered bread." GROFF, *Snow Flake Cook Book*, 38.

NUT SANDWICHES

"Grate equal parts of parmesan cheese and English Walnuts (unblanched), and mix together with salt. Cut bread into thin slices, butter and spread with the mixture." GRAY, *Cook Book*, 65.

*POUNDED CHEESE

1 pound cheddar cheese, grated, or 1 pound soft cheddar

⅛ tsp. cayenne   **⅛ tsp. black pepper**

¼ to ½ cup butter   **2 tsp. prepared mustard**

½ tsp. curry powder

Work the butter into the cheese until both are well mixed. Add the seasonings and the mustard and blend well into the cheese mixture. Taste must determine the amounts of each seasoning. The recommendations above furnish a guide, but caution suggests it is best to start with a small portion. LEE, *Complete Library*, 47.

*SPICED SALT

Take ¼ tsp. grated nutmeg and same of cloves, ⅛ tsp. of white pepper, same of allspice, mace, bay leaf, basil and thyme (these three latter herbs should be dried in an oven). Put these all into a mortar, and pound them to an impalpable powder, and sift it. Take one cup fine salt and mix with it the spices; amalgamate them thoroughly; keep the spiced salt in a tin box, which will shut perfectly closed. Use it in the following proportion: ¼ tsp. to a pound of boned veal. LEE, *Complete Library*, 181.

*CHEESE STRAWS

Have ice cold ¾ of a cup of butter, chop fine into two cups of flour, mix with ½ cup ice water a little at a time using a fork to mix it. Flour board and pin. Turn out dough and roll to the thickness of a silver dollar; sprinkle well with grated sharp cheddar cheese and salt; roll it up like a newspaper and roll out about six inches in width and as long as the dough will admit; cut in strips ¼ inch wide, place in unbuttered pan, sprinkle with cheese and coarse salt. Bake at 450 degrees for 12 minutes. DAYTON AVENUE PRESBYTERIAN CHURCH, *Cook Book*, 114.

*BURNT ALMONDS

2 cups almonds	¼ cup water
shelled and skinned	1 cup sugar

Boil water and sugar until clear and thick enough to run slowly off a spoon. Add almonds and stir with a wooden spoon until you hear the nuts crack. Take off the fire, but keep stirring them; and when dry put in a wire sieve and sift all the sugar from them. Now put that sugar on to boil again, adding about 3 teaspoons of water and ½ teaspoon cinnamon, if you like. When this boils add the almonds and keep stirring until dry. Take off the fire, cool, and pack in a glass jar. *"Aunt Babette's" Cook Book*, 362.

*PLUM CATSUP

3 pounds Santa Rosa	½ tbsp. cinnamon
or wild plums	¼ tsp. cloves
3 cups sugar	¼ tsp. pepper
¼ cup cider vinegar	¼ tsp. salt

Boil the plums in a cup of water for twenty minutes, then strain through a colander. Put in all the ingredients except the vinegar, which add just before it is done. Boil one-half hour. Bottle. Yield: about 3 cups. FIRST BAPTIST CHURCH, *Tried and True*, 33.

*ENGLISH WALNUT PICKLES

1 cup walnuts, shelled   1¼ cups water
4 tbsp. coarse salt

Boil water to dissolve salt, pour over walnuts. Allow the nutmeats to stand in the brine for a total of nine days, replacing the old brine with fresh every three days. At the end of nine days, drain walnuts again and spread them in a shallow pan to dry in a preheated oven at 300 degrees for about 15 minutes.

Vinegar solution:

¾ cup cider vinegar   ¼ tsp. pepper
¾ cup water   ½ tsp. mustard seed
½ tsp. mace   1 or 2 slivers gingerroot
½ tsp. cloves

Add spices to vinegar and water, steep for 15 minutes; bring to a boil and pour over nutmeats without straining. Drain and reboil the seasoned liquid each day for three days, pouring the hot spicy vinegar over the nuts. Allow the nuts to stand undisturbed in the liquid for a week. Drain and spread the walnuts in a shallow pan. Dry them in a 250-degree oven until they are crisp. BUTTERICK, *Perfect Art of Canning*, 24.

TOMATO VINEGAR

"A very superior quality of vinegar may be made by taking ripe tomatoes, scalding them, pressing out the juice, and adding to every four gallons one gallon of rain water, if you add to this quantity one-quarter pound of sugar, you will have good vinegar in ten days. I consider this vinegar superior to cider in quality, as there is no danger of its loosing its strength or dying. I tried it last fall, and think it a good way to use tomatoes after the season for marketing is over." *Farmer and Gardener*, 1:185 (June, 1861).

Reference Notes

Chapter 1 — INTRODUCTION — Pages 1–34

[1] Susan M. Hazeltine Adams Diary, April 5, 22, 23, 1856, in Andrew W. Adams and Family Papers, Minnesota Historical Society.

[2] Harriet Griswold to Father and Mother, March 30, September 14, [1858–59]; Florence R. Griswold to Grandma, December 19, 1859, in Harriet Griswold Papers, Minnesota Historical Society. The full names of the Griswolds' correspondents are not known, nor are the complete dates of some letters. The probable dates, appearing in brackets, have been supplied by the cataloger.

[3] Harriet Griswold to Brother Henry, April 29, [1858–59]; to Father and Mother, September 14, [1858–59], in Griswold Papers. On the Panic of 1857, see Theodore C. Blegen, *Minnesota: A History of the State*, 208 (Minneapolis, 1963).

[4] Harriet Griswold to Father and Mother, March 30, [1858–59], December 19, [1859]; to Father, June 27, [1858–59], in Griswold Papers.

[5] "Autobiography of Mary Jane Hill Anderson, Wife of Robert Anderson," 16, 19, 20, 29, in Minnesota Historical Society manuscripts division.

[6] Mary E. Carpenter to Cousin Laura, August 18, 1871, in Mary E. Lovell Carpenter and Family Papers, Minnesota Historical Society.

[7] Developments in Minnesota during the 1850s are described in Blegen, *Minnesota*, 166–210.

[8] *Minnesota Pioneer* (St. Paul), March 27, 1850; Joseph A. Wheelock, *Minnesota: Its Place among the States*, 125, 126 (Minnesota Bureau of Statistics, *First Annual Report* — Hartford, Conn., 1860); *United States Census*, 1900, *Population*, part 1, p. 25.

[9] United States, *Statutes at Large*, 12:392–394; on the history and results of the Homestead Act, see William W. Folwell, *A History of*

Minnesota, 2:331–333 (Reprint edition, St. Paul, 1961); *Rochester Republican*, June 25, 1862.

[10] Editorial comment on immigrants entering Minnesota in the 1860s found frequent expression in the press; see, for example, *Pioneer and Democrat* (St. Paul), September 4, 1859, June 19, 1861, July 15, 1862; *St. Paul Daily Press*, June 30, 1861, May 12, 1863, July 28, August 2, 1865, June 13, 1867; *Mankato Semi-Weekly Record*, May 21, 1861, June 4, 1864; *Sauk Rapids Frontierman*, October 27, 1859; see also Blegen, *Minnesota*, 175.

[11] *St. Paul Daily Press*, June 19, 1866; *Daily Pioneer and Democrat*, September 4, 1859; *Minneapolis Tribune*, January 30, 1868.

[12] On the development of roads, see Arthur J. Larsen, "Roads and Trails in the Minnesota Triangle, 1849–60," in *Minnesota History*, 11:387–411 (December, 1930); Bertha L. Heilbron, *The Thirty-Second State: A Pictorial History of Minnesota*, 100, 161 (Revised edition, St. Paul, 1966); Blegen, *Minnesota*, 252, 295. The early overland routes to St. Paul from Galena, Illinois, and from Dubuque, Iowa, brought not only settlers, but also supplies to Minnesota during the winter months.

[13] *Daily Minnesotian* (St. Paul), May 20, 1857.

[14] Lucy L. W. Morris, ed., *Old Rail Fence Corners: The A. B. C.'s of Minnesota History*, 173, 295 (Second edition, Austin, 1914).

[15] *St. Paul Daily Pioneer*, April 2, 1865.

[16] Mrs. Joseph Ullmann, "Saint Paul Forty Years Ago: A Personal Reminiscence," 14, 15, typed copy in Minnesota Historical Society manuscripts division.

[17] *Minnesota Pioneer*, April 28, May 12, 1849, September 1, 1853.

[18] Elizabeth Steere to sister, December 20, 1855, in Isaac Steere and Family Papers, Minnesota Historical Society.

[19] Here and below, see "House Account," 1857, vol. 1 in Abby Abbe Fuller and Family Papers, Minnesota Historical Society.

[20] *Minnesota Pioneer*, February 6, 1851; *St. Paul Daily Democrat*, December 11, 1854; *St. Paul Pioneer*, September 11, 1867. For more on market hunters in Minnesota, see David and Jim Kimball, *The Market Hunter*, 39–52, 67–72, 93–112 (Minneapolis, 1969).

[21] *Daily Minnesotian*, August 10, 1854; Morris, ed., *Old Rail Fence Corners*, 104. In Minnesota it was legal to snare or net passenger pigeons until 1891; by 1895 few pigeons remained in the state, and in 1914 the last surviving passenger pigeon in the nation died in a zoo. On the passenger pigeon, prairie chicken, and other game, see W. J. Breckenridge, "A Century of Minnesota Wild Life," in *Minnesota History*, 30:223, 224 (September, 1949); Mary W. Berthel, "Hunting in Minnesota in the Seventies," in *Minnesota History*, 16:259–271 (September, 1935).

[22] *Minneapolis Tribune*, November 30, 1885.

[23] Grace Lee Nute, "American Fur Company's Fishing Enterprises," in *Mississippi Valley Historical Review*, 12:491, 497 (March, 1926); Evadene A. Burris, "Frontier Food," in *Minnesota History*, 14:384 (December, 1933); *Daily Pioneer*, June 15, 1854; T. B. Sheldon Day Book, March 16, [1876], vol. 37, in T. B. Sheldon Papers, Minnesota Historical Society; Sidney Smith Grocery Store, Order Book, September 8, 23, 25, 1875, in Minnesota Historical Society; *Rochester Post*, May 25, June 15, 1867, January 11, 1868; June D. Holmquist, "Commercial Fishing on Lake Superior in the 1890s," in *Minnesota History*, 34:243–249 (Summer, 1955).

[24] Burris, in *Minnesota History*, 14:384; June D. Holmquist, "Fishing in the Land of 10,000 Lakes," in *Minnesota History*, 33:254 (Summer, 1953).

[25] *Minnesota Democrat* (St. Paul), July 15, 1851; *Daily Minnesotian*, August 23, 1855; *Pioneer and Democrat*, December 27, 1855.

[26] *Red Wing Sentinel*, April 2, 1859; Morris, ed., *Old Rail Fence Corners*, 110.

[27] *Weekly Pioneer and Democrat*, December 3, 10, 1857; Merrill C. Jarchow, *The Earth Brought Forth: A History of Minnesota Agriculture to 1885*, 191 (St. Paul, 1849). For the estimated value of exportable surpluses in 1860, see Folwell, *Minnesota*, 2:65n; exports included grain, potatoes, lumber, furs, ginseng, hides, cranberries, and other items.

[28] *Minnesota Pioneer*, June 10, 1852; Ullmann, "Saint Paul Forty Years Ago," 14.

[29] Sarah Fuller to Elizabeth Fuller, June 18, 1855, in Fuller Papers; *Weekly Pioneer and Democrat*, April 22, 1858.

[30] *Minnesota Pioneer*, February 20, May 2, 1850, May 27, June 3, 1852.

[31] Sesyle Joslin, "The Ice Cream of Rome," in *Travel and Leisure*, August, 1975, p. 30; a copy of the menu is in the Fuller Papers.

[32] Ullmann, "Saint Paul Forty Years Ago," 31; Morris, ed., *Old Rail Fence Corners*, 119; Mrs. Alexander Ramsey to Marion Furness, October 6, December 26, 1875, roll 21, frames 647, 764–765, in Alexander Ramsey Papers, Minnesota Historical Society; Sarah G. Baird Dairy, April 18, 1882, in Sarah G. Baird Papers, Minnesota Historical Society.

[33] Morris, ed., *Old Rail Fence Corners*, 132; Ann L. North to parents, November 25, 1849, January 6, February 9, 1850, roll 1, John Wesley North and Family Papers, copies in Minnesota Historical Society. Originals of the North Papers are in the Henry E. Huntington Library and Art Gallery, San Marino, California; they are used here with permission. On Ann North, see Lucile M. Kane, "A Bride's Home on Nicollet Island," in A. Hermina Poatgieter and James T. Dunn, eds., *Gopher Reader II*, 200–202 (St. Paul, 1975).

[34] Morris, ed., *Old Rail Fence Corners*, 118, 244, 289.

[35] Morris, ed., *Old Rail Fence Corners*, 262; Fred L. Israel, ed., *1897 Sears Roebuck Catalogue*, 115, 125, 135, 300 (Reprint edition, New York, 1968). For a good description of home life in the 1850s, see Evadene A. Burris, "Keeping House on the Minnesota Frontier," in *Minnesota History*, 14:263–282 (September, 1933).

[36] Israel, ed., *1897 Sears Roebuck Catalogue*, 23, 101, 104, 134, 139; Lucile M. Kane, *The Waterfall That Built a City*, 142 (St. Paul, 1966); Blegen, *Minnesota*, 572; Heilbron, *The Thirty-Second State*, 107.

[37] Philip D. Jordan, *The People's Health: A History of Public Health in Minnesota to 1948*, 148, 175 (St. Paul, 1953); Robert C. Alberts, *The Good Provider: H. J. Heinz and His 57 Varieties*, 49, 168 (Boston, 1973); United States, *Statutes at Large*, 34:768–772.

[38] Jordan, *People's Health*, 149, 158, 160, 163, 170.

[39] Jordan, *People's Health*, 148, 150, 158; *Daily Pioneer Press* (St. Paul and Minneapolis), November 20, 1880.

[40] Jordan, *People's Health*, 152, 175.

[41] Jordan, *People's Health*, 113, 115–119.

[42] James H. Collins, *The Story of Canned Foods*, 218 (New York, 1924).

[43] Butterick Publishing Co., *The Perfect Art of Canning and Preserving*, 10 (*Metropolitan Pamphlet Series*, vol. 3, no. 3 — London and New York, 1891); Eliza Leslie, *Miss Leslie's New Cookery Book*, 568 (Philadelphia, 1857).

[44] Coverage of the Pure Food Show appears in the *Minneapolis Journal*, October 2–6, 9, 11, 13, 15, 1894; the exhibits are described in the issue of October 9, 1894.

[45] Mrs. Rorer gave 12 demonstration lectures between October 2 and 13, 1894. The *Minneapolis Journal* printed full accounts of her appearances, including the recipes used, in the issues cited above. Her talks on keeping warm and on butchering and marketing meat (during which a woman fainted at the sight of blood) are reported in the *Journal*, October 4, 5, 1894, respectively.

Chapter 2 — BREAD–THE VISIBLE SYMBOL — Pages 35–57

[1] Morris, ed., *Old Rail Fence Corners*, 170, 171; Julia K. S. Hibbard, Reminiscences, 11, typed copy in Hibbard Papers, Minnesota Historical Society. For a "Johnnycake" recipe, see chapter 9, p. 210, below.

[2] Morris, ed., *Old Rail Fence Corners*, 166, 171, 270, 274. For information on early flour milling, see Paul W. Klammer, "Some Water-

Powered Gristmills of Pioneer Minnesota," in Poatgieter and Dunn, eds., *Gopher Reader II*, 157–162.

³ Morris, ed., *Old Rail Fence Corners*, 62, 118, 244.

⁴ Maria Parloa, *Miss Parloa's New Cook Book*, 54 (Boston, 1880); Leslie, *New Cookery Book*, 433; Dayton Avenue Presbyterian Church (St. Paul), *A Cook Book Compiled by the Ladies of Dayton Avenue Presbyterian Church*, 8 (St. Paul, 1892). Fresh homemade bread was often the hospitable gift to new neighbors just as it is today. A St. Paul woman, for example, wrote of receiving a loaf, still warm from the oven, from the Nathaniel P. Langford family in the late 1890s. See Polly Caroline Bullard, "Reminiscences of Things Past," 26, typed copy in the Minnesota Historical Society manuscripts division.

⁵ *Tried and Approved. Buckeye Cookery, with Hints on Practical Housekeeping*, 8 (Minneapolis, 1881), hereafter cited as *Buckeye Cookery*. Another rather messy test of quality was to "Throw a little lump of flour against a dry, smooth perpendicular surface; if it adheres in a lump, the flour has life in it; if it falls like powder, it is bad"; *Red Wing Republican*, October 16, 1857.

The Buckeye Publishing Company issued a series of cookbooks beginning in 1877 with *Buckeye Cookery and Practical Housekeeping: Tried and Approved, Original Recipes*, which was published in Minneapolis. A "second edition" entitled *Tried and Approved. Buckeye Cookery and Practical Housekeeping* was published in Marysville, Ohio, the same year. Under variations of these titles, additional editions are known to have been published in Minneapolis in 1881, 1883, 1884, 1887, and 1894, and in St. Paul in 1896, 1904, and 1905 (the last three by different publishers). The later editions were edited by Estelle W. Wilcox. In 1883, the word "Buckeye" was dropped from the title to disassociate the book from its state of origin, but it was restored in 1904. See Eleanor and Bob Brown, *Culinary Americana: Cookbooks Published in the Cities and Towns of the United States of America during the Years from 1860 to 1960*, 119, 120, 238 (New York, 1961). The Minnesota Historical Society library has copies of editions dated 1877, 1881, and 1904. Citations in the present volume refer to the 1881 edition except where noted. See also p. 183, below.

⁶ Kane, *Waterfall That Built a City*, 105; John Storck and Walter D. Teague, *Flour for Man's Bread*, 188, 338, 339, 340 (Minneapolis, 1952); George D. Rogers, "History of Flour Manufacture in Minnesota," in *Minnesota Historical Collections*, 10:46, 47 (St. Paul, 1905).

⁷ Parloa, *New Cook Book*, 54; *Buckeye Cookery*, 413; Storck and Teague, *Flour for Man's Bread*, 340. As early as 1868, Minneapolis was considered "a flour city" in which "nearly every family manufactures its own bread"; *Minneapolis Tribune*, February 21, 1868.

[8] *Buckeye Cookery*, 54; Dayton Avenue Presbyterian Church, *Cook Book*, 8.

[9] *Buckeye Cookery*, 55–58. Hop culture spread from Wisconsin into Minnesota, reaching its peak about 1869 after which it abruptly declined; Edward V. D. Robinson, *Early Economic Conditions and the Development of Agriculture in Minnesota*, 73 (University of Minnesota, *Studies in the Social Sciences No. 3* — Minneapolis, 1915).

[10] *Buckeye Cookery*, 58. On the various grades of sugar, see chapter 3, note 12, below.

[11] *Buckeye Cookery*, 57.

[12] *Buckeye Cookery*, 54, 55.

[13] *Buckeye Cookery*, 8, 55, 57.

[14] *Buckeye Cookery*, 7, 9.

[15] *Buckeye Cookery*, 10, 12.

[16] *Buckeye Cookery*, 10.

[17] For material here and in the following paragraph, see *Buckeye Cookery*, 11, 12.

[18] *Buckeye Cookery*, 25; Storck and Teague, *Flour for Man's Bread*, 340.

[19] *Buckeye Cookery*, 25; Morris, ed., *Old Rail Fence Corners*, 51. After seven vain attempts to produce salt-rising bread, the author can heartily agree that success comes to a chosen few.

[20] *Buckeye Cookery*, 12, 13. For the vagaries of stoves, see chapter 7, below.

[21] *Buckeye Cookery*, 12; Juliet Corson, *Miss Corson's Practical American Cookery and Household Management*, 488 (New York, 1886).

[22] *Buckeye Cookery*, 14, 15.

[23] *Buckeye Cookery*, 13; Corson, *Practical American Cookery*, 487.

[24] *Buckeye Cookery*, 13; Leslie, *New Cookery Book*, 435.

[25] Leslie, *New Cookery Book*, 434.

[26] *Buckeye Cookery*, 17.

[27] First Baptist Church (St. Paul), *The Tried and True Cook Book*, 45 (St. Paul, 1881).

[28] *Buckeye Cookery*, 41.

[29] *Buckeye Cookery*, 28.

[30] *Webster's Dictionary*, Second edition; Westminster Presbyterian Church (Minneapolis), [*Valuable Recipes*], 33 (Minneapolis, 187?).

[31] *Buckeye Cookery*, 35; Corson, *Practical American Cookery*, 504; Dayton Avenue Presbyterian Church, *Cook Book*, 30; "Doughbellies" is the name given to fried bread by at least three generations of a family dating well back into the 19th century; conversation of the author with Jean A. Brookins, June, 1975.

[32] Recipes for several varieties of toast are in *Buckeye Cookery*, 34, 35.

[33] Leslie, *New Cookery Book*, 423, 606.

[34] Leslie, *New Cookery Book*, 607; Catherine E. Beecher and Harriet Beecher Stowe, *The American Woman's Home or Principles of Domestic Science*, 481, 485, 488 (New York, 1869). Miss Leslie also condemned the use of tartaric acid and soda for cakes; see *New Cookery Book*, 423.

[35] A. W. Chase, *Dr. Chase's Third, Last, and Complete Receipt Book and Household Physician*, 366 (Detroit, Mich., and Windsor, Ont., 1891); Mary F. Henderson, *Practical Cooking and Dinner Giving*, 69 (New York, 1881); Parloa, *New Cook Book*, 59.

[36] Westminster Presbyterian Church, [*Valuable Recipes*], 28, 31; Methodist Episcopal Church (Buffalo), *The Christmas Cook Book*, 16 (Buffalo, Minn., 1899).

[37] Irma S. Rombauer and Marion R. Becker, *The Joy of Cooking*, 501 (Revised edition, Indianapolis and New York, 1953); Mrs. Simon Kander, *The Settlement Cook Book:Treasured Recipes of Six Decades*, 101 (Revised edition, New York, 1965).

[38] Charles R. Groff, *The Snow Flake Cook Book: A Collection of Practical Recipes*, [3], (St. Paul, 1881). The Pure Food and Drug Act of 1906 successfully cracked down on baking powder manufacturers, forcing them to eliminate lead and arsenic from the product; Richard O. Cummings, *The American and His Food: A History of Food Habits in the United States*, 103 (Chicago, 1941).

[39] *Buckeye Cookery*, 33; Chase, *Receipt Book*, 624.

[40] *Buckeye Cookery*, 31–54; Ascension Church (Stillwater), *Family Friend*, 139 (St. Paul, 1893); Leslie, *New Cookery Book*, 432. For a wide variety of Minnesota recipes for "Breakfast and Tea" specialties, see First Baptist Church, *Tried and True*, 47–51; Westminster Presbyterian Church, [*Valuable Recipes*], 27–35; Methodist Episcopal Church, *Christmas Cook Book*, 10–14; Dayton Avenue Presbyterian Church, *Cook Book*, 22–32. See also page 208, below, for additional bread recipes.

[41] *Buckeye Cookery*, 7, 14, 16.

Chapter 3 — A COOL DRY PLACE — Pages 59–76

[1] See Burris, in *Minnesota History*, 14:272; A. J. Russell, *Loring Park Aspects*, 45 (Minneapolis, 1919); *Daily Pioneer and Democrat*, July 6, 1859.

[2] Conversation with Brookins, June, 1975; *Freeborn County Standard* (Albert Lea), February 11, 1869.

[3] Morris, ed., *Old Rail Fence Corners*, 279; *Freeborn County Standard*, January 14, 1869.

[4] *Buckeye Cookery*, 457; Catherine E. Beecher, *Miss Beecher's Domestic Receipt-Book: Designed as a Supplement to Her Treatise on Domestic Economy*, 218 (Third edition, New York, 1858).

[5] *Buckeye Cookery*, 455; *Stillwater Gazette*, January 12, 1881.

[6] *Freeborn County Standard*, December 30, 1869.

[7] *St. Paul Daily Press*, April 19, 1863; John W. North to George S. Loomis, October 13, 1850, in North Papers; Catherine E. Beecher, *A Treatise on Domestic Economy*, 279 (New York, 1847); *Buckeye Cookery*, 458; Jarchow, *Earth Brought Forth*, 94. A "Copperas Solution," described as a disinfectant, consisted of "Sulphate of iron (copperas) dissolved in water in the proportion of 1½ lbs. to 1 gal.," according to Chase, *Receipt Book*, 68.

[8] Conversation of the author with June D. Holmquist, July, 1975.

[9] Theodore C. Blegen, "The Day of the Pioneer," in *Minnesota History*, 14:141 (June, 1933). The storing of such a large quantity of butter was not unusual; most housewives considered making butter for the family a regular chore, one that they had learned to do as children. For the inexperienced buttermaker, however, *Buckeye Cookery*, 438, included explicit directions, from milking cows to storing butter rolls in crocks of brine "kept in a clean, sweet place."

[10] Beecher, *Domestic Receipt-Book*, 223.

[11] Beecher, *Domestic Receipt-Book*, 217, 219, 220; Morris, ed., *Old Rail Fence Corners*, 51; *Buckeye Cookery*, 428.

[12] There were, for example, 11 different grades of soft brown sugar manufactured from molasses by a refinery in Maine in the 1860s and later. Grocers in St. Paul in 1852 advertised "Common Brown, Refined, A, B, and C. Crushed and Powdered, by the barrel"; *Minnesota Pioneer*, November 11, 1852. In 1868 a Hastings grocer announced that 5 lbs. of "Crushed Sugar" cost $.85, "Granulated Sugar" 3 lbs. for $.51, and "Brown Sugar" 5 lbs. for $.50. Sugar molds varied in size from 11 to 22 inches high, 5 to 10 inches in diameter, and in weight from about 5 to 35 pounds.

With the development of the centrifugal machine about 1870, refineries were able to produce a pure white granulated sugar previously unknown. Frederick G. Holcomb, *The Sugar Refining Industry of New England*, 35, 41 (Denver, 1954); Noel Deerr, *The History of Sugar*, 2:465 (London, 1950); *Chambers's Encyclopaedia: A Dictionary of Universal Knowledge for the People*, 9:192 (Philadelphia, 1879). When the Civil War cut off sugar supplies from the South, Minnesotans experimented with growing sorghum and manufacturing their own syrup, as they had always done with maple syrup. Production of sorghum increased until about 1880, but the industry never attained real importance in the region. Robinson, *Development of Agriculture in Minnesota*, 73, 275.

[13] Morris, ed., *Old Rail Fence Corners*, 166; *Minneapolis Tribune*, May 29, 1870; Beecher, *Domestic Receipt-Book*, 220; *Buckeye Cookery*, 428. Rock salt from Michigan was considered to be the form most free of impurities; *Encyclopaedia Britannica*, 14th edition, 19:897. Along with rock salt, some brands sold by Minnesota grocers included Kanawha from West Virginia, Saginaw, Turk's Island, an import, and Solar, made by the sun-evaporation of salt brine in New York. A Red Wing grocer sold salt by the sack ($.15 in 1875) and by the barrel ($3.15 for Solar in 1868 and $4.50 for dairy in 1874); a St. Paul supplier sold it by the bushel ($1.00) in 1854; at Rochester the price of a barrel of salt in 1867 was $4.25; *Daily Pioneer*, June 15, 1854, December 4, 1864; T. B. Sheldon Journal, 1868–75, vol. 20, in T. B. Sheldon Papers; *Rochester Post*, June 15, 1867; *Duluth Minnesotian*, January 6, 1872; Arthur G. Peterson, *Glass Salt Shakers: 1,000 Patterns*, 7, 8 (Des Moines, Ia., 1970).

In the 1870s unsuccessful attempts were made to develop salt production in Minnesota, especially at Belle Plaine in Scott County and an area in Stevens, Otter Tail, and Wilkin counties; *Minneapolis Tribune*, May 29, September 7, 1870, January 1, February 8, 1871; *Daily Pioneer*, August 21, September 6, 1870; *Daily Press*, September 6, 1870, March 13, August 18, 1872; Folwell, *Minnesota*, 4:479–481 (St. Paul, 1930).

[14] Beecher, *Domestic Receipt-Book*, 219; Morris, ed., *Old Rail Fence Corners*, 80; *Buckeye Cookery*, 428. The standard barrel holding 196 pounds of flour remained in use in Minnesota well into the 20th century; Storck and Teague, *Flour for Man's Bread*, 271.

[15] Beecher, *Domestic Receipt-Book*, 219.

[16] Beecher, *Domestic Receipt-Book*, 219, 220. Some Minnesotans made their own molasses from maple sap; see Burris, in *Minnesota History*, 14:383.

[17] Morris, ed., *Old Rail Fence Corners*, 71.

[18] Leslie, *New Cookery Book*, 613; *Buckeye Cookery*, 150. Describing the cellar of his boyhood home in Cloquet about 1906, Walter O'Meara recalled a large crock of eggs stored in water glass, a common name for sodium silicate. O'Meara, *We Made It Through the Winter: A Memoir of Northern Minnesota Boyhood*, 48 (St. Paul, 1974).

[19] Chase, *Receipt Book*, 549–552. In 1894 a Mazeppa, Minnesota, housewife kept eggs for two months by packing them in "dry, old oats"; she succinctly concluded that "They may be sold as fresh eggs . . . at a much higher price"; *The Country Kitchen: The Northwestern Farmer Recipe Book*, 52 (St. Paul, 1894).

[20] On pickling, see chapter 5, below; Morris, ed., *Old Rail Fence Corners*, 76, 119.

[21] Jarchow, *Earth Brought Forth*, 181; Morris, ed., *Old Rail Fence Corners*, 127, 128. For a full discussion of "The Grasshopper Invasion,

1873–77," see Folwell, *Minnesota*, 3:93–110 (Reprint edition, St. Paul, 1969).

²² Juliet Corson, *Cooking School Text Book, and Housekeepers' Guide to Cookery and Kitchen Management*, 49 (New York, 1879); Corson, *Practical American Cookery*, 10; *Buckeye Cookery*, 459.

²³ Corson, *Practical American Cookery*, 11; Mrs. N. K. M. Lee et al., *Complete Library of Cookery*, 237 (Chicago, 1890); *Buckeye Cookery*, 458, 459.

²⁴ Corson, *Practical American Cookery*, 11; Lee, *Complete Library*, 237.

²⁵ Conversation with Brookins, June, 1975.

²⁶ *Minnesota Farmer and Gardener*, 1:361 (December, 1861).

²⁷ Lee, *Complete Library*, 237; *Freeborn County Standard*, October 14, 1869; Corson, *Cooking School Text Book*, 46; Corson, *Practical American Cookery*, 11; *Buckeye Cookery*, 459.

²⁸ Corson, *Cooking School Text Book*, 49; Corson, *A Course of Lectures on the Principles of Domestic Economy and Cookery*, 89 (Minneapolis, 1886); Corson, *Practical American Cookery*, 11. The word "vitamin" was coined by Casimir Funk in 1912; vitamin A was pinpointed in 1913.

²⁹ On canning and drying, see chapter 4, below; *Buckeye Cookery*, 458.

³⁰ Beecher, *Domestic Receipt-Book*, 217.

Chapter 4 — CANNING AND DRYING FRUITS AND VEGETABLES — Pages 77–96

¹ *Buckeye Cookery*, 159; Lee, *Complete Library*, 236.

² Butterick, *Perfect Art of Canning*, [1].

³ For brief accounts of the contributions of John L. Mason and Lewis R. Boyd to the home-canning industry, see Julian H. Toulouse, *Fruit Jars*, 342–347, 350–352, 541 (Camden, N.J., 1969).

⁴ *Farmer and Gardener*, 1:219 (July, 1861).

⁵ Here and below, see Henderson, *Practical Cooking*, 245. The words "hearth" and "fire" in Mrs. Henderson's recipe refer not to an open fire or fireplace but to a cookstove; in 1881 cookstoves were fitted with a shelf and a door at the side next to the firebox.

⁶ Here and below, see *Buckeye Cookery*, 119, 121. The jar sealed with wax or putty undoubtedly developed from a grooved-ring wax sealer patented in 1855 by Robert Arthur for use with tin cans, pottery jars, or "vessels formed in a plastic state," which would include glass. Central to his design was the vertical inner wall of the groove and a close-fitting

right-angle rim that surrounded the metal lid. The inner wall was intended to prevent the differences in the cooling of the wax and of the jar contents from pulling any of the wax into the container. It also prevented air inside the vessel from blowing through the incompletely hardened wax seal and destroying its effectiveness. See Toulouse, *Fruit Jars*, 341.

7 Toulouse, *Fruit Jars*, 417, 420, 421, 422, 464–490.

8 *Buckeye Cookery*, 119.

9 *Buckeye Cookery*, 119; Butterick, *Perfect Art of Canning*, 8.

10 Butterick, *Perfect Art of Canning*, 10; *Buckeye Cookery*, 121.

11 *Buckeye Cookery*, 121.

12 Henderson, *Practical Cooking*, 248; *Buckeye Cookery*, 119, 181, 182; Lee, *Complete Library*, 152; Beecher, *Domestic Economy*, 350. Preserves had not enjoyed wide popularity in the decades preceding 1850, being used primarily as food for those who were ill. "They are unhealthy, expensive, and useless to those who are well," wrote Lydia M. Child, in *The Frugal Housewife*, 81 (6th edition, Boston, 1831).

13 *Buckeye Cookery*, 181, 182; Lee, *Complete Library*, 152; Butterick, *Perfect Art of Canning*, 2, 5, 6, 10.

14 Henderson, *Practical Cooking*, 248; Baird Diary, July 27, 30, September 11, 13, 1882, in Baird Papers.

15 Ascension Church, *Family Friend*, 113; Lee, *Complete Library*, 152; *Buckeye Cookery*, 182; Butterick, *Perfect Art of Canning*, 6; Beecher, *Domestic Receipt-Book*, 153. Bladder covers were the washed bladders of butchered animals. They were stored in salt brine and used primarily to cover crocks and jars, although occasionally they substituted for sausage casings and were also used to store headcheese. As covers, the bladders had to be brushed with salt water every other day to keep them from shrinking. They could be used again to cover a smaller vessel if the dried and stiffened portions were trimmed off. Conversations of the author with Alex Weiss, St. Paul, and Jerome F. Bechtold, St. Joseph, July 25, 1975, and Alfred G. Muellerleile, St. Paul, July 11, 1975. Mr. Muellerleile also recalled that children on the farms around Madison Lake, Minnesota, made balloons from the bladders. Paraffin wax was commercially available by the mid-1850s; *Encyclopaedia Britannica*, 11th edition, 20:752–756.

16 Elizabeth Steere to parents, December 18, 1855, in Steere Papers; *Minnesota Pioneer*, February 20, 1850, April 6, 1854; *Daily Pioneer and Democrat*, October 21, 1857. For Minnesota recipes for jams and jellies, see First Baptist Church, *Tried and True*, 62–65; Ascension Church, *Family Friend*, 113–115; Westminster Presbyterian Church, [*Valuable Recipes*], 62; Central Presbyterian Church (St. Paul), *The "Central" Cook Book: A Collection of Household Recipes*, 55, 61, 62 (St. Paul,1900); *Buckeye Cookery*, 182–189.

[17] Morris, ed., *Old Rail Fence Corners*, 195, 198.

[18] Morris, ed., *Old Rail Fence Corners*, 68, 71, 141; *New Era* (Sauk Rapids), June 28, 1860; Burris, in *Minnesota History*, 14:380.

[19] Morris, ed., *Old Rail Fence Corners*, 20, 91, 123; *Farmer and Gardener*, 1:283 (September, 1861).

[20] Central Presbyterian Church, *Cook Book*, [59]; Ascension Church, *Family Friend*, 139.

[21] Ascension Church, *Family Friend*, 113; First Baptist Church, *Tried and True*, 62. For the quince recipe below, see *Tried and True*, 64.

[22] *Buckeye Cookery*, 122.

[23] *Buckeye Cookery*, 122.

[24] *Buckeye Cookery*, 123–125.

[25] Butterick, *Perfect Art of Canning*, 8–10.

[26] Lee, *Complete Library*, 19, 61.

[27] *Buckeye Cookery*, 250.

[28] *Buckeye Cookery*, 250.

[29] Leslie, *New Cookery Book*, 543; Lee, *Complete Library*, 65. On grades of sugar, see chapter 3, note 12.

[30] *Buckeye Cookery*, 182, 245.

[31] *New Buckeye Cook Book*, 157–159 (St. Paul, 1904).

[32] *New Buckeye Cook Book* (1904), 158.

[33] *New Buckeye Cook Book* (1904), 158.

[34] Butterick, *Perfect Art of Canning*, 11. Rhubarb was so popular a pie filling that it was often referred to simply as "pieplant." See recipe on p. 257, below.

[35] Butterick, *Perfect Art of Canning*, 29.

[36] Butterick, *Perfect Art of Canning*, 29.

[37] *Buckeye Cookery*, 282 (Minneapolis, 1877); Butterick, *Perfect Art of Canning*, 29.

[38] Butterick, *Perfect Art of Canning*, 29; Lee, *Complete Library*, 237.

[39] Butterick, *Perfect Art of Canning*, [1].

Chapter 5 — THE USEFUL ART OF PICKLING — Pages 97–114

[1] Butterick, *Perfect Art of Canning*, 21.

[2] Corson, *A Course of Lectures*, 38; Leslie, *New Cookery Book*, 116, 424; First Baptist Church, *Tried and True*, 41; Ascension Church, *Family Friend*, 42, 43, 129; Groff, *Snow Flake Cook Book*, 29; Parloa, *New Cook Book*, 49; Lee, *Complete Library*, 240–242.

[3] Leslie, *New Cookery Book*, 608.

[4] Lee, *Complete Library*, 241.

[5] *Buckeye Cookery*, 362, 533.

⁶Lee, *Complete Library*, 241; Chase, *Receipt Book*, 578. By the 1860s honey was commonly found on pioneer dinner tables; see Burris, in *Minnesota History*, 14:383.

⁷Jarchow, *Earth Brought Forth*, 243; *Farmer and Gardener*, 1:273, 275 (September, 1861). The Chatfield editor's remarks are reprinted in *Farmer and Gardener*, 1:309 (October, 1861). On the Wealthy apple and other northern varieties developed in Minnesota, see Edgar C. Duin, "Peter M. Gideon, Pioneer Horticulturist," in *Minnesota History*, 44:96-103 (Fall, 1974). Lacking apples, potatoes soaked in vinegar were used to make an imitation apple pie filling, according to Burris, in *Minnesota History*, 14:389.

⁸Mrs. Ramsey's book, in the Ramsey Papers, is a collection of cooking formulas, some written in longhand and others clipped from newspapers and pasted onto the pages; *Northwestern Farmer and Breeder*, 11:382 (January 1, 1893).

⁹*Buckeye Cookery*, 362; Mrs. William H. C. Folsom's undated recipe, in the William H. C. Folsom Papers, Minnesota Historical Society; Morris, ed., *Old Rail Fence Corners*, 96. The popularity of maple sugar on the Minnesota frontier is discussed by Burris, in *Minnesota History*, 14:383.

¹⁰*Northwestern Farmer and Breeder*, 8:171 (June 15, 1890). Genuine mincemeat was "a special treat" in pioneer Minnesota, according to Burris, in *Minnesota History*, 14:389, and mock mincemeat was made locally by soaking pumpkin in vinegar with dried grapes.

¹¹*Buckeye Cookery*, 254, 255; Butterick, *Perfect Art of Canning*, 20. Eliza Leslie suggested lining the pickling kettle with vine leaves to make cucumbers green; Leslie, *New Cookery Book*, 576.

¹²*Buckeye Cookery*, 254, 255.

¹³First Baptist Church, *Tried and True*, 31; Ascension Church, *Family Friend*, 119, 120; Central Presbyterian Church, *Cook Book*, 93, 95; Dayton Avenue Presbyterian Church, *Cook Book*, 158; Westminster Presbyterian Church, [*Valuable Recipes*], 20; Methodist Episcopal Church, *Christmas Cook Book*, 10. Recipes for dill pickles, which were considered a German favorite, appeared only in two books in the Minnesota Historical Society's collection: Central Presbyterian Church, *Cook Book*, 95, and *"Aunt Babette's" Cook Book: Foreign and Domestic Receipts for the Household*, 417, 418 (Cincinnati and Chicago, 1889); Frederick Converse Beach, ed., *Encyclopedia Americana*, "Dill," vol. 5, n.p. (New York, 1903–05).

¹⁴*Buckeye Cookery*, 254; Ascension Church, *Family Friend*, 117–125. For recipes for pickled vegetables and fruits, see Westminster Presbyterian Church, [*Valuable Recipes*], 14, 19–22; Dayton Avenue Presbyterian Church, *Cook Book*, 155–162; First Baptist Church, *Tried and True*, 30–32; *Buckeye Cookery*, 257–269.

[15] *Buckeye Cookery*, 265, 266; Butterick, *Perfect Art of Canning*, 20.

[16] Westminster Presbyterian Church, [*Valuable Recipes*], 22.

[17] Ascension Church, *Family Friend*, 117; Parloa, *New Cook Book*, 48.

[18] Methodist Episcopal Church, *Christmas Cook Book*, 8.

[19] Butterick, *Perfect Art of Canning*, 25, 26; Corson, *Practical American Cookery*, 259.

[20] For recipes here and in the four paragraphs below, see First Baptist Church, *Tried and True*, 30; Ascension Church, *Family Friend*, 122, 124; *Buckeye Cookery*, 260.

[21] Ascension Church, *Family Friend*, 118, 119. Other chowchow recipes are in the First Baptist Church, *Tried and True*, 31; Dayton Avenue Presbyterian Church, *Cook Book*, 159; Westminster Presbyterian Church, [*Valuable Recipes*], 19. Chowchow is the Chinese name for a mixed pickle originally imported from China; Sidney Morse, *Household Discoveries: An Encyclopaedia of Practical Recipes and Processes*, 577 (Petersburg, N.Y., 1909).

[22] Henderson, *Practical Cooking*, 258. "Indian pickle" refers to India, not American Indians.

[23] Butterick, *Perfect Art of Canning*, 22; Leslie, *New Cookery Book*, 581. Leslie also suggested combining nasturtium flowers with peppergrass for a summer salad.

[24] Leslie, *New Cookery Book*, 578; *Buckeye Cookery*, 264.

[25] Lee, *Complete Library*, 139; *Buckeye Cookery*, 254.

[26] *Buckeye Cookery*, 254; Butterick, *Perfect Art of Canning*, 21.

[27] Lee, *Complete Library*, 214. In the 1860s and later, custom sauerkraut makers in St. Paul "every fall are called on to visit the houses of numerous citizens to cut up cabbage and turn it into krout." See *Daily Press*, September 24, 1870.

[28] Corson, *Practical American Cookery*, 422; R. T. Trall, *The New Hydropathic Cook-Book; with Recipes for Cooking on Hygienic Principles*, 91 (New York, 1873); Collins, *Story of Canned Foods*, 199.

[29] For material on pickling meats and fish here and in the paragraphs below, see *Buckeye Cookery*, 157, 203; Lee, *Complete Library*, xxxv, 144, 145, 180; Leslie, *New Cookery Book*, 116, 315; Maria Parloa, *Miss Parloa's New Cook Book and Marketing Guide*, 124 (Revised edition, Boston, 1908).

[30] *"Aunt Babette's" Cook Book*, 41. This book contains numerous other German and Jewish recipes; see also p. 182, below.

Chapter 6 — THE CHALLENGE OF MEAT, FISH, AND POULTRY — Pages 115–141

[1] Morris, ed., *Old Rail Fence Corners*, 262.

[2] Morris, ed., *Old Rail Fence Corners*, 154, 156; Abby Fuller to "Aunt Trotwood," December 10, 1860, in Fuller Papers. For charts showing various cuts of beef, veal, pork, and mutton, see *Buckeye Cookery*, 432.

[3] For the material here and below, see Lee, *Complete Library*, 181.

[4] Jarchow, *Earth Brought Forth*, 195; Morris, ed., *Old Rail Fence Corners*, 143, 296. Salt pork sold for $18 a barrel in St. Paul in 1854 and for 18 cents a pound in Rochester in 1867; a barrel probably held a hundred pounds. *Daily Pioneer*, June 15, 1854; *Rochester Post*, June 15, 1867.

[5] Adams Diary, April 22, 1856, in Adams Papers; commercial porkpackers, who also cured hams, were established in Minneapolis by the 1870s; see *Minneapolis City Directory, 1874*, 88, *1878–79*, 393, front and back covers (Minneapolis, 1874, 1878).

[6] *Buckeye Cookery*, 435. Similar but less detailed directions for curing pork appear in the *Saint Croix Monitor* (Taylors Falls), November 1, 1862.

[7] Henderson, *Practical Cooking*, 160; Leslie, *New Cookery Book*, 225.

[8] *Buckeye Cookery* (1877), 371.

[9] Baird Diary, February 9, 10, 11, 1886, in Baird Papers. "There is no romance or poetry in making boiled soap, only patient hard work," according to *Buckeye Cookery*, 454, which offered a lengthy description of the process.

[10] Here and below, see First Baptist Church, *Tried and True*, 40.

[11] First Baptist Church, *Tried and True*, 41; Lee, *Complete Library*, 193; see also *Buckeye Cookery*, 434, 435.

[12] Here and below, see Leslie, *New Cookery Book*, 231, 251.

[13] Leslie, *New Cookery Book*, 232; Morse, *Household Discoveries*, 597.

[14] *Buckeye Cookery*, 434.

[15] Chase, *Receipt Book*, 411. The melted lard acted as a sealer, much as paraffin does in jellymaking today.

[16] Leslie, *New Cookery Book*, 246; Parloa, *New Cook Book*, 48.

[17] Parloa, *New Cook Book*, 48.

[18] Westminster Presbyterian Church, [*Valuable Recipes*], 13; *Buckeye Cookery*, 433. See also [*Valuable Recipes*], 14, for a "Recipe for Red Round" contributed by Charlotte O. Van Cleve, a well-known pioneer who had arrived at Fort Snelling in 1819 and eventually penned her autobiography, "*Three Score Years and Ten*," *Life-Long Memories* (Minneapolis, 1888).

[19] *Buckeye Cookery*, 436, 437.

[20] Morris, ed., *Old Rail Fence Corners*, 195; Francis H. Buzzacott, *The Complete American and Canadian Sportsman's Encyclopedia of Valuable Instruction*, 27 (Revised edition, Chicago, 1905).

[21] Leslie, *New Cookery Book*, 148; Corson, *Practical American Cookery*, 328, 329.

[22] *New Buckeye Cook Book* (1904), 1046; Morse, *Household Discoveries*, 595.

[23] For material here and in the following paragraph, see the *North Branch Review*, December 11, 1891. The article was reprinted from *Prairie Farmer*, a magazine published in Chicago.

[24] *New Buckeye Cook Book* (1904), 1046.

[25] Corson, *Practical American Cookery*, 327–329.

[26] Leslie, *New Cookery Book*, 149.

[27] *Buckeye Cookery*, 433.

[28] Recipe in Rudolph H. Fitz and Family Papers, in Minnesota Historical Society.

[29] *Buckeye Cookery*, 436.

[30] Leslie, *New Cookery Book*, 236, 237; *Buckeye Cookery*, 437.

[31] *Buckeye Cookery*, 433, 437.

[32] Morris, ed., *Old Rail Fence Corners*, 71, 95.

[33] *Buckeye Cookery*, 423.

[34] *Buckeye Cookery*, 424; Chase, *Receipt Book*, 429, 430. Butter to be treated in the potash mixture needed to be sliced, washed, rinsed, remolded, wrapped in muslin, and covered over with a "nice brine." A cloth dipped in the dissolved potash mixed in a ratio of one teaspoon of the solution to one cup of water was also recommended as a treatment for burns and bruises and to drive away flies.

[35] Burris, in *Minnesota History*, 14:384; Morris, ed., *Old Rail Fence Corners*, 142; Groff, *Snow Flake Cook Book*, 76. Fish from Lake Superior were sent to market in 200-pound barrels and 100-pound half-barrels. As early as 1872 frozen fish were shipped from the Great Lakes, and after 1900 a Duluth company shipped via parcel post fish frozen in blocks of ice. See Holmquist, in *Minnesota History*, 34:249. Commercial canning of fish began in the eastern United States early in the 19th century, and in 1860 food packing plants opened in the central states. Their primary products were fish, oysters, and seafood, with fruits and vegetables a later sideline. See Edith E. Swank, *The Story of Food Preservation*, 69 (n.p., 1943); Collins, *The Story of Canned Foods*, 12.

[36] Fred Miller, "Fishing with Early Minnesota Indians," in *Minnesota Conservationist*, May, 1939, p. 4. On recipes for pickling fish, see chapter 5, p. 112, above.

[37] Corson, *Practical American Cookery*, 222.

[38] *New Buckeye Cook Book* (1904), 257.

[39] Lee, *Complete Library*, 180.

[40] Burris, in *Minnesota History*, 14:385. For a vivid eyewitness account of an autumn buffalo hunt in 1850 and the butchering process followed by the Indians, see a letter from the Rev. George A. Belcourt to Henry H. Sibley printed in *Spirit of the Times*, 20:546 (January 4, 1851).

[41] Morris, ed., *Old Rail Fence Corners*, 15.

[42] Morris, ed., *Old Rail Fence Corners*, 15; Edwin T. Denig, *Five Indian Tribes of the Upper Missouri*, 12 (Norman, Okla., 1961); Grace L. Nute, *The Voyageur*, 54 (Reprint edition, St. Paul, 1955).

[43] On disappearing game, see "[Henry H.] Sibley as a Wild Game Conservationist," in *Minnesota History*, 18:417 (December, 1937); [O. J. Niles], "Up in this Neck of the Woods," in *Grand Rapids Herald-Review*, April 11, 1945. Walter O'Meara clearly recalls snaring, hunting, and eating rabbits as a youngster at Cloquet about 1900; see *We Made It Through the Winter*, 37, 40, 66.

[44] Here and the following paragraph, see Morse, *Household Discoveries*, 598.

[45] *Farmer and Gardener*, 1:87 (January, 1861); *Buckeye Cookery*, 457, 458.

[46] *Buckeye Cookery*, 457, 458.

[47] Jordan, *People's Health*, 105; John R. Cummins Diary, February 3, 4, 1858, in John R. Cummins Papers, Minnesota Historical Society.

[48] *Buckeye Cookery*, 458.

Chapter 7 — KITCHENS AND KITCHENRY — Pages 143–171

[1] Morris, ed., *Old Rail Fence Corners*, 320; Mary E. Carpenter to Laura, June 1, 1873, Carpenter Family Papers; Hibbard, Reminiscences, 8, 9. For general background on the evolution of kitchens and kitchen utensils, see Earl Lifshey, *The Housewares Story*, 125–195 (Chicago, 1973).

[2] For material here and in the following two paragraphs, see Hibbard, Reminiscences, 9, 12; *Buckeye Cookery*, 399; Beecher, *Treatise on Domestic Economy*, 262, 267, 269; Corson, *Practical American Cookery*, 6; interview with Janis Obst, curator of historic houses, Minnesota Historical Society, September, 1975.

[3] Beecher, *Treatise on Domestic Economy*; June D. Holmquist and Jean A. Brookins, *Minnesota's Major Historic Sites: A Guide*, 11, 53 (Revised edition, St. Paul, 1972); John W. North to G. S. Loomis, October 13, 1850, in North Papers; interview with Obst.

[4] *Buckeye Cookery*, 398; *Farmer and Gardener*, 1:217 (July, 1861); Corson, *Practical American Cookery*, 2; Hibbard, Reminiscences, 9; Evadene A. Burris, "Building the Frontier Home," and "Furnishing the Frontier Home," in *Minnesota History*, 15:46, 184 (March, June, 1934).

[5] Beecher, *Treatise on Domestic Economy*, 317.

[6] *Buckeye Cookery*, 398, 403.

[7] On stoves and refrigerators, see p. 149, 161, below; *Buckeye Cookery*, 398.

[8] Burris, in *Minnesota History*, 14:270–272; Jordan, *People's Health*, 101–129.

[9] Beecher, *Treatise on Domestic Economy*, 316.

[10] Corson, *Practical American Cookery*, 3; *Buckeye Cookery*, 403. On copperas water, see chapter 3, note 7, above.

[11] On the lack of fireplaces in frontier Minnesota, see Burris, in *Minnesota History*, 15:47, 192; p. 12, above. For material on the Norths, here and below, see Ann North to parents, November 12, 25, 1849, February 3, 1850, in North Papers.

[12] Ann North to parents, November 25, 1849, January 6, February 9, 1850, in North Papers. On North, see Carlton C. Qualey, "John Wesley North and the Minnesota Frontier," in *Minnesota History*, 35:101, 110–116 (September, 1956).

[13] Morris, ed., *Old Rail Fence Corners*, 115, 300.

[14] Morris, ed., *Old Rail Fence Corners*, 70.

[15] Burris, in *Minnesota History*, 15:186, 191; *Minnesota Pioneer*, September 1, 1853; *Minneapolis Daily Tribune*, May 25, 1867.

[16] St. Paul Branch, Cleveland Co-Operative Stove Co., *Catalogue of Cooking and Heating Stoves, Ranges and Hollow Ware*, 16 ([Cleveland, 1881]).

[17] Cleveland Co-Operative Stove Co., *Reduced Net Wholesale Price List*, 11 (Cleveland, April 1, 1885).

[18] Cleveland Co-Operative Stove Co., *Catalogue of Cooking and Heating Stoves*, 1, 11–16, 21, and *Reduced Net Wholesale Price List*, 10, 11.

[19] *Excelsior Manufacturing Company* [Catalog], 13, 14 (St. Louis, January, 1887).

[20] Cleveland Co-Operative Stove Co., *Reduced Net Wholesale Price List*, 22, 23, 24; Israel, ed., *1897 Sears Roebuck Catalogue*, 128.

[21] On the problems of stoves and comparative values of wood, see Beecher and Stowe, *American Woman's Home*, 66–76; Corson, *Cooking School Text Book*, 19; *Buckeye Cookery*, 64, 346, 401, 429. The latter also discussed soft and hard coal. On the use of hay, straw, and sunflowers as fuel, see *Daily Globe* (St. Paul), April 28, September 19, 1878. A large machine that made hay or straw into bales of 10 to 15

pounds each was included in the price of a stove exhibited in 1878 at the Northwestern Exposition in Minneapolis. It was said that two men using the machine could "bale enough fuel in six days to last one stove for a whole year." See *Daily Pioneer Press*, August 10, 1878.

The use of coal as a fuel in Minnesota began in 1870 with the first large shipments by railroad; before that "hardly any coal was brought to St. Paul except what was consumed by the St. Paul gas-works and some eight or ten gentlemen who used it as a fuel." Reflecting its availability, the number of coal-burning stoves sold in St. Paul jumped from 104 in 1869 to 436 in 1870. See "The Coal Trade of St. Paul," in *Daily Press*, December 20, 1870.

[22] *Buckeye Cookery* (1877), 44. By 1908 Minnesotans could buy stoves fitted with oven thermometers from the St. Paul mail-order firm of G. Sommers & Co. Although not considered extremely accurate, such thermometers, placed in the oven door, were of some "benefit to the painstaking woman, as she can get a good idea of the heat of the oven without allowing it to escape by holding the door open." G. Sommers & Co., *Our Leader*, no. 193, p. 358 (Fall, 1908); Juniata L. Shepperd, *Hand-Book of Household Science*, 118 (St. Paul, 1908). In 1913 an elementary oven regulator was invented; see Kathleen Ann Smallzried, *The Everlasting Pleasure: Influences on America's Kitchens, Cooks and Cookery, from 1565 to the Year 2000*, 229 (New York, 1956).

[23] Child, *The Frugal Housewife*, 53 (Boston, 1829).

[24] *Buckeye Cookery*, 401.

[25] Corson, *Cooking School Text Book*, 17. Bath brick dust, pumice and rottenstone, as well as sifted wood or coal ashes, all materials of a gritty consistency, were recommended for cleaning steel knives. Morse, *Household Discoveries*, 141.

[26] Abbie T. Griffin, Diary, May 28, 1882, in Abbie T. Griffin Papers, Minnesota Historical Society. On chimneys as "One of the most serious evils in domestic life," see Beecher and Stowe, *American Woman's Home*, 76–79.

[27] Parloa, *New Cook Book*, advertisement, [67]; *Buckeye Cookery*, 522.

[28] Here and in the paragraph below, see Israel, ed., *1897 Sears Roebuck Catalogue*, 115–118.

[29] Israel, ed., *1897 Sears Roebuck Catalogue*, 115, 116; *Minneapolis Journal*, August 8, 1894.

[30] "Rochester News," in *Daily Globe*, November 23, 1880; Israel, ed., *1897 Sears Roebuck Catalogue*, 20; United States, *Statutes at Large*, 35:1131. The fire test, a safety measurement for petroleum products, was first required by Minnesota in 1876. Primarily a test for illuminating oils used in lamps, it was applied to other petroleum products to measure the ignition point (or temperature) in Fahrenheit degrees at

which the liquid would burn continuously. Petroleum distillation in those days was rather inexact, and the term gasoline was an indefinite one covering products now more rigidly defined. The inefficiencies of early petroleum processes often left lighter components in heavier oils, raising their ignition points and making them more dangerous to handle. Gradually the fire-test laws were tightened. By the 1890s 150 degree fire-test oil was common, although Minnesota still required only 120 degrees as late as 1894. See Harold F. Williamson and Arnold R. Daum, *The American Petroleum Industry: The Age of Illumination 1859–1899*, 575 (Evanston, Ill., 1959); Minnesota Department of Oil Inspection, *Report, August 1, 1909 to July 31, 1914*, 8 ([St. Paul, 1914]); Minnesota, *Statutes*, 1894, pp. 452–458.

[31] Israel, ed., *1897 Sears Roebuck Catalogue*, 117. Kerosene was available in Minnesota as early as the 1850s. See Burris, in *Minnesota History*, 14:266.

[32] Montgomery Ward & Co., *Catalogue and Buyers' Guide No. 57, Spring and Summer, 1895*, 423 (Reprint edition, New York, 1969); Burris, in *Minnesota History*, 14:267, 268.

[33] Beecher, *Domestic Receipt-Book*, 267. On various "refrigerators" of the day, see Burris, in *Minnesota History*, 14:273.

[34] *Pioneer and Democrat*, July 21, 1856.

[35] For the information here and below, see Minnesota Refrigerator Co., *Illustrated Catalogue for 1888–9*, 4, 9, 25, 27, 29 (St. Paul, 1888).

[36] Ann North to parents, December 23, 30, 1849, in North Papers; Morris, ed., *Old Rail Fence Corners*, 141; Anderson, Autobiography, 30.

[37] Beecher, *Treatise on Domestic Economy*, 319–321; Leslie, *New Cookery Book*, 615. A list of kitchen utensils and kitchen luxuries appears in *Buckeye Cookery*, 414–417. See also Burris, in *Minnesota History*, 15:184, 189.

[38] Morris, ed., *Old Rail Fence Corners*, 49; Beecher, *Treatise on Domestic Economy*, 320; Lee, *Complete Library*, xx.

[39] Corson, *A Course of Lectures*, 11, 12; Beecher, *Treatise on Domestic Economy*, 319; J. R. Dolan, *The Yankee Peddlers of Early America*, 113–152 (New York, 1964).

[40] *Buckeye Cookery*, 402; chapter 1, note 33, above.

[41] For material here and below, see *Buckeye Cookery*, 63, 415, 416, 417.

[42] Ann North to parents, November 12, 19, 1849, in North Papers; entries for May 9, July 8, August 15, 19, 1857, and p. [53] in "House Account," 1857, vol. 1, in Fuller Papers. See also Burris, in *Minnesota History*, 15:188.

[43] *Buckeye Cookery*, 414–416; Parloa, *New Cook Book*, advertisement, [64].

[44] Here and below, see Leslie, *New Cookery Book*, 615.

⁴⁵ See advertisements in *Minnesota Pioneer*, March 18, 1852; for a history of coffee mills, see William H. Ukers, *All About Coffee*, 575–581, 598 (New York, 1935); Lifshey, *Housewares Story*, 253.

⁴⁶ Ukers, *All About Coffee*, 598; *Buckeye Cookery*, 137; *Minnesota Pioneer*, June 3, 1852; *St. Paul Pioneer*, January 4, 1863; Leslie, *New Cookery Book*, 596; Lee, *Complete Library*, 53. Ukers, 130, 131, lists over 40 kinds of coffee by their market names, which were derived from the areas of production and which implied differences in taste, color, and potency.

⁴⁷ For material here and below, see *Buckeye Cookery*, 138, 139, 141.

⁴⁸ *Buckeye Cookery*, 403, 408.

⁴⁹ *Buckeye Cookery*, 369, 397.

⁵⁰ Morris, ed., *Old Rail Fence Corners*, 50.

Chapter 8 — MINNESOTA COOKBOOKS OF THE 19TH CENTURY — Pages 172–202

¹ Morris, ed., *Old Rail Fence Corners*, 130.

² Thomas K. Gray, *T. K. Gray's Cook Book*, [7] (Minneapolis, 1896).

³ Lincoln, *Boston Cooking School Kitchen Text-Book* (Boston, 1887); Farmer, *The Original Boston Cooking-School Cook Book, 1896* (Facsimile reprint edition, New York, 1973). Brief biographical sketches of Farmer and Lincoln are in *Dictionary of American Biography* (1928), 6:276, 11:265, respectively.

⁴ Eleanor Lowenstein, *Bibliography of American Cookery Books, 1742–1860*, 1 (Worcester, Mass., and New York, 1972).

⁵ Lowenstein, *American Cookery Books*, 4, 25, 31, 74; Simmons, *American Cookery: Or, the Art of Dressing Viands, Fish, Poultry, and Vegetables* (Hartford, 1796, and Facsimile reprint edition, New York, 1958). A copy of the 1814 edition is in the Minnesota Historical Society collection. Simmons called herself "An American Orphan" and claimed her recipes were adapted to America and "all grades of life." On Child, who was also a widely known abolitionist, see *Dictionary of American Biography* (1928), 4:67–69. An earlier survey of the Minnesota Historical Society's cookbook collection may be found in Kreidberg, "Corn Bread, Portable Soup, and Wrinkle Cures," in *Minnesota History*, 41:105–116 (Fall, 1968).

⁶ Lowenstein, *American Cookery Books*, vii, 24; on authors named, see *Dictionary of American Biography* (1928), 2:125 (Beecher); 4:454 (Corson); 11:185 (Leslie); *Notable American Women, 1607–1950*, 3:16–18 (Parloa), 193–195 (Rorer) (Cambridge, Mass., 1971); on Henderson, see John H. Brown, ed., *Lamb's Biographical Dictionary of the*

United States, 4:5 (Boston, 1901); Kramer is identified in Brown and Brown, *Culinary Americana*, 46, 171.

[7] First Baptist Church, *Tried and True*, 77.

[8] *Buckeye Cookery*, 404.

[9] Beecher, *Domestic Economy*, [5], 155; *Domestic Receipt-Book*, 217.

[10] For material here and in the following paragraph, see Beecher, *Domestic Receipt-Book*, 283.

[11] Leslie, *New Cookery Book*, xxviii; Parloa, *New Cook Book*, [3].

[12] Leslie, *New Cookery Book*, xxv, 418–421.

[13] Leslie, *New Cookery Book*, 35, 68.

[14] Leslie, *New Cookery Book*, 51, 53, 66, 328.

[15] Leslie, *New Cookery Book*, 139, 140. On the French influence on American cooking, see Evan Jones, *American Food: The Gastronomic Story*, 28–47 (New York, 1975).

[16] Henderson, *Practical Cooking*, [9], 30, 219, 359–364. The book was first published in 1876 and was reissued at least four times by 1882. The Minnesota Historical Society collection has a copy of the 1881 edition. See Brown and Brown, *Culinary Americana*, 158, 159, 160.

[17] Henderson, *Practical Cooking*, 320, 334, 337, 338.

[18] For material here and below, see Corson, *Cooking School Text Book*, iii, 25, 66, 103, 143. Food prices in 1879 can be judged by Corson's per-dish cost: a 6-pound beef roast with vegetables and seasonings, $1.00; apple pie, 19 cents; 3-pound chicken sautéed with mushrooms, wine, flour, oil, and seasoning, 74 cents; 3 eggs scrambled in butter, 5 cents.

[19] Corson, *Practical American Cookery*, title page.

[20] Corson, *Practical American Cookery*, 219, 299, 305, 309, 323, 405, 430. For "Chicken Quenelles" recipe, see p. 242, below.

[21] Corson, *Cooking School Text Book*, iii; Parloa, *New Cook Book*, [3], 43; for an example of Parloa's explicit directions, see her recipe for "Gâteau Saint Honore," 43. The copy of Parloa's *New Cook Book* in the society's library is stamped "Compliments of Washburn, Crosby Co.," indicating it was given away to the milling concern's customers. General Mills, Inc., Minneapolis, successor to Washburn, Crosby, issued a facsimile reprint of the book in 1974 with different advertising and pagination.

[22] Parloa, *New Cook Book*, 7, 10, 15, 20, 21, 22.

[23] For material here and in the following paragraph, see Corson, *A Course of Lectures*, [3], 21, 26; the report was issued separately and as "Appendix to Supplement I," in University of Minnesota, Board of Regents, *Fourth Biennial Report* (1886).

[24] *"Aunt Babette's" Cook Book*, 5, 25, 62, 71, 76, 77, 452–466. "In order to govern and command the respect of your servants and to show them that you are not ignorant of the duties you expect them to per-

form," she wrote, "you must first learn the management of a household yourself."

[25] *"Aunt Babette's" Cook Book*, 52, 128, 199, 222, 235, 293.

[26] *"Aunt Babette's" Cook Book*, 300, 301, 396, 484–489.

[27] *Buckeye Cookery* (1877), [iii], v; on various editions, see chapter 2, note 5, above. A publisher's notice in the 1883 edition stated that over 100,000 copies had been sold since 1880. Another indication of its popularity is the appearance of "Buckeye" recipes in the manuscript cookbooks of Minnesota housewives. See, for example, Griffin Diary, 1882–85, in Griffin Papers.

[28] *Buckeye Cookery* (1877), 343, 419.

[29] *Buckeye Cookery* (1881), 25, 147, 171, 197, 348, 374, 382, 384, 385, 394, 396, 445, 446, 453, 460, 477, 484, 492, 503, 518, 521. Many recipes from *Buckeye Cookery* are included in chapter 9, below.

[30] *Buckeye Cookery* (1877), 330, 331.

[31] *Buckeye Cookery* (1881), 346.

[32] Farmer, *Boston Cooking-School Cook Book*, 27.

[33] Groff, *Snow Flake Cook Book*, title page; chapter 2, p. 55, above.

[34] For coffee recipes, see Groff, *Snow Flake Cook Book*, 19–23, 70–73; see also Beecher, *Domestic Receipt-Book*, 217–223.

[35] For material here and in the following two paragraphs, see "Ellen Gray," *The Orange Blossom Cook Book*, [2], 6, 47 (St. Paul, 1885). The practical if romantic tale comprised 45 pages, broken into 11 chapters.

[36] For material here and in the following two paragraphs, see E. M. May & Son, *Catalogue*, [4], [5], 10, 11, 14, 24, 39, 49, 94, 96, 127, 129, 141 (Minneapolis, 1887).

[37] Gray, *Cook Book* (1896), [5]. The Minnesota Historical Society library has copies of all five editions.

[38] Gray, *Cook Book* (1896), 25, 63, 83, 97. For these cake recipes, see p. 245, 247, below.

[39] Lee, *Complete Library*, title page. Mrs. Lee is identified as "A Boston Housekeeper."

[40] Lowenstein, *American Cookery Books*, 32; Lee, *Complete Library*, title page, vii–xxvi, xxxiii–xlvii, 251–256, 278, 291.

[41] For material here and in the following two paragraphs, see *Our Chef's Best Receipts*, [3], 52, 112 (Chicago and New York, 1899).

[42] Margaret Cook, *America's Charitable Cooks: A Bibliography of Fund-Raising Cook Books Published in the United States (1861–1915)*, 139, 141 (Kent, Ohio, 1971); Ascension Church, *Family Friend*, [3], 10. The Minnesota Historical Society library has copies of the 1874 and 1893 editions.

[43] Here and below, see Westminster Presbyterian Church, [*Valuable Recipes*], 13, 60, 63, 66.

[44] First Baptist Church, *Tried and True*, 43, 48, 55, 61, 95, 96.

⁴⁵ For material here and below, see Dayton Avenue Presbyterian Church, *Cook Book*, 4–8. Clara S. Hays, a graduate of Iowa Agricultural College, was professor of domestic science at the North Dakota Agricultural College and Experiment Station, Fargo, from 1889 until her death in 1892. Marion D. Shutter and J. S. McLain, *Progressive Men of Minnesota*, 156 (Minneapolis, 1897); *Who Was Who in America with World Notables*, 4:422 (Chicago, 1968).

⁴⁶ Methodist Episcopal Church, *Christmas Cook Book*, 20, 24, 26. For "Christmas Pudding" recipe, see p. 262, below.

⁴⁷ Central Presbyterian Church, *Cook Book*, 71.

⁴⁸ *Northwestern Farmer: A Literary-Home-Journal for Farmers*, 11:368 (October 15, 1893).

⁴⁹ *Country Kitchen*, cover; *Northwestern Farmer*, 11:368, (October 15, 1893); Margaret Landin, ed., *Country Kitchen Cook Book*, iv, v (St. Paul, 1973).

⁵⁰ Thomas M. Newson, *Pen Pictures of St. Paul, Minnesota*, 209 (St. Paul, 1886); Mrs. Anna Ramsey's account book, January, 1880, in Ramsey Papers, roll 47, frames 543–553.

⁵¹ Morris, ed., *Old Rail Fence Corners*, 159.

⁵² *Minneapolis Journal*, October 10, 1894.

⁵³ *Daily Minnesota Pioneer*, August 6, 1855.

⁵⁴ See, for example, Methodist Episcopal Church, *Christmas Cook Book*, 22; Central Presbyterian Church, *Cook Book*, 52; First Baptist Church, *Tried and True*, 60.

⁵⁵ Baird Diary, September 4, 1886, in Baird Papers; Morris, ed., *Old Rail Fence Corners*, 73, 142; *Goodhue County Republican* (Red Wing), April 26, 1867; *Mankato Weekly Record*, April 16, 1870; *Stillwater Gazette*, April 5, 1876.

⁵⁶ Chapter 7, p. 169, above; Morris, ed., *Old Rail Fence Corners*, 115, 117, 199, 244; on currant tea, see Child, *Frugal Housewife* (1829), 15; on sassafras, see First Baptist Church, *Tried and True*, 82; on ginseng, see William E. Lass, "Ginseng Rush in Minnesota," in *Minnesota History*, 41:249–266 (Summer, 1969). Teas sold by Minnesota grocers included Japan, green, black, Oolong, Gunpowder, and mixed. Smith Grocery Store, Order Book, 1875; *Rochester Post Bulletin*, June 15, 1867, January 11, 1868, October 17, 1879.

⁵⁷ Virginia Huck and Ann H. Andersen, eds., *Minnesota Centennial Cookbook: 100 Years of Good Cooking* (Reprint edition, St. Paul, 1970).

⁵⁸ Conversations of the author with Carlton C. Qualey, director, Minnesota Ethnic History Project, Minnesota Historical Society, September, 1975.

⁵⁹ On Mrs. Kander and various editions of *The Settlement Cook Book*, see Cook, *America's Charitable Cooks*, 268.

⁶⁰ First Baptist Church, *Tried and True*, [5].

[61] Westminster Presbyterian Church, [*Valuable Recipes*], 34; First Baptist Church, *Tried and True*, 97.

Chapter 9 — SELECTED RECIPES — Pages 203–274

[1] Dayton Avenue Presbyterian Church, *Cook Book*, 36, 38.

[2] For an especially broad selection of wild-fowl recipes, see Washburn, Crosby Co., *New Cook Book*, 26.

[3] Leslie, *New Cookery Book*, 344, 365.

[4] For material here and in the following paragraph, see Leslie, *New Cookery Book*, 384; Parloa, *New Cook Book*, 25. Leslie, p. 383, identifies Sidney Smith, the "inventor" of the first salad recipe given below, as a minister "whose genius as a writer and a wit is well known on both sides the Atlantic."

[5] Morris, ed., *Old Rail Fence Corners*, 37, 100, 130; Corson, *Course of Lectures*, 45; on syrup produced from sugar cane, see Clara and Ditus Day to Lucia Hendryx, October 5, December 12, 1858, in Schuyler V. R. Hendryx Papers, Minnesota Historical Society; on Japan apple-pie melon, see *Stillwater Messenger*, October 8, 1861; *Farmer and Gardener*, 1:182, 333 (June, November, 1861). For instructions on using the hand-cranked ice cream freezer, see Parloa, *New Cook Book*, 39.

[6] Morris, ed., *Old Rail Fence Corners*, 152.

General Index

Blueberries, wild, 87, 199; recipes, 208, 255, 260
Blue Earth, 25
Bohemians, 9, 167
Boiling, popularity, 22, 23, 25, 181, 194, 214, 218, 225
Boston (Mass.), 173, 174, 185, 189, 258
Botulism, 30, 117
Boyd, Lewis R., 78
Brandy, 14, 23, 24, 85, 91, 183, 246, 250, 256, 263, 266, 268; recipe, 269
Brass, 158; utensils, 31, 83, 102, 164, 165
Bread, making, 1, 3, 7, 12, 20, 38–57, 120, 150, 156; importance, 36–38, 43, 57, 87; yeast, 40–53, 208; salt-rising, 45–47; quick, 53–57, 208. *See also* Recipe Index
Breakfast, 52, 56, 121, 192, 208; recipes, 223, 232, 243, 244
Brick dust, 113, 158, 170
Brooklyn Center, 16
Brooms, oven tests, 49, 52, 156
Buckeye Cookery, quoted, 38, 40, 47, 57, 63, 66, 81, 110, 120, 127, 128, 130, 134, 136, 139, 144, 154, 156, 165, 169; recipes, 50–52, 92, 94, 102, 104, 112, 209, 210, 212, 214, 221–223, 225–227, 229, 231, 233, 235, 239, 241, 243, 265, 267, 268; described, 183–185
Buckwheat, 20, 36, 64, 68; recipe, 212
Buffalo, 137, 154, 177, 178
Buffalo (Minn.). *See* Methodist Episcopal Church

Butchers and butchering, 15, 16, 27, 29, 117, 118, 120, 138
Butter, prices, 5, 13, 15; supplies, 14, 20, 25, 27, 60, 64, 67; uses, 43–45, 49, 51, 70, 125, 178
Butterick Publishing Co., *Perfect Art of Canning*, 274

CABBAGE, 4; uses, 64, 71, 73, 75, 102, 103, 106–108, 191, 198, 234; recipes, 207, 230, 235. *See also* Sauerkraut
Cakes, 39, 156, 198; bakery, 22; kinds, 22, 24, 25, 120, 172, 188, 193, 194, 208; baking, 154; recipes, 194, 212, 245–250
California, 131, 150
Cambridge, 4–6
Candles, 27, 64, 144
Candy, 14, 98, 187, 189
Canning, 3; commercial, 28, 30, 32, 135; vegetables, 30, 77, 79, 82, 92–94; jars and utensils, 78–85, 88, 89, 110, 113, 138; fruits and berries, 79, 83, 84, 89–92; methods, 89, 92; meats, 138
Cannon Falls, 150
Capers, 22–24, 109, 114
Carbolic acid, 63, 184
Carpenter, Mary E., quoted, 7
Carrots, 4, 21, 72, 73
Catering service, 187
Catsups, 15, 71, 80, 104–106, 110, 178; recipes, 104, 105, 273
Cauliflower, pickled, 103, 108, 109
Celery, 73, 106, 234, 238
Cellar, importance, 3, 26, 59; root, 61, 150; underground, 62, 70, 72–76, 96, 110

Central Presbyterian Church (St. Paul), *Cook Book*, 194, 206, 209, 210, 213, 215, 221, 233, 235, 238, 244, 248, 249, 250, 253, 254, 260, 261, 263–265
Charcoal, uses, 65, 69, 129, 134
Chase, Dr. A. W., *Receipt Book*, 70, 134
Chatfield, 100
Cheese, 10, 14, 60, 190; recipes, 270, 272, 273
Cherries, wild, 85, 87, 90, 104; recipes, 208, 261
Chicago (Ill.), 174, 189, 196
Chicken, 11, 22, 64, 124, 181, 218, 234. *See also* Recipe Index
Child, Lydia M., author, 173
Chili sauce, 200, 243
Chocolate, 14; recipes, 250, 267
Chokecherries, wild, 87
Chowchow, 108
Christmas, foods, 24, 86, 116, 194, 262
Cider, apple, 90, 100, 113, 266
Cisterns, 30, 60, 63, 145, 148
Cleveland Stove Co., models, 151–153
Coal, fuel, 26, 48, 153, 154
Codfish, 14, 135, 170; price, 15; salted, 17, 136, 181, 197, 214; recipes, 206, 215
Coffee, 24; supplies, 13, 15, 27, 169, 186, 199, 200; mills, 36, 169; pots, 167, 169, 170; making, 169; recipes, 169, 170, 213, 247, 266
Coleslaw, popular, 191, 198, 234; recipes, 235, 239
Cookies, 24, 25, 187, 196, 245; recipes, 252–254

Recipe Index

The Illustrations

THE LINE ENGRAVINGS appearing in this volume were selected to give readers a sense of the times as well as to clarify the text. Illustrations such as these were commonly used by 19th-century publishers to enhance their books and catalogs. The reproduction of photographs by the halftone process used in printing today was unknown until late in the 19th century and was not widely used until the 1900s.

Many of the illustrations appearing here were chosen from cookbooks — largely those mentioned in the text and reference notes — and 19th-century catalogs in the collections of the Minnesota Historical Society library. Others are from contemporary sources that reprint old-fashioned engravings. The latter are *The Handbook of Early Advertising Art* (New York, 1956) by Clarence Hornung; *The Growth of Industrial Art* (Reprint edition, New York, 1972), compiled by Benjamin Butterworth with an introduction by Mark Kramer; *Old Engravings and Illustrations*, volumes 1 and 2 (Minneapolis, 1965), and *Uncensored Situations* (Minneapolis, 1966), both by former Minneapolis artist Dick Sutphen.